SIDELINED

SPORTS, CULTURE, AND BEING
A WOMAN IN AMERICA

JULIE DiCARO

DUTTON

For Auntie

(1908–2004)

DUTTON

An imprint of Penguin Random House LLC
penguinrandomhouse.com

Previously published as a Dutton hardcover in March 2021
First trade paperback edition: March 2022

THE LIBRARY OF CONGRESS HAS CATALOGED THE
HARDCOVER EDITION OF THIS BOOK AS FOLLOWS:

Names: DiCaro, Julie, author.
Title: Sidelined : sports, culture, and being a
woman in America / Julie DiCaro.
Description: [New York, New York] : Dutton, [2021] |
Includes bibliographical references. | Identifiers: LCCN 2020041049 (print) |
LCCN 2020041050 (ebook) | ISBN 9781524746100 (hardcover) |
ISBN 9781524746117 (ebook)
Subjects: LCSH: Sex discrimination in sports—United States. |
Feminism and sports—United States. | Sports—Sociological aspects. |
Sports for women—Social aspects—United States. | Women's rights—
United States. | Sports journalism—Social aspects—United States. |
Women sportswriters—United States—Social conditions. |
Women athletes—United States—Social conditions.
Classification: LCC GV706.32 .D54 2021 (print) |
LCC GV706.32 (ebook) | DDC 796.082—dc23
LC record available at https://lccn.loc.gov/2020041049
LC ebook record available at https://lccn.loc.gov/2020041050

Printed in the United States of America
1st Printing

Dutton trade paperback ISBN: 9781524746124

BOOK DESIGN BY LAURA K. CORLESS

Praise for *Sidelined*

"Sharp and insightful, *Sidelined* shows us the way forward in a culture that has often been resistant to women's advancement. It's an illuminating look at sexism in sports, and in America."
—Billie Jean King, sports icon and *New York Times* bestselling author

"*Sidelined* is the feminist sports book we've all been waiting for. Whether you're a sports enthusiast or not, Julie DiCaro's work will captivate you."   —Jessica Valenti, author *Sex Object: A Memoir*

"[A] remarkable window into what American sports culture—a powerful and enduring distillation of masculine power and privilege—tells us about the state of inequality in America. A must-read."
—Soraya Chemaly, author *Rage Becomes Her*

"Shame on the public and the press for treating sexism and misogyny in women's sports as a game. This book digs deep into why and how it happens and how it can be stopped."   —Soledad O'Brien

"A writer, a lawyer, a columnist, a friend, Julie DiCaro has fearlessly taken on homophobia, racism, and sexism in *Sidelined*, connecting with anyone who's been carelessly hurt or needlessly slandered. She's the teammate who makes everyone better."
—Lesley Visser, Hall of Fame sportscaster

"If there is any justice, *Sidelined* will become a cornerstone text for everyone who works in—or cares about—sports media. The level of insight that Julie DiCaro provides holds the key for making us more open-minded and empathetic about the sexism that pervades the industry. It is also written with a snappy flair that reads like the best sports writing."
—Dave Zirin, sports editor at *The Nation* and host of the *Edge of Sports* podcast

"There's no other current book that captures the challenges women face in sports media, and DiCaro does this masterfully. Bringing a feminist lens to the world of sports, this book sets itself apart with its reporting and relevancy." —*Library Journal* (starred review)

"Journalist DiCaro debuts with a sweeping takedown of misogyny in America's sports media and professional leagues. . . . [Her] investigative journalism chops shine through in her insightful interviews, and she crafts engrossing narratives out of historical events, like the battle to get female reporters access to locker rooms after games. Ultimately, DiCaro believes that if media outlets, teams, and fans want to address the deeply entrenched culture of inequality in the way women are treated in sports, they need to 'grow the f*** up.' This bracing call to arms is a step in that direction." —*Publishers Weekly* (starred review)

"A gifted writer, [DiCaro] moves deftly between her own experiences and the voices of other women. . . . *Sidelined* delivers a powerful call to action for women and men within the industry, as well as sports fans, who can also play a role in cultivating diversity and ending misogyny."
—*Booklist*

"Through anecdotes, interviews, and focused research, [DiCaro] shows the myriad ways these problems are structural and institutional, while highlighting female athletes and reporters who continue to break barriers by refusing to be sidelined." —*Shelf Awareness*

CONTENTS

'd love to open this note with a reflection on how much surrounding women in sports has changed since *Sidelined* was originally published in March of 2021. I wish I could talk about a massive push for investing in women's sports, more equality for women in broadcasting and writing, and sports media finally getting its #MeToo moment. Unfortunately, none of that has happened in any meaningful way. At least not yet.

This is not for lack of work on the part of women in the industry and their allies. Sites dedicated to covering women's sports, like Just Women's Sports, did see infusions of cash from high-profile athletes like Kevin Durant, Elena Delle Donne, Hilary Knight, and Arike Ogunbowale. We saw terrific reporting on sexual harassment in Major League Baseball from reporters like Katie Strang and Britt Ghiroli over at the Athletic. Serena Williams's daughter, Alexis Olympia, joined her mom in becoming a part owner of the new

National Women's Soccer League team Angel City FC; the mother and daughter are joined by a host of other celebrities, such as Jessica Chastain, Eva Longoria, Natalie Portman, Billie Jean King, and members of the 1999 US Women's National Soccer Team. Across sports media, it became clear that if women wanted to make gains in leagues like the WNBA, NWSL, and the newly minted Premier Hockey Federation, they were going to have to do it themselves.

There were also gains in the broadcast booth: In September 2021, Kate Scott was named the new play-by-play announcer for the Philadelphia 76ers, and Lisa Byington got a similar gig with the Milwaukee Bucks. Major League Baseball, an organization that loves to see women in the booth on International Women's Day but hardly any other time, saw Jessica Mendoza and Melanie Newman call a game on a regular ole Wednesday night—the first time ESPN ever aired an all-women broadcast for a men's professional baseball, football, or basketball game. And an all-women broadcast team covered the ShopRite Classic on the Golf Channel in another first, this time for the Ladies Professional Golf Association. Still, it begs the question of why it took until 2021 for women to entirely take over a broadcast for any of these leagues.

And yet, when it comes to examining how women are still treated in the sports world, there are plenty of incidents out there that send my heart racing with fury and indignation. Ahead of the 2021 collegiate Women's Basketball Championship, elite players entered their workout room only to discover a single rack of barbells and some yoga mats. The Norwegian women's beach handball team was fined for refusing to wear skimpy bikini bottoms at the European Championships, opting instead to wear the same shorts as the men's teams. It was a fight they continued to wage during the Summer Olympics in Tokyo, where swim caps designed for and to protect natural Black hair were also disallowed. So were *literal babies*: Athletes who were nursing their babies were initially told that no family members would be allowed to travel to the games, including their infants, until women fought back publicly and the International Olympic Committee was forced to reverse their original decree. And while we saw Simone Biles and Naomi Osaka hailed by some for choosing to put their mental health first and drop out of huge competitions, there were also plenty of detractors, both on social media and in the press.

It wasn't a great year for alleged misconduct either. Dodgers ace Trevor Bauer was accused of sexual assault by two different women and was only placed on administrative leave by the MLB and his team after an outcry from fans and media. Houston Texans quarterback Deshaun Watson was accused of various forms of sexual misconduct during massages by twenty-two separate women during the off-season, yet he was eligible to play when the NFL season kicked off in September 2021. Tampa Bay Buccaneers wide receiver Antonio Brown settled a sexual assault lawsuit during his off-season, and it was only fifteen minutes into the NFL season when broadcaster Al Michaels referred to Brown having a "whole host of issues" and then went on to wax poetic about what a great friend quarterback Tom Brady was for standing by him. Over in the NWSL, Carolina Courage coach Paul Riley was finally fired, six years after players originally came forward with allegations of sexual harassment and misconduct. Alas, too much seemed to remain the same.

Off the field, sports media remains overwhelmingly white and male. The Associated Press Sports Editors 2021 Sports Media Racial and Gender Report Card bumped the industry up to a B+ when it came to overall racial hiring but continued to give sports media an F when it came to gender hiring. According to the report, 77.1 percent of sports reporters in 2021 were white and 85.6 percent were men, yet another indicator of sports reporting's failures when it comes to women in general, but especially Black women and other women of color. It's clear we still have miles to go before we sleep.

When interviewing women for *Sidelined* in 2019 and early 2020, I heard over and over again that "we're doing this for those coming behind us." It's a laudable goal. After all, had it not been for the women I mention in Chapter 1—the first women into men's professional sports locker rooms—it's unlikely I'd be able to work as a sports columnist and reporter in 2021. Yet it got me thinking: How many generations of women have to sacrifice themselves for the *next* generation? When do we ever get to see the fruits of our own work? Forty years after Melissa Ludtke's groundbreaking lawsuit against Major League Baseball, we're still working for the women yet to enter the industry, in hopes that everything will be better for them than it is for us. Fifty years from now, will women in sports media still be saying the same? I can feel my blood pressure going up just thinking about it.

Speaking of blood pressure, let's talk about online harassment, specifically Twitter. I had hopes that once Donald Trump was de-platformed by Facebook and Twitter following the 2020 election and January 6 insurrection, things might return to some semblance of normalcy, given that so much harassment of women seems to be done by guys with #MAGA in their Twitter bios. That's not to say there are not plenty of guys there who purport to be huge fans of Vice President Kamala Harris and the kindness and positivity of Ted Lasso, who then spend their days shit-posting on women's timelines, blissfully unaware that Ted Lasso wouldn't think they were very nice people at all. God, I wish I had a Roy Kent in my life to help me deal with men like that.

There are basically two issues when it comes to being on Twitter for women in sports media. The first is criminal harassment: death threats, rape threats, doxing. The kind of Twitter posts that make your blood run cold and your friends urge you to contact the police. The second kind is the daily deluge of shit-posting, constantly doubting everything a woman says, calling her names, criticizing her looks. Both have a devastating impact on one's mental health—and, frankly, at this point, I'd swap the occasional death threat for getting rid of the shit-posters any day of the week and twice on Sundays. Death threats I can handle. Fifty guys dedicated to telling me how much I suck in ten different ways every single day has become much harder to deal with.

I expected a certain amount of backlash once *Sidelined* was published. I knew for certain I would never work in radio in Chicago again. I felt that I'd aired too much of our dirty laundry in a market that rewards people for keeping quiet and waiting for another chance. I wasn't interested in doing that and made peace with leaving radio, as much as I loved it, before the book even came out.

What I wasn't prepared for was men I had worked with in the past, and whom I considered friends if not allies, joining in with my trolls and accusing me of lying about some of the things that they damn well *know* happened in our workplace. When one former coworker accused me of lying for the book about men saving pictures of women in lingerie on work computers and leaving evidence of watching porn on work computers, I was dumbfounded. I told him I knew who the responsible party was and had screenshots to prove it. "Then you have a [horny-on-main coworker's name] problem, not a problem with the rest of us," he sneered in a #NotAllMen moment for the ages. "It was only a few guys so it doesn't count as sexual harassment" is not and has never been the rule, but my dedicated trolls took the episode as the proof they've been seeking that I'm a liar who can't be trusted. That I somehow make things harder for the women who *really* experience harassment.

I hadn't used names when talking about my experiences working in sports talk radio because, to me, it didn't matter who these men were. I wasn't looking for revenge or to call anyone out. I only wanted to illustrate what it's like for many women who work in male-dominated spaces, both in sports and out. But now the mob screamed for names. "Give us names and proof or you're a liar" more than one man screeched at me on Twitter. And again, that is not and has never been the rule.

What followed my former coworker's allegations that I had lied to make something sound good for the book was a Twitter storm of epic proportions. My core group of trolls, which has grown substantially since they initially found me in 2015, exploded all over my timeline. Such is the world of Twitter. If you fight back against false allegations, it only makes things worse. If you protest on your own behalf, it gets worse. If you do anything but try to go about your day like a normal person who is unaware of the firestorm around you, it gets worse. One of my online friends, a pro wrestler with a sizable following, publicly supported *Sidelined* on Instagram and Twitter. The mob came for him, too, which was especially bold of them given that he could literally kick these guys' asses into next week.

I spent days more or less unable to function. My Fitbit put my resting heart rate at over one hundred beats per minute. I barely slept for days, unable to relax my mind or body enough. If you've never felt deeply, mortally wronged and felt helpless to do anything about it, I highly recommend staying that way.

For the past couple of years, I've been envious of every woman I saw who was able to leave Twitter and maintain her career. The fantastic Lindy West is a model for leaving the hellscape of social media behind and becoming even more successful afterward. But how many of us are as talented as Lindy West? For those of us who crave a steady flow of information and interaction with like-minded people (especially in the midst of a global pandemic that sees us all isolated at home), it's incredibly difficult to stay away. As discussed at length in the outstanding documentary *The Social Dilemma*, social media has changed our brains, and going back feels impossible.

As much as I complain about Twitter (in a few short years I've gone from being a complete Twitter evangelist to begging everyone in my life to get as far away as possible from the platform), the deeper problem that stalks women wherever they go is that we are *still* punished for speaking out about how we are treated, both on the field and in the office. The backlash may not come in the form of being terminated. Instead, it comes in getting the cold shoulder from male colleagues who feel as if you've made them look bad. It may not come from your direct supervisor; it might, instead, come from the nameless faceless misogynists on Twitter. But it always comes in one form or another. For nearly every woman who speaks out on her own behalf, there's an accompanying story of abuse and harassment, and a toll on her mental health. The law can only protect us in so many ways; the backlash has become a legal, alternative way of silencing women.

I've tried to leave Twitter in the past, and taken multiple extended breaks, but it's never really stuck. I've felt too out of the loop when it comes to industry news, to world news, and even to the constant stream of in-jokes and low-stakes controversies drummed up on the site each day. But after this latest wave of harassment, something in me broke. I asked a few people, including my agent, Noah Ballard, for advice. Could I leave Twitter? If not forever, for a substantial period of time? Months? Half a year? And still be able to push my work out to my followers? Would everyone stop reading my writing? Would I lose the ability to market future work? Would I lose my voice?

In the end, it didn't matter. I'd recently returned to therapy to deal with the constant misogyny online and in the industry and talking through my feelings with my therapist made it clear that remaining in a space that was so damaging to me personally wasn't negotiable. I officially decided to leave the site while listening to the "Cancel Culture" episode of the podcast *You're Wrong About*. The episode touched upon the "cancellation" of YouTuber Natalie Wynn, who infamously said that she'd been sexually assaulted and canceled, and that being canceled was worse. It was a sentiment I unfortunately agreed with, though my experiences with online abuse pale in comparison to hers. I don't think I've been canceled, though there are certainly people who don't like me and say so loudly whenever they can. But I've been harassed to within an inch of my sanity. It has affected my mental health and therefore the lives of my husband and sons and my parents and siblings. Enough was enough. It was time. After all, if Simone Biles and Naomi Osaka can drop out of major international competitions to focus on their mental health, I can certainly log off Twitter.

As of the time of writing this note, I've been off Twitter for five days, which feels more like five months. I feel completely out of the loop when it comes to Twitter sports controversies. I feel out of touch when it comes to what's going on in the world minute by minute. I don't know who the unfortunate soul is today whose name tops the "Trending" sidebar. But as I slowly acclimate to life without the constant stream of information, each day it becomes more and more okay. I am sleeping again. My heart rate has come back down to its previous level, and then seven beats per minute lower than that. More important, I have time to do things like reading and writing and walking my dogs. Simple things that often felt more like chores due to the constant doom-scrolling I was doing at all hours of the day and night. Everything feels lighter, softer, more manageable. I can feel the desire to create slowly coming back.

So yeah, the last year has been a journey, one with more ups and downs than I could have imagined. And, without Twitter, I'm going to have to learn new ways to fight because, for so long, screaming into the void on Twitter *felt* like fighting for something. And in a small way, it was. But I'm no longer interested in small victories. It's time for *big* victories. Ones that matter. And no one is better at fighting the big fights than the women who surround me in this industry.

—October 2021, Chicago

SPORTS AREN'T JUST ABOUT SPORTS

n this introduction, I'm supposed to tell you why I wrote this book. So let's see. I wrote it, I think, because of all the things I felt I couldn't say working in sports media, and all the times other women have whispered things to me—important things—and sworn me to secrecy . . . and then checked in on me multiple times to make sure I kept my promise and didn't tell anyone.

I wrote it because there are only 240 characters in a tweet, and every time a troll rolls up on me, I have to weigh my mental health against the burning desire to tell him off, and because there are never enough characters in the world to say all the things I want to say. No one should have as many bad days as women who work in media do.

I wrote it because working in sports talk radio, in many ways, is like working in a frat house. But you can't say that, not publicly, unless you want everyone at work to be furious with you.

I wrote it for all the women in sports and sports media, as well as for all the women who work in male-dominated industries, who go to work every day and have to bite their tongues and swallow their cutting retorts to the men around them. Because, knowing what I know, they have every right to let those retorts fly.

I wrote it for the woman on Twitter who told me that I seem to see everything through the lens of sexual discrimination, because yes, that will happen when you work in an industry with almost no women that is, actually, rife with sexual discrimination. Sometimes you're a hammer and everything actually is a nail.

Mostly, though, I wrote it because I realized, somewhere around year two of my six years working in sports media, that whatever issues women have in society in general, they're amplified by a factor of about a million in sports. Women who work in the industry swim in a toxic stew of gender inequality. Often it seems as if no one cares.

As such, this is a book about sports that's not really about sports. It's about women. Sports is merely the lens through which we'll look at problems that permeate being a woman in the United States and likely everywhere else in the world.

We'll talk about Serena Williams crying at work, but we've all cried at work before, right? We'll talk about the history of sexual harassment at ESPN, but we'll do so knowing that the Worldwide Leader in Sports is far from the only corporation where gender harassment is said to be endemic. We'll talk about how men (and other women) contribute to a culture of white male supremacy, knowing that it's an issue in every industry in America and likely beyond.

Sports talk radio is a bizarre industry. It sounds like the best job in the world (and I'll give you this: it beats spending the morning trying to control your client in divorce court), but it's populated by some of the meanest and most miserable people (men) I've ever met. People who love radio really love radio, and I really did. But there's something about the off hours, the deluge of people calling or texting in to yell at you all the time, the backbiting competitiveness of it, that makes people hard and cynical and sometimes nasty.

It's also an industry where you can listen all day and never hear a woman's voice, maybe not even in commercials. When I fell assbackward into my first radio job after practicing law for more than ten years, I couldn't believe it had actually happened. I'd been raised on Chicago's WGN Radio during its golden years, listening to "Uncle Bobby" Collins on the way to school with my dad and catching the end of Spike O'Dell on my way home from soccer or gymnastics practice. I went into radio feeling like the luckiest woman on the planet, but I left feeling disillusioned and sad. And yet, I miss my microphone and my weeknight show terribly. I didn't want to leave the industry; I just wanted to industry to grow the fuck up.

Even though many radio stations have beat reporters on staff, it exists in a weird place where sales rule. As such, there's not much editorial freedom. The station can shut down a story just because they don't want to upset an important team or client. In a tough media climate with mass layoffs lurking around seemingly every corner, I found myself always looking over my shoulder and obsessing about making a mistake. Focused like a laser on not saying the wrong thing. And yet I always seemed to find the wrong thing to say. Those wrong things were nearly always social justice issues, talking about Colin Kaepernick or violence against women or racial injustice. Yet those were the things that made sports interesting to me: the interplay between political tensions in our society. But those same issues brought down a world of hurt on me, both online and in my career. There are so many obstacles for women in sports radio to navigate, but, by and large, we navigate them alone.

Radio is a sink-or-swim business, meaning there's no real formal training. Sure, you might do a bunch of score updates or work in the producer's booth, but there's really not much to prepare you for the first time you host a show, especially if you don't have a co-host. While I'm sure it's also a daunting task for men, there's a whole extra level of toxicity for women to learn to handle.

In some ways, the sports media industry shows us what America might look like if we'd never passed Title VII or the Equal Pay Act. If those who did the hiring were simply left to their own devices, relying on the old trope of hiring the best candidate, no matter what race, gender, or creed. Except, as in every other industry, the "best candidate" almost always turns out to be white and male. Sports talk radio is one of the least diverse fields in media (more on that later), and it's only getting worse.

Recently there's been a push in sports for men to disclose their salaries with their female colleagues (if they have any), in order for women to assess if they're being underpaid (we are) and by how much (a lot). I never had the guts to ask any of my male colleagues what they earned, but I made $25 an hour as an update anchor and got bumped up to $50 an hour when I began hosting my show. This is where you picture me swimming through piles of money like Scrooge McDuck. That might sound like a decent salary, but my show was only two hours every night. By the time I drove to the city (I got off at midnight), parked, and got a drink or snacks for the show, I was making around $75 a night. I can't prove it, but while I worked on an hourly basis with no benefits, I'm certain most of the male hosts at my station had multiyear contracts worth hundreds of thousands of dollars. It's not only the US Women's soccer team and the WNBA players fighting for equal pay for equal work.

When the global pandemic claimed my job, a group of women who had also been laid off by my employer reached out to me to share stories. That led to me talking to several attorneys, all of whom were appalled by the lack of women working full-time in radio at my station's parent corporation, Entercom. I was far from the only woman who had run smack into a brick wall, unable to rise above a part-time, after-hours show. I was advised to go to the Equal Employment Opportunity Commission (EEOC), but I decided not to. Going to the EEOC would have meant the start of a legal action, which likely would have ended with a settlement and a nondisclosure agreement. I couldn't risk having to sign an NDA when I had so much to say. So I agreed not to sue the company, took my paltry severance, and decided to work through my feelings in this book.

Though "stick to sports" is the current rallying cry to silence those who see sports as a means to achieving social justice, sports have always been a microcosm of society and a lens through which to view gender inequality. From gold medalist Aly Raisman to world champion Serena Williams to broadcasters Jessica Mendoza and Beth Mowins, women are waging battles for fairness on the field, in the booth, and in the stands.

Truth be told, there still aren't many places where women in sports can speak honestly about unfair treatment, sexual harassment, social justice issues, and the fight to make it in an industry still dominated (and controlled) by men. In fact, women in sports just aren't asked about these topics all that often, and, when the issues are raised, their responses are often taken out of context and presented in isolation. While every woman in the sports world has a different experience, many of their stories overlap and intersect in profound ways. It's time to take a holistic look at how the sports world treats women and how high-profile women in the industry are fighting to level the playing field.

As the world continues to struggle with the implications of unequal wages, violence against women, and the fallout of #MeToo, the world of sports, as always, is leading the charge in forcing Main Street, USA, to take a good, long look at how women are treated in today's society, on and off the field. During my time as a sports radio host and in my current career as a journalist, I've had a front-row seat to the sexism and misogyny that pervade amateur, college, and pro sports and the media that covers them.

I'm grateful to every single woman who talked to me for this book, some on the record, and some off. The truth is, many of the women who spoke to me did so knowing they'll suffer harassment or blowback from current and former colleagues. While I would never purport to speak for all women, this is the story of many women, as well as my own.

CHAPTER 1

BEHOLD: SMASHERS OF GLASS CEILINGS

Inside the Original Struggle over On-the-Ground Sports Reporting

loved pro sports growing up. The summer after my fourteenth birthday, I plastered every inch of my bedroom walls with posters and pictures of the Chicago Cubs, covering up the rainbow-and-doves wallpaper I had so lovingly picked out only a few years before. I spent Sundays in the fall with my friend Emily; we'd ooh and aah over which Chicago Bears players were the cutest, but also complain about how far the defense had fallen since Buddy Ryan left for the Philadelphia Eagles. And, of course, there was Michael Jordan, looming over all of it from a poster that took up the entire length of my door.

I don't know why sports journalism never seemed like a serious career path to me back then, but it probably didn't help that I didn't see many women doing it. Secretly, I used to practice calling play-by-play for the Cubs in my head (sometimes, I still do), but when it came time to decide what I wanted to study in college, I told people

I wanted to go into journalism, not sports journalism, or law, not sports law. I often wonder if that would have been different if I had grown up seeing as many women covering sports on TV as I do now.

The women I *did* see covering sports? Legends. I was fascinated by Melissa Isaacson covering the Bulls for the *Chicago Tribune*. I envied Lesley Visser on CBS TV, on the court after games, getting to talk to all our college basketball heroes. Cheryl Miller, one of my idols, got to cover the NBA and its players, not only as a broadcaster but as a peer. Miller, having led the USC Trojans to back-to-back NCAA championships and her USA teams to Olympic and International Basketball Federation (FIBA) gold medals, was already more accomplished than many of the NBA players she covered. By the time the WNBA was announced in 1996, Miller had already moved on to coaching, heading up the Phoenix Mercury for a few years. Miller never got to play in the NBA, but she continues to loom large as one of the greatest Americans, male or female, ever to play the game.

I'd always assumed the first group of women through the door got there because of their preexisting fame. Phyllis George, who smashed through the glass ceiling to work on *The NFL Today*, had been Miss America; her time in a very different kind of national spotlight gave her unique leverage as she built a career in TV. Cheryl Miller had ridiculous credentials: She was a college basketball giant, both in stature and in reputation. But there was a group of women I didn't know about because they took up the fight long before Barbies and stuffed animals fell away in favor of soccer balls and baseball mitts in my life. It didn't occur to me then how many "regular" women, who hadn't been superstar college athletes or pageant winners, had fought to make way for the rest of us. It was only later in life, when facing my own challenges as the only woman working at my radio station, that I began to delve into their stories.

It's tough to say who the first woman across the threshold into a pro sports locker room was, as several women were pushing for access in different sports in the mid-1970s. In 1975, Robin Herman, a twenty-three-year-old reporter for the *New York Times*, had been trying to get NHL teams to grant her access to locker rooms for a year, with no success. Back then, almost all sports reporters were men, and access to the players as soon as they came off the ice was important to every sportswriter. That's when they got the most genuine and emotional reactions from the guys who had just played the game.

Not that being *in* the locker rooms was always easy or fun. Sports are weird in that they are the only beat in which reporters are expected to interview subjects who are in various states of undress. And the rooms themselves are usually cramped, smelly, humid—definitely not the kind of place anyone would choose to hang out.

For women covering sports, going in the locker room was never about nudity. It was about that all-important access to the players. And, sometimes, also about basic human dignity. At Fenway Park in the 1970s, the women were not allowed to eat in the same area as the male sportswriters, even though they were doing the same job. In 2019, the Chicago Cubs were roundly criticized for putting up a historical press credential outside the press box, presumably to show how times had changed. The credential read NO WOMEN ADMITTED and had a picture of a pink poodle on it.

According to ESPN's excellent documentary on the first women in pro sports locker rooms, *Let Them Wear Towels*, it was during the 1975 NHL All-Star Game that everything changed. Before the game got underway, a reporter asked the two coaches at the pregame press conference if they were going to allow women into the locker room. The coaches looked at each other, shrugged, and said, "Sure, they can come in." So into the locker room went Robin Herman and her colleague Marcel St. Cyr.

Herman, formerly an assistant dean of research at Harvard's School of Public Health, wrote in a 1990 *New York Times* op-ed that, looking back, she was only allowed access that night because "responsibility was diffuse." The All-Star Game meant two coaches managing what wasn't *quite* an actual game with players they didn't usually coach. Herman believed that the coaches allowed them into the locker room "on a whim," maybe even a "dare." But that whim literally opened the door for women in sports writing.

As soon as the two women got into the room, Herman told ESPN, the cameras and microphones immediately swung in her direction, with someone yelling, "There's a girl in the locker room!" Though she insisted the game, not she, was the story, it was hard to convince her male colleagues that was the case. Said Herman, "The game was boring. A girl in the locker room was the story."

Of course, the response from some of the players was less than ideal. As Herman interviewed player Denis Potvin, another player yanked off Potvin's towel, leaving him completely exposed.

Still, Herman said later, "My post–locker room quotations showed patience and good cheer. I was twenty-three years old and fairly new to my job, and not yet beaten down by the abuse and slamming of doors that would follow this one-time opening."

Unfortunately, the All-Star Game didn't set the precedent Herman hoped it would. Owners and coaches in other cities continued to block locker room access to women, sometimes physically, sometimes using police. But once the barrier was broken, things started to change for women in sports.

At the same time that Herman—the only woman in the sports department at the *New York Times*—was breaking the NHL barrier,

Jane Gross was doing the same with NBA teams while covering the New York Nets. The daughter of a sportswriter, Gross admitted in *Let Them Wear Towels* that she likely got her job as the result of nepotism, but her timing was astute. In 1974, women filed a class action lawsuit against the *New York Times*, titled *Elizabeth Boylan et al. v. The New York Times*. It's well worth reading the whole story behind the lawsuit in Nan Robertson's excellent book *The Girls in the Balcony*. Robertson wrote:

> *There were forty women reporters to three hundred and eighty-five men reporters, and eleven of those women were in family/style. Of twenty-two national correspondents, not one was a woman. Of thirty-three foreign correspondents, only three were women. There was only one woman bureau chief, just appointed to Paris. In the Washington bureau, with thirty-five reporters, only three were women; the number had not gone up in nine years, although the staff had nearly doubled in that time. There were no women photographers. Of thirty-one critics in culture news, only four were women. Reviewers of drama, music, movies, television, and books were all male. The sports department had one woman and twenty-three men. There were no women on the editorial board, which had eleven members. There were no women columnists. Of the seventy-five copy editors on the daily paper, four were women. Almost all the lower-paying, lower-ranking jobs were confined to women.*

That suit was eventually settled in 1978, and the *Times* was forced to hire more women. Reading the writing on the wall, other newspapers began hiring women as well, and some of those women wanted to write about sports. Major League Baseball's obstinance aside, by the mid-1970s, newspapers were resigned to the fact that they had to hire women reporters across the board, and that led to the hiring of some of the true giants in the industry, women like Christine Brennan, Lesley Visser, Claire Smith, and Michele Himmelberg.

But back to the locker rooms. To this point, no one had challenged MLB to open up their locker rooms to women. Enter *Sports Illustrated*'s Melissa Ludtke. Melissa grew up in a family of five children, with a baseball-loving mother and college-football-loving father. In 1977, Ludtke was assigned by *Sports Illustrated* to cover the World Series between the New York Yankees and Los Angeles Dodgers. Concerned about having access to players immediately following the games, Ludtke had been slowly and quietly lobbying the players for access to the locker room in the World Series. She had secured permission from the Yankees, and then Dodgers pitcher Tommy John took Ludtke's case to the Dodgers' locker room on her behalf. John told Ludtke, "I'm not going to tell you it was unanimous, but we know you have a job to do, so come on in."

John, an affable guy who loved to tell stories, tended to minimize his role in helping women break through the literal barrier of the locker room door. When I asked him about Ludtke, he said, "I was a player rep for the Dodgers, and I was the union guy. We're in the World Series, and they came and said, 'Would you guys have a problem if Melissa Ludtke comes into the locker room?' My question to the people that asked it, I said, 'Is she licensed? Does she have credentials?' And they said, 'Oh yeah.' I said, 'Then why not?'"

John told me he took the case to his teammates, asking, "'You guys, would you have a problem if there is a female reporter in the locker room before and/or after the game?' and they said, 'No.' But then everybody was panicking in the Dodger front office: 'Oh, we've got to get cover-ups. We've got to get a wraparound for all you guys.' I told the general manager, and I told Peter O'Malley, 'Peter, I don't walk around in front of my teammates naked, so why would I do that with somebody I don't know?'"

I t's worth noting that, until this time, women sportswriters, typically made up of a grand total of one at any given game, were forced to wait in the hallway outside the locker room while their colleagues talked to players immediately following the game. The women had to request access to players, then wait for a team PR rep to bring the players out to speak to her, usually quite a long time after the player had spoken to male sports reporters. And after they had already told their story at least once to other reporters. As Betty Cuniberti, the first woman in the Dodgers' press box, said in *Let Them Wear Towels*, "Half the human race was shut out of this profession for no good reason." She went on to point out that, at the time women were trying to gain locker room access, there were no women in the US Senate and no women on the US Supreme Court. Any room with any kind of power at all was usually all men.

John, who played for the Dodgers off and on for six seasons, agreed that keeping women out of the locker room was nothing more than sexism. "People feel that baseball is a man's sport. No, it's not. It's a people sport," he told me.

Yankees manager Billy Martin had been allowing Ludtke to enter the locker room through a side entrance and sit on the couch in his office, which Ludtke later described as being like having a bleacher seat to what was going on at the players' lockers.

In *Let Them Wear Towels*, Ludtke said the 1977 Yankees locker room was filled with drama and large personalities, like Billy Martin, George Steinbrenner, and Reggie Jackson. The ongoing name-calling and war of words *was* the story in 1977. And all that was taking place in the locker room—making access to the players immediately postgame vital to covering the team. In a 2018 podcast interview, Ludtke told me other women had been in NHL and NBA locker rooms by 1976, saying, "Both professional hockey and professional basketball had very much moved further down the line, due to their commissioners pushing those leagues to provide equal access to women who were reporting on sports."

MLB commissioner Bowie Kuhn got word that Ludtke had been lobbying teams for access. Even though MLB hadn't been directly challenged on their locker room policies, it was clear they'd been thinking about how to handle it when they were.

To back up a second, Ludtke already had a relationship with the Yankees, and she'd been taking baby steps to slowly work on getting the same access to the players male sportswriters had. "I spent a lot of time around the Yankees and, by the end of the season, I had worked under the radar very, very closely with the PR people at the Yankees," she told me. "So the last two games of that year, 1977, the Yankees left me a clubhouse pass for the last two games. I had made enormous progress by taking a sort of gradual approach.

"So when we get to the '77 World Series and the Yankees are in it, I feel I'm all set with the Yankees, this is no longer an issue," Ludtke said. "I went over and wanted to make an effort with the Dodgers, because I had never covered them, to be sure they knew I might be coming into their locker room after [the game]. I had a pass that said I had access to the clubhouse. I was going above and beyond what I needed to do, but it's what I felt I should do, just prepare them and sort of get ready. So in doing that, the Dodgers ended up taking a team vote, a majority of them said, 'Listen, we understand she has a job to do, fine. We get it.' And that is what led to me being banned from the locker room."

The commissioner's office made a preemptive call to Ludtke, telling her they didn't care what the Yankees and Dodgers said, they controlled the locker rooms and she would not be allowed in post–World Series. Instead, she would wait in another area and players would be brought out to her after they had dressed—putting her at a huge disadvantage in covering the team. When she asked why the commissioner's office was making that decision, she was told the commissioner's office hadn't polled the players' wives about allowing women into the locker room and that the players' children would be ridiculed at school. Publicly, Commissioner Kuhn said that having women in the locker room was unfair to players, other reporters, and fans. Kuhn's office said only he could grant permission for Ludtke to enter the locker rooms, and since he hadn't granted it, she never had it.

And, just like that, Melissa Ludtke was shut out from the biggest sporting event of the year.

John blames Kuhn for blowing the entire thing out of proportion, telling me that having a woman in the locker room was never a big deal to the players. "Bowie Kuhn was a buffoon and an asshole, and I'm giving him the benefit of the doubt, seriously," he said. "He was so ill-equipped to take that job. The stuff that happened under his watch, it was horrible for baseball."

In Game 6 of the World Series that year, the Yankees' Reggie Jackson, who had been sparring with coaching and management all season, hit three home runs on three consecutive pitches. Ludtke stood in the hallway and watched as all her colleagues made their way into the locker room for the postgame reaction. For an hour and forty-five minutes, Ludtke waited for Jackson to be brought to her for an interview. When Jackson finally did emerge from the locker room, he was dressed. He told Ludtke, "Melissa, I'm exhausted, I'm going downtown. Sorry."

Ludtke's bosses at *Sports Illustrated* decided they weren't going to allow Kuhn's decision to stand. In 1977, they filed a lawsuit in federal court, under the title *Melissa Ludtke and Time Inc., Plaintiffs, v. Bowie Kuhn, Commissioner of MLB et al.* (Time Inc. was the parent company of *Sports Illustrated*.) There's great video in *Let Them Wear Towels* of a twenty-six-year-old Melissa Ludtke sitting with Howard Cosell and explaining why she needed access to locker rooms.

The decision came down on September 25, 1978, with the federal district finding that Kuhn's decision violated Ludtke's Fourteenth Amendment rights of equal protection and due process, including her right to pursue her profession. The court held that Ludtke had been treated differently from her colleagues based solely on her gender. That decision applied only to the New York Yankees and Yankee Stadium, but it put other MLB teams on notice that their policies had to change. When Peter Ueberroth took over as commissioner in 1984, he opened up MLB locker rooms to women across the board.

Though pro sports leagues were starting to mandate that women have locker room access, that didn't mean the players were on board. And while pro sports teams had to allow women into the locker rooms, they didn't control what happened once they got in there.

"It was baseball that made the decision that interviews took place in the locker room," Ludtke told me. "If they don't want anyone in the locker room, including the men reporters, that's okay with me. My lawsuit was about equal access. It wasn't about whether I got to go into the locker room or not. It was saying that whatever access they gave to the male reporters, they had to give that same access to the women reporters.

"It means how the men report the story is how the women report the story. So baseball had a tradition that the male reporters were in the locker room. That's where they went to interview the players. And so if you wanted to get the immediacy of responses, if you wanted to see what was happening between players on the team after the game is over, if you want to have exposure to that, you're in the locker room," Ludtke continued. "When most people pick up their newspaper or they see a broadcast, they don't know how that reporter has gotten the story. They don't really think much about how that happens."

Ludtke's point was that, for all those who accused her of wanting to see naked men, she wasn't allowed in the locker room before the game started, when the players were all fully dressed in their uniforms. If that were truly MLB's motivation, it was a simple fix, but one they declined to make. "The only way the male reporters wanted to play this story up and the way baseball wanted to play it was to sort of question my morality in wanting to be in a place where I might see a man who was naked. I was accused of wanting to leer at men's bodies. But there were no bodies to leer at in between batting practice and the game starting, so why wasn't I allowed in then? But that wouldn't have been as sexy of a story, and I wouldn't have been portrayed as sort of this wanton woman," Ludtke told me.

But as I said, once women made it into the locker rooms, pro sports pushed back by often making no effort to control what happened in those locker rooms.

While playing for the Detroit Tigers in 1990, pitcher Jack Morris infamously said to the *Detroit Free Press*'s Jennifer Frey, "I don't talk to people when I'm naked, especially women, unless they're on top of me or I'm on top of them." Before her death in 2016, Frey would tell friends of other run-ins with Morris, including the times he called her a bitch and the time Kirby Puckett allegedly had to keep him from physically attacking her in the Minnesota Twins locker room. After his baseball career ended, Morris went on to a broadcasting career and was elected to the Baseball Hall of Fame by the Modern Era Committee in 2018.

Lisa Saxon, who covered the then-California Angels for the *Los Angeles Daily News*, told Boston radio station WBUR, "Going in the locker room, knots would get in my stomach. It actually is a physically uncomfortable thing to do because you didn't know what you would face. And at the very least you would have jockstraps thrown at you and dirty undergarments. And that was an everyday occurrence, and then you would just build onto that what might happen. And you just hoped for the best when you went in."

The wonderful Claire Smith, the first woman in America to have an MLB beat (she covered the Yankees for the *Hartford Courant*) and the first woman writer and only the fourth African American writer to be inducted into the Baseball Hall of Fame, told a story in *Let Them Wear Towels* about standing in the hallway crying after being sworn at and physically pushed out of the San Diego Padres' locker room in 1984 while up against a deadline.

Smith told ESPN that being denied access was "humiliating," saying being barred from the locker room made it look and feel like she was trying to get into someplace she didn't have a right to be, which was obviously not the case. She also told a heartwarming story about first baseman Steve Garvey riding to her rescue—coming out into the hallway to give her the quotes she needed and vowing to stay as long as she needed him—as long as she stopped crying.

Utility player Dave Kingman dumped buckets of cold water over Jane Gross's head on two separate occasions in the locker room, and he once sent a rat in a corsage box to Susan Fornoff of the *Sacramento Bee*. The first woman sportswriter for the New York *Daily News*, Lawrie Mifflin, was called "a cunt" by NHL player Tiger Williams, who then picked her up and forcibly removed her from the locker room.

And things weren't any better for the women covering the NFL and college football. Lesley Visser, who began covering sports in 1974 and who was the first woman to ever have an NFL beat, recalled that one of her credentials said right on it that it was invalid if presented by a woman or child. San Francisco 49ers head coach Bill Walsh refused to allow women into the locker room and, when asked why, told Michele Himmelberg of the *Sacramento Bee* that she was "interfering with his season." Himmelberg also had to go to court in 1981 to get access to the 49ers' locker room.

Eventually, male newspaper editors backed their women reporters. And they began lobbying NFL and college teams to allow women the same access to players as the men had. Under pressure from the same papers that covered their team and gave them free advertising, the NFL was forced to give in.

Of course, once women were allowed into locker rooms in any given sport, columnists, cartoonists, and the general public had a field day at their expense, portraying them as shameless women who just wanted to get a look at some naked guys. In truth, though, women never asked to go into locker rooms—they simply asked to have the same access to players that their male colleagues did. It was the sports organizations themselves that decided postgame interviews should take place in the locker room, with lots of naked men roaming around.

If you think this issue was settled after these few turbulent years, think again. In 1990, Lisa Olson, who was covering the New England Patriots for the *Boston Herald*, went public about being harassed by Patriots players in the locker room. Olson was confronted by several naked players, one of whom said, "This is what you want. This is what you need. Want to take a bite out of this?" I'm leaving out the names of the players at Lisa's request—she doesn't want their reputations forever tarred because of that one bad day, in her words, which is more generous than I would be able to be in her shoes.

Olson sued the team, which earned her being called a "classic bitch" by Pats owner Victor Kiam. But Olson was vindicated when the players and team were fined by the league for their conduct. What followed for Olson were insults and death threats so severe, she wound up fleeing the country for Australia. She wasn't alone: many of the women at the forefront of this effort for equal workplace treatment were subjected to such poor treatment by coaches, players, and their colleagues that they went on to pursue other beats—leaving sports altogether.

USA Today's Christine Brennan, the first woman to cover Washington's NFL team in 1984, said in *Let Them Wear Towels* that women in locker rooms had to smile and laugh and be "a little bit deaf and a little bit blind." Stories persist to this day of players, some beloved by fans off the field, still engaging in harassing behavior toward women in the locker room. In the whisper network that exists among women sports reporters, everyone knows who those guys are, though the general public would probably be shocked at some of the names.

These issues still haven't really gone away, and women remain a minimal presence in locker room reporting. In 2015, Graham Watson, a writer for Yahoo! Sports, was barred from entering the Jacksonville Jaguars' locker room in Indianapolis by a male usher. And in 2017, Carolina Panthers quarterback Cam Newton pointed out in a press conference that he felt it was "funny" to hear a woman asking him a question about routes following an interaction with sportswriter Jourdan Rodrigue.

Bleacher Report's Mirin Fader, one of the best features writers alive today, told me, "Being one of the few—or only—women in the locker room is difficult. You're looked at sometimes like you shouldn't be there, like you don't belong. Sometimes there are remarks said out loud, but other times it's more covert. You can feel it."

The Athletic's Maggie Hendricks shares Fader's unease in some locker rooms. "It's incredibly intimidating, particularly in baseball . . . I tried to make myself invisible, which seemed to work because once the Dodgers' Joc Pederson almost hit me in the face with a water bottle he was throwing in the garbage. He wasn't throwing it at me; it was literally that he didn't see me. And the open clubhouse time is so long, and then you have to squeeze into the managers' office for his pregame. It's just a whole lot. Since there aren't many other women, there's no one to build any solidarity with."

One woman, who asked not to be identified, told me she was sent into an NFL team's locker room by her media outlet to ask players questions for a feature compilation. She said, "Basically, I had to ask at least twenty players questions off the record. [The team center] was right next to a player I was talking to. I focused on rookies because a lot of the older players were either pretending they didn't hear me, or were running out of the locker room, or whatever. [The center] had said no, which was fine. He was in just a towel, so I turned away from him. But then he stood next to me as I was asking another player questions, rubbing his junk with a towel. I just ignored him, but on the inside, I was terrified." Probably worth noting that there's another story about a particularly beloved NFL player shaking his genitals at a veteran female sportswriter. Football fans would be shocked to hear about this noted "great guy" harassing women in the locker room, but those of us covering the NFL have all heard the story.

I asked Ludtke if we'd made as much progress by 2021 as she would have thought after she won her lawsuit back in 1977. "Yeah, we can measure progress," she said. "We have women in the broadcast booth in a number of sports doing a fantastic job. And so that is enormous progress. We have any number of women, particularly at ESPN, behind the camera doing production, being sports producers. That is a major role to play."

Certainly, there are more women working in sports today than there were back in 1976. But how is it that fifty years after Robin Herman became the first woman on staff for the *Princetonian*, I was the only woman with a regular weekday show on my station, 670 The Score in Chicago? Chicago is so sports-mad that we have *two* full-time sports talk radio stations. When I lost my show (and my job) due to the COVID-19 pandemic in 2020, it meant there was not a single woman host on either station. During my call with the Chicago market manager (also a woman) who fired me, I asked her if she was comfortable removing the only woman left at the station. She got upset and told me she didn't take gender into consideration when making hiring and firing decisions. Maybe she should start.

"On the other hand," Ludtke told me, "the numbers [of women in sports media] are going down, not up, and staying small in terms of the number of women who are in sports departments doing sports journalism. I often say to people that I had it a lot easier than women do today. And by that I meant yeah, it wasn't fun being the target of a columnist and the people who were writing the things they were writing at the time. I was twenty-six years old, no one had ever known my name, and suddenly I was sort of this target and symbol of all these things the people hated about pushy women."

Forty-five years after Ludtke "pushed" her way into an MLB locker room, women forcing men to accept them in a space where we aren't welcome is still a major theme for women working in sports and sports media. In *Let Them Wear Towels*, *New York Post* sportswriter Maury Allen said he feared that the "impact of women in sports will diminish the joy of the sport." If my station's text line is any indication, that sentiment is still shared widely by male sports fans.

"I took the hits for [being in the locker room]" Ludtke continued, "but none of the hits were anything like what you all face today. And the major difference is that the columnists had to have their byline on it and they often had their picture at the top, which had a certain constraint on the characterizations they made of me and the words they used. [Women working in sports today] face a lot more today than I ever did. It absolutely floors me that because women state an opinion about sports, they become targets and sexual objects. What is it about sports that turns people into these monsters that use the kind of language they do and issue death threats?"

So we find ourselves more than forty years after the first group of women sportswriters made their way into locker rooms and maybe not all that much has changed. There are more women working in sports, but not nearly as many as there should be after forty years of progress. Women still feel uncomfortable in locker rooms. And oh, by the way, women are still struggling to be taken seriously.

A few years ago, I sat on a panel with one of the old-guard female sportswriters. When a young woman asked her for advice on how to handle herself in a locker room, she told her to carry felt-tip pens because they still worked when you hold your notepad in front of your eyes. I suppose this advice is practical, but it's also pretty cynical. Forty years on, should women still have to deal with players intentionally trying to make them uncomfortable with their nudity? For that matter: Why, in the name of all that's holy, are we even still *doing* interviews in locker rooms? It seems like something that should have gone out of style with smoking in the dugout and driving relievers in on golf carts. Can we really do no better than this?

In the forty years since the first women smashed through the glass door and into pro sports locker rooms, it feels like we should be further along. I meet a lot of young women who aspire to work in sports when I speak at colleges and universities. Like me, they undoubtedly look up to the women they see on their TVs (or, more likely in 2021, on their phones). All too often, they tell me that the fear of being bullied, online or in locker rooms, is funneling them off into sports-adjacent careers, like PR or social media managements, rather than into reporting. God knows there were plenty of times on the air, watching intentionally nasty texts flood my computer screen while my producers tried to stem the tide of sexism on the phone lines, that I asked myself, "Why am I even here? This is never going to get any better. I should do something else." There were plenty of times when I felt lonely.

I often wonder what kind of mental toll it takes on those of us who are the sole women in workplaces full of males. I asked Nicole Bedera, who studies gender equality at the University of Michigan. "When men are in almost exclusively female spaces, there is something called the 'glass escalator' effect. They are valued more highly than the women around them, and that benefits them. They get more promotions and power until they are seen in their rightful place at the top of the hierarchy," she said. Women, it turns out, don't get the same benefit for being in the minority, according to Bedera. "Instead, researchers have found that they have to act like men to fit in. This can make the moments where their gender is undeniable especially painful—moments of sexual harassment or sexual violence included. It can also make it harder for them to seek out the services they need when they are wrapped up in needing to be as tough as the other men and twice as put together and independent."

When I did a podcast back in 2018 on the first women in pro sports locker rooms, I was lucky enough to get to talk to some of the women who, like Ludtke, fought their way through to make it easier on the next generation. Their stories give me hope, but, more than that, they give me strength. More than once, I've been on the verge of tears over some casual remark by some caveman in the industry, only to hear Melissa Ludtke telling me her story, Claire Smith talking about crying outside a locker room, or Lisa Olson describing what it feels like to be chased out of the country by a Neanderthal team owner and his rabid fan base.

That's when I bite back the tears, draw myself up, square my shoulders, and get ready to fight back. For the women coming behind me.

CHAPTER 2

WOMEN CALLING THE SHOTS

Power and Pushback on Women's Voices

When I broke into sports talk radio at the age of forty, I had no idea I'd spend so much time worrying about the sound of my voice. After a career as a lawyer and as a writer for outlets like *Sports Illustrated*'s The Cauldron, and the *Chicago Tribune*'s *RedEye*, I had long since learned to speak with confidence, and I knew my stuff. It hadn't crossed my mind that my voice would hold me back.

Of course I knew I'd have to warm it up before shows, enunciate, and, like Veronica Corningstone—Ron Burgundy's coanchor in the movie *Anchorman*—work on my nonregional diction. But I'd long since given up the put-on, little-girl voice so many of my friends and I used in our twenties. By 2014, I had finally managed to lose the vocal fry and uptalking that followed—though I arguably shouldn't have had to do so. If you still roll your eyes at the way young women talk, you really should check out Amanda Montell's book *Wordslut*, which explores how women use language (including all those "likes" and vocal fry), to build community and put their listeners at ease. Montell makes a great case for ending the policing of women's voices, and reading it made me regret all the times I suggested that women should "sound more authoritative." In other words, sound more like men.

But back to my voice. Deeper than some, sometimes a little scratchy, but rich and full, with a hint of West Side Chicago that I blame on my dad. When I started working in sports radio, I was comfortable just sounding like me. Speaking too quickly has always been a problem for me, and I still squeak a little when I get excited, but other than working on slowing down and enunciating, I was happy with how I sounded; I actually *liked* my voice.

But there was a significant group of people who did not like my talk radio voice and weren't shy about letting me know: male sports fans.

During my first few weeks on the air, I would spend my time between top- and bottom-of-the-hour scores and news updates watching the comments roll in to the station's text line.

Shrill!
Annoying!
Sounds like my wife nagging me!

One brutally honest texter even wrote: *I tune in to sports radio to get AWAY from women. Why do I have to listen to one telling me scores?*

Whenever I hear men say something like this, and believe me, I've heard it quite a bit, I wonder what their relationships are like with the women in their lives. Because I'm guessing they're not all that healthy. I've had plenty of days when I'm sick of men (and white men in particular), but I don't take it out on Anderson Cooper just because he happens to be between me and the day's news. I'm not sure where men got the idea that sports is solely their domain, but it's as antiquated an idea as men going to college while women go to finishing school. We won the "should women do a sports?" argument back in the 1970s: We're here to stay. Get on board or get bent.

At first, I was devastated and became increasingly insecure about the way I sounded. I spent hours at home reading text out loud to myself, trying to sound like someone else. My voice role model was Sigourney Weaver, who has a voice so soothing and lovely she was chosen to narrate the original episodes of *Planet Earth* for Discovery Channel. Eventually, I got to a place where I could do a pretty good impression of her, as long as I was reading text that I didn't care about. But as soon as I got back into the studio and the mic was on, I went right back to sounding like myself, no matter how much I concentrated on lowering my register or rounding out my vowels. (It's easier to sound like Sigourney when reading about the mating habits of seals than when speaking extemporaneously about why the Cubs need to move Javier Báez up in the batting order.)

As my first year in radio went on, male listeners continued to complain about my voice, and I continued to go home each day and practice sounding like Sigourney. I tortured myself by relistening to my worst moments on the radio over and over again, beating myself up for sounding like, well, me. I had started to make stupid mistakes, mispronouncing names or inverting scores. The excessive scrutiny—both from fans and from my own internal monologue—

made me even more nervous for each and every update, which came through in my voice.

I began dreading going to work. Who wants to go to a place every day where you have to listen to strangers tell you how much you suck? And what if you start to believe it?

I tried to take the criticism constructively, but it was hard to figure out exactly what was so objectionable about my voice. According to my amateur vocal coaches on the text line and social media, it was simultaneously too high, too low, too shrill, too girly, too raspy, and, my favorite, "too sexy."

Even when I asked men who complained about my voice on social media to pinpoint the problem, they could only describe it as "irritating" or "annoying." They struggled to identify anything specific. The only time I got regular compliments on how I sounded was when I returned to work after a bout with bronchitis and sounded like a cross between Lauren Bacall and Kathleen Turner. But unfortunately, I recovered after a few days.

As one does these days, I looked to the internet for advice. Just what was it that I was doing that was alienating so many male listeners? What could I do to get out of my own head, shake off my nerves, and find a voice that people would want to hear?

It didn't take long before I realized I wasn't alone in having men insult my voice. As I looked around, I began to notice that every time a woman was involved in a breakout role in broadcasting sports, men online would immediately start piling on complaints about the sound of her voice. Whether it was longtime sports reporter Erin Andrews on the sideline for FOX's NFL coverage, Jessica Mendoza in the booth for *Sunday Night Baseball*, Beth Mowins doing play-by-play for *Monday Night Football*, or Doris Burke calling the NBA on ESPN, the nasty, unrelenting insults about their voices were the same as the texts about my voice. It didn't matter that none of us sound even remotely alike.

It wasn't that the women working in sports broadcasting have annoying voices. In fact, there are so many barriers for women getting into the upper echelon of sports broadcasting that no one with a truly terrible voice could come within shouting distance of a broadcast booth in her career. No, what men were complaining about was something much more intractable about our voices.

They were complaining that we sounded like women.

By now, I bet you can guess why men lose their shit when they hear a woman making sports words with her mouth. Sports media is one of the last remaining industries where men outnumber women significantly. In the workplace (and, not surprisingly on sports talk radio), men still think it's acceptable to insult another man by comparing him to a woman, and it's where, for a certain generation of men, it's still a surprise to see a woman pop up from time to time, even in very tiny numbers, even in a very limited number of roles.

Still, while women in sports media broadcasting are vastly outnumbered, our presence is hardly a new phenomenon. Suzyn Waldman has been doing color commentary for the New York Yankees on the radio since 2005. Michele Smith was in the TBS booth for an Atlanta Braves–Los Angeles Dodgers game back in 2012. The first woman to call an NFL game was Gayle Sierens, who did TV play-by-play for the Seattle Seahawks–Kansas City Chiefs game back in 1987. The next woman to walk through the door that Sierens kicked down? It was Beth Mowins, thirty years later. For those counting at home, that was in *2017*. How many other industries have three decades in between the first and second women to perform the same job? And yet the fact that women, for thirty years, did not call football games on national TV was simply accepted by athletes, fans, and broadcasters. In the year of our lord 2018, sports media continued to be one of the last holdout industries, a place where diversity was neither valued nor sought.

"I think it's partially comfort," Jessica Mendoza told me when I asked her about the criticism she's received. Mendoza, a former Olympic softball player, had recently signed a multiyear deal with ESPN, making her the lone female color commentator on *Sunday Night Baseball* (until she was replaced heading into the 2020 season) alongside Alex Rodriguez, Matt Vasgersian, and Buster Olney. "I heard [legendary Dodgers announcer] Vin Scully forever because I grew up in LA, and there's something to the sport that has a specific voice, and that's across all sports. It has to be this deep, very manly voice, but also soft enough that it's easy to listen," she said.

"Having a female voice, being more high-pitched, it's just harder to digest when [the fans] haven't heard it a ton, I'm guessing," Mendoza said. "But I've never heard a female voice and stopped and gone, 'Ewww!' For every man—and woman—who says, 'I can't handle a woman's voice,' there are men and women who stop and go, 'Oh my gosh, this is really freaking cool!'

"I think the day when no one stops is the day we're all looking for."

Mowins said that she, too, is looking forward to the day when the sound of women's voices is unremarkable and less important than how they cover a game. "For some guys, for whatever reason, I think a lot has to do with whether or not you grew up with women in your life. You just don't hear a woman's voice. I used to hear a lot,

'Well, it's not authoritative.' I just had to kind of win people over," Mowins said. "'Hey, give me a chance, listen to the content as much as the quality and the sound of it.' And I have to try and win people over that way."

If Hollywood had wanted to set the movie *Anchorman* in contemporary times, all they would have had to do to make it believable was place Veronica in a sports media outlet. And unfortunately for us Veronicas, the backlash doesn't come just from the meatballs sitting on the couch at home furiously tapping into their smartphones. It also comes from within the industry.

Women in sports learn quickly that men will allow us into their little corner of the world as long as we play by their rules. The rules are extensive and constantly changing, but they generally encompass being physically attractive, wearing what men think you should wear, sticking to the roles men think you should have (sideline reporter, panel "moderator," social media expert). Roles that, you know, require women to regurgitate facts or repeat what a man has told them. Roles that don't necessarily require any input from the women themselves. The unspoken rules mandate that women should never be the centerpiece of a sports broadcast, should not be outspoken or controversial in any way, should not be too big a part of the broadcast, and should not challenge the way things are and have always been. Abide by the rules and you can stay.

One need look no further than former FOX Sports Radio host Mike North, and Atlanta sports radio host Mike Bell, who felt the need to weigh in on Jessica Mendoza's first appearance on *Sunday Night Baseball*—and the first time any woman had taken that seat on the show. Bell, who, like many men working in sports, has a Twitter avatar in which he resembles a thumb, tweeted out: "yes tell us Tits McGhee when you're up there hitting the softball you see a lot of 95 mile an hour cutters?"

Mike North, who once worked at my old radio station and is best known for calling a Korean Cubs pitcher "a Chinaman" and the fact that he was a hot dog vendor before landing his own radio show (tell me again how women aren't qualified to talk about sports?), said on FOX Sports Radio, "ESPN's Jessica Mendoza is the worst. If she were a man, she'd already be fired by now." FOX Sports Radio pushed out North's comment via tweet, then deleted the tweet quickly after the righteous backlash bubbled up. In case you're wondering, North looks exactly like you think he would.

In an interview with ABC News, Mendoza said she had no doubt that Bell—an adult male who wears a sports jersey to work at a desk—had come after her because she was a woman. Bell was ultimately suspended. He later apologized for his flaming-hot take, and Mendoza graciously accepted.

North, too, quickly walked back his comments in the manner he's become accustomed to.

After Beth Mowins's debut on *Monday Night Football* was subjected to the same complaints about the sound of her voice, veteran NFL reporter Andrea Kremer told me she wasn't surprised about the backlash these women received.

"I have no doubt that 'hating the sound of her voice' is code for 'I hate that there was a woman announcing football,'" Kremer said. "Remember, as women in high-profile sports broadcasting jobs, we get criticized from head—and hair!—to toe. We are in a most subjective business, but the haters are always going to find something they don't like about us because they don't want us there."

Feminist author and Fulbright Scholar Rebecca Martínez, who researches women's and gender studies at UC Irvine, calls bullshit on the idea that dragging women's voices isn't rooted in misogyny: "The negative online reaction to Mowins's play-by-play calling football games is steeped in sexism," she said. "The comments, mostly from men, have focused on her voice being annoying to the point of not wanting to listen to her. They'll focus on the naturally higher pitch of women's voices and 'shrillness,' all the while claiming their critiques of higher pitch have nothing to do with sexism. Women who have high visibility, particularly in settings that are traditionally male, will experience backlash."

All this probably sounds familiar to any woman who works or even just spends time in male-dominated spaces. Following Mowins's *Monday Night Football* debut, I wrote a piece for the *New York Times* on women in sports broadcasting and the criticism their voices get. I filed the piece and promptly forgot about it until it ran as the main story on the front page of the sports section a few days later. I was thrilled it resonated with so many women, but the real shock came later that night, when a friend texted me. She was at an event at the 92nd Street Y in New York, and Hillary Clinton mentioned my piece in her speech.

Apparently, Hills was used to having her voice criticized, too.

I've talked to a lot of women over the years about why it's so difficult for more of us to get into the broadcasting booth. It's not a question of talent or even merit. We've seen a number of sons and grandsons of famous broadcasters rocket right to the top of the profession with relatively little experience. FOX Sports broadcaster

Joe Buck, son of the legendary St. Louis Cardinals announcer Jack Buck, even called his autobiography *Lucky Bastard* as a direct reference to his heir apparent status.

We all get by now that it isn't *really* about any objective quality of voice, either. I mean, there are men infamous for terrible broadcasting voices. Howard Cosell, one of the most famous and successful sportscasters of all time, was imitated not for his breadth of knowledge or wonderful content but for his truly terrible voice.

And it's not a function of personal experience on the field or the court. Some of our most cherished broadcasters, men like Vin Scully, Harry Caray, Bob Costas, and Al Michaels, never played the sports they called, even at the college level.

Rather, what seems to be stopping women cold from getting into the broadcast booth is the men doing the hiring, plain and simple. With few exceptions, those who have the power to put more women onto national broadcasts are men. And almost always older white men. While I was in environments with a lot of diversity in my time as a lawyer, actual, meaningful diversity doesn't seem to be a major concern to many sports media outlets.

Think of the teams you see on national sports broadcasts: largely a white man doing play-by-play, perhaps a Black man doing commentary (usually a former athlete), and the women are relegated to the sidelines or back in the studio. It's a formula that has served sports media well: any deviation from the formula is a risk, and when one's job is to maximize the amount of money coming in, risk is, literally, a four-letter word.

As one coworker told me, "Bosses hire what they know. And what white male bosses know is white males."

Amy Lawrence, the host of *After Hours with Amy Lawrence* on CBS Sports Radio, is one of a handful of women to rise to the level of hosting a national sports talk radio show. And still, despite the years of experience Amy has honing her skills and beating out lesser men for jobs, she deals with constant complaints about her manner.

"I battle an inherent double standard on a nightly basis with callers to my show. It's a no-win situation for a female host whose audience is at least eighty-five percent male," Amy told me. "When a caller expresses a view or opinion that deviates from my own, I listen long enough to get the gist and then typically lay out the reasons why I see things differently. I rarely ever yell or get heated, hardly ever raise my voice; yet I still get lambasted on social media for being 'arrogant,' 'rude,' 'mean,' and 'abrasive.'" Pretty funny, considering how many men in sports talk radio have a reputation for yelling back at their listeners. And yet it's not funny at all.

All the women in the industry I've spoken with believe the same thing: there won't be more women in sportscasting until more women are doing the hiring and firing. To a woman, listening to another woman call a football game doesn't seem like such a risk.

And whether or not a certain faction of male sports fans wants to hear it, women make up at least a third of the fan base in every single pro sport, and they are inching closer to 50 percent with every passing season. The NFL, for example, has experienced a growth in the fan base over the last few years only because of female fans, who now comprise a whopping 47 percent of NFL viewers, according to the league themselves. Miraculously, women have come to football, despite the NFL's fixation on machismo, playing through head injuries, barely caring about domestic violence, and a weird obsession with a CGI robot named "Cleatus." In any other industry, marketing would grab on to a new demographic like grim death and do everything possible to exploit it. But in sports, the existence of millions of female fans rarely ever even

merits soliciting women's opinions, let alone putting them anywhere near the spotlight.

There will always be men who complain about women invading
their space. That narrative has been around ever since the Little
Rascals wouldn't let Darla into their clubhouse. And it probably
isn't going away anytime soon. But the goal has to be getting more
young women in the broadcasting pipeline along with their male
counterparts so they can someday replace the Doris Burkes, Andrea
Kremers, and Jessica Mendozas who are leading the way for female
broadcasters.

And there may still be hope for women who dream of calling
pro or college sports on a national platform without waiting for the
next generation to take over programming, though. And it's via the
route that allowed women to get a foothold in all major media outlets: opportunity. Every woman who told me about her journey to
the booth mentioned at least one person who believed in her and
pushed her forward, even if she didn't feel she was 100 percent
ready. After all, men are given the chance to learn and grow in the
booth all the time, as anyone who listened to Jason Witten on *Monday Night Football* can attest.

Whatever the reason for the constant complaints about women
in the broadcast booth from fans and men in the industry, women
are making their way there from the sidelines. On September 27,
2018, Andrea Kremer and Hannah Storm became the first all-
women broadcasting team to call an NFL game. The alternative
broadcast, which was audio only, didn't get nearly the marketing
launch it deserved, and Amazon Prime, which hosted the feed,
made it incredibly difficult for fans to find their broadcast. But despite the early missteps, Kremer and Storm struck a chord among

fans, especially women. Marie Donoghue, vice president of Global Sports Video for Amazon, told *Variety* that customer feedback was so positive after their first season, they brought the women back for 2019.

In 2018, Jenny Cavnar became the first woman since 1993 to call play-by-play for an MLB game during a prime-time matchup between the Colorado Rockies and the San Diego Padres. And in 2018, Katy Winge became the first woman to hold the role of analyst for Altitude TV, which carries Denver Nuggets games, at the age of just twenty-five. Emma Tiedemann is the first female play-by-play broadcaster in the South Atlantic League, where she's the voice of the Lexington Legends, the Class A affiliate of the Kansas City Royals. Brooke Weisbrod regularly does color for ESPN broadcasts of men's college games.

With so many new and expansive ways to find and grow talent, there's no reason the sports media shouldn't accurately reflect the sports fan base. If the broadcast is successful and finds an audience, perhaps some of these new, nontraditional outlets will continue to expand and feature women broadcasters. Perhaps we'll get an all-women MLB or NBA broadcast. Eventually, those numbers will get big enough to boost women onto the mainstream media stage.

I'm asked all the time if I think more women will enter sports broadcasting in the years to come. I would love to believe so. After all, three generations of women have now grown up post–Title IX, with access to playing sports in ways their grandmothers couldn't have dreamed of. At the same time, twenty-four-hour sports stations on TV and radio have become ubiquitous. Regardless of the path it takes, the good news for the next future of women in sports media is that many women who have succeeded on the sidelines and in the broadcast booth feel an obligation to kick down doors for the next generation.

"I feel a responsibility [to women]," Mendoza said when we spoke. "It can also come in the form of a lot of pressure. I probably didn't sleep the first year of *Sunday Night Baseball*. I was just a mess with exactly that: I can't mess up. I have to study, and study, and study. And then to be honest, I wouldn't speak, a lot of times, until I knew, *Okay, I'm not going to screw this up*. So, I'm going to talk. Because I know this isn't just about me."

Veteran NFL sideline reporter Laura Okmin, who holds coveted roles for both NFL on FOX and Westwood One radio, created GALvanize, an organization that helps teach young women the skills they need to succeed in sports media. Through her regional boot camps, Okmin has trained hundreds of young women in the art of covering the NFL. ESPN's LaChina Robinson has a similar program for women called Rising Media Stars.

But perhaps the quickest and most effective way to get more women into the broadcast booth is for female fans to demand representation in the sports they love from the networks that bring them into our homes. Given the incredible diversity of pro sports fan bases across the board, there are zero reasons for us to continue to be subjected to two white men in a broadcast booth in perpetuity. Recently at a fan convention, I witnessed a young girl, no more than eight, stand up in front of a room full of adults and demand that Cubs president Theo Epstein explain why there weren't more women working in baseball. Let's all be that eight-year-old girl.

It's important for fans to be effusive and vocal in their support for women who have made it into the booth, letting teams and media outlets know that not only do they like hearing women broadcasters calling sports, they want to hear *more* of them. Remember, many of the people making the decisions to have women calling games view it as an experiment. Tell them their experiment is working. Programming directors and powers that be love hearing how much fans enjoy their talent. Tweeting, emailing, and sending Facebook messages to media outlets, and specifically to those in charge of choosing which broadcasters fans get to hear, matters, especially for local flagship stations that are constantly looking for new ways to bring in an audience. Fans can also support women in the booth by amplifying their platform on social media. When Andrea Kremer and Hannah Storm announce their next season calling NFL games on a streaming platform, fans should share that news and help it reach a wider audience.

But even more importantly, fans can help women in the booth by watching and listening when they're on air. When it comes to TV and radio, ratings are the name of the game. Make it a point to turn on your TV when Beth Mowins is calling an NFL game, even if you're busy with something else in the background. Set a reminder to check out Jessica Mendoza or Jenny Cavnar calling an MLB game. Look up which NBA games Doris Burke is calling and watch them. If possible, have them on while your sons and daughters are around. Help make women in the broadcasting booth a humdrum, everyday occurrence.

In her interview with Kremer on *Real Sports*, Doris Burke was almost optimistic about the backlash against women's voices. "I could tell you of people, men, who have come up to me and said, 'When I first heard you, I'm thinking, *What is she doing there?* But then I listened. And you're okay.'"

With any luck (or, let's be real, with a lot of work), boys and men won't learn to question women's voices at all. I remember watching Beth Mowins's *Monday Night Football* debut with my sons, who were fifteen and sixteen at the time. I turned on the game, sat back on the couch, and waited for them to notice that a woman was calling the game.

They never did.

CHAPTER 3

NOW, FROM THE SIDELINES

The Fight for Respect in Sports Reporting

never wanted to be an update anchor. Not really. Update anchors mostly sit quietly in a remote studio, waiting for the top and bottom of the hour, at which point they have something like ninety seconds to tell listeners the most up-to-date scores and news for that hour. Sometimes the hosts talk to you for a few minutes, sometimes they don't. In my first job in radio, I had an open mic during the show, meaning I could jump into conversations with the hosts whenever I wanted, and the hosts were great and welcoming about me tossing in my two cents on whatever they were talking about. Other shows I worked on wanted me to do my updates and sit quietly until it was time for my ninety seconds again.

The thing I hated most about updates, though, is that there was little room for me to inject any thoughts or feelings or analysis. In ninety seconds, you can do a couple of scores and a couple of headlines. That's it. What I hated more about updates was that, when it came to sports talk radio, this was a job that seemed to be reserved for women. At the first sports station I worked at, they hired three women at the same time. Amazing, right? Except we were all up-date anchors. They hired ten men at the same time, all as hosts, some of whom had never had a significant on-air role before. At my second radio job, I replaced the previous update anchor, also a woman, when she left for greener pastures. Update anchor was the job women were allowed to have. And, obviously, you couldn't have more than one woman on air at any given time! How ridiculous of you to suggest otherwise.

The longer I sat in the update studio, the more I listened to the men who had been anointed as the chosen "hosts," the more I came to resent the position. All day, I listened to men hold court on topics I knew just as much about as they did—and some that I knew more about, like the law and the dynamics of violence against women. One host used to routinely swing by the update studio before his show, ask my opinion on a topic, then parrot exactly what I had told him as if he'd come up with it all on his own. I'll never forget sitting there silently, clenching my teeth, while four men weighed in on the likelihood of Peyton Manning having sexually harassed a trainer while at the University of Tennessee, or whether a woman would lie about being sexually assaulted by Derrick Rose, without seeking input from a single woman, especially not the one sitting fifteen feet away in front of a microphone. In sports radio, be-ing loud and confident in your opinion is often confused with being good at your job. If you're a man, that is.

The climb from update anchor to host was a long slog, and one that I was lucky to have made at all. In fact, if our station hadn't eliminated score updates altogether, I'd likely still be stuck behind the update anchor desk. The update anchor job, or other iterations of the same role, are usually sold to women as something we have to go through to hone our "on-air presence," build an audience, and work on our radio voice. But I couldn't help but notice that there were plenty of men in the industry who were allowed to skip this step, jumping from behind-the-scenes roles to on-air positions without having to put in any time behind the anchor desk. When I used to complain about the limits of my job, one of my friends often told me: "A million women would love to have your job." It wasn't lost on me that he didn't say "a million men" would love to have my job.

Even the men who *did* have my job went about it differently. They didn't hesitate to prolong their ninety seconds bantering with the hosts, or to jump in with their thoughts before someone cut their mic. Even when I had my own show, I once had a rookie producer cut me off midsentence to bring up a completely different topic.

One of the side effects of being the only woman in a male-dominated workplace is that you start to adopt the "I'm just lucky to be here" attitude. I felt that keenly. A million women probably *would* have loved to have my job. So I tried my best to keep my updates to ninety seconds, follow all the rules, not overstep my place, not show up the hosts. In an industry where so many men distinguish themselves by not following the rules, I held on to them for dear life. As I got more confidence in my on-air persona, I got bolder about telling producers to turn on my microphone because I wanted to jump in with a comment. But even then, I tried to limit how often I weighed in. I was told enough times in grade school that nobody likes a know-it-all.

To be fair, spending time as an update anchor *was* how I got my foot in the door in radio, how listeners became familiar with my voice, and it forced me to spend countless hours listening to more established hosts so that, when I finally got my own chance to host, I had some idea of what to do. But it was never my ultimate goal. I was lucky in that Amy Lawrence, a national host on CBS Sports

Radio, had already smashed through the glass ceiling of a woman hosting her own show. Amy had befriended me, and we spent countless hours commiserating about the industry. Because of Amy, I knew a woman could host a successful show. And that was what I wanted for myself.

But let's be honest, there aren't a ton of women hosting their own sports shows in any medium. And when it comes to live sports, too many women are foisted off on the sidelines. You often see sideline reporters—who, by the way, hustle their asses off as much as anyone else covering the game—when there's a lull in the action and the guys in the booth throw to the (always pretty) woman in a winter coat standing on the field. Or a sideline reporter might catch a coach headed to the locker room for a quick comment before halftime. Or after a game, where you see a lone woman fighting through a mass of testosterone-laden humanity to get to the coach or star quarterback. Sideline reporting is a hard job and a necessary job. It just shouldn't be the only job for women.

The tragedy is that many young women entering the field aspire for that limited role.

Don't get me wrong. Women like Andrea Kremer, Pam Oliver, and Laura Okmin have elevated sideline reporting to an art form, getting information to viewers by the sheer force of their reporting chops and the respect they command from the coaches and players they cover. Kremer has branched out to doing color commentary to Hannah Storm's play-by-play on Amazon's *Thursday Night Football* in addition to her duties as a correspondent for HBO's *Real Sports*. Oliver is often tasked with in-depth interviews with players that air before or during games. And Okmin, in addition to being one of the most prolific sideline reporters in history, has dedicated her limited free time to advancing other women in the sport she loves.

No one knows better than Okmin the rigors of being a successful sideline reporter in the NFL. Even so, she bristles at so many women entering sports media aspiring to the same role. "Most women don't even know about other positions. All they know is 'when I think about women in sports, I think about them on the sideline.' I'm in no way criticizing the role; I've been very blessed by it for a very long time. And I get so much out of it. But before last year, I would have said I know my ceiling in sports. We all see it. Now that's changing. Now I see, okay, can you go into coaching? Can you go into being an executive in the building?" And while Okmin loves the view from the sidelines, she wants to make sure younger women understand their value.

"I want women to understand that, at the end of a Sunday, I've worked just as hard as any of my teammates. I've been in every meeting. I've had every conversation with every player and every coach that my play-by-play guys and my analyst have had. And yet they get three-plus hours to talk about it and I get a minute and a half. That can really make you question your value, and it can really make you question your work."

It's a point I understand only too well. When you sit around and argue sports with your friends, no one argues about who has the better facts. You argue about who has the better opinion. Whose take is right. Whose take is horrible. And the most limiting thing about being an update anchor or a sideline reporter is that, at the end of the day, you're being trusted to report the facts, but not being trusted to give your opinion on what those facts mean. And, ultimately, a lot of what women in sports media want to do is the same thing that men entering the field want to do: we want to talk about what those facts mean.

"I don't judge myself by how much time I get," Okmin said, "but I did when I was younger. And I want women to understand that the sideline reporter is a side of mashed potatoes. And it's awesome. I love mashed potatoes, and I love filling up on them. I love to eat mashed potatoes, but it's not my filet mignon. It's not what's sustained me for nearly thirty years in the business. I've had to work on a lot of other things to feel fulfilled, to feel my value. If you look at Pam and you look at Erin Andrews and you look at Lisa Salters, you will see that we define ourselves by a whole lot more than being a sideline reporter."

One of the great ironies of throwing women new to the industry into sideline reporter roles is that it's one of the toughest jobs in sports to do well. As part of her GALvanize boot camps, Okmin tries to prepare young women for everything the job throws at them. "I started seeing all of these young woman get put into positions where I was like, 'Thank God I wasn't put into that position.' I love seeing women getting opportunities, but I started seeing them get them so early in their lives, so early in their careers," she said. Okmin remembers one NFL head coach telling her: "How do you think it makes me feel when I'm at the most stressful point of my job, my career, my life, and I'm down twenty-one points at halftime and I have an adorable young girl who reminds me of my daughter interviewing me, but she's asking me questions that I don't understand? And when I try to give her something so she has some information, and she doesn't understand me? How do you think that makes me feel?"

"I feel so horrible for these women, and I felt so protective because all I kept thinking was 'What if I was twenty-five and covering the NFL?'" Okmin said. "I wasn't ready, and I'm so glad I got to learn; I'm so proud I got to build relationships. I'm so glad that, by the time I got to NFL on FOX, I had my feet wet. I started thinking about what I could do to help these young women, because I didn't have that when I was younger."

Even Beth Mowins, the first woman to call an NFL game in thirty years, remembers being foisted into sideline roles early in her career. "Most of the men that were doing the hiring wanted to turn me into a sideline reporter," she said. "And so I had to do sideline reporting in addition to the things I wanted to do; I had to do sideline reporting to get my foot in the door. Then I could convince people that I could do play-by-play." It's the TV equivalent of having to be an update anchor before being able to host a show. Mowins is thrilled to see other play-by-play jobs opening up for women. "We're starting to see more women attracted to that role, to being the driver of a bus, to be *the* voice. I hope that as we get more and more women's opinions out there, we sort of start to break things down."

Of course, sports aren't the only area in which women's opinions are only grudgingly accepted. According to the Women's Media Center (WMC), women at the four biggest US newspapers wrote only about 15 percent of guest-writer op-eds on international issues from 1996 to 2016. When it comes to editorial positions, where decisions are made about what topics are going to be covered and by whom, the *Columbia Journalism Review* found in 2018 that editors of the nation's 135 most widely distributed newspapers were overwhelmingly white and male. That disparity gets even worse for media involving sports, which have always been considered the province of men. Per the WMC, sports desks at seventy-five of the nation's newspapers and online news sites earned a B+ for racial diversity; a D+ for gender and racial diversity, combined; and a sixth consecutive F for lack of gender equity, according to the "Racial and Gender Report Card," commissioned by the Associated Press Sports Editors (APSE). Additionally, when it comes to print media, women report on sports 10 percent of the time; which means 90 percent of the time sports are reported on by men. That 10 percent number skyrockets to a whopping 21 percent when we look at women reporting on sports in the digital medium.

One of the roles I've seen women thrust into lately is that of the studio host. Making a woman the "host" of a round table show is a convenient way to make it look like *a* woman is in the mix—it's never more than one woman unless we're talking about women's sports—while still relegating her to a role where her opinions don't come into play. The studio host may control the conversation, but it's her job to solicit opinions from the men around the table, not to offer her own thoughts and analysis. And while the host may guide the conversation, you never see any of the men turn the tables and ask her what she thinks.

For women working in sports, the concept of men not believing us until what we say is corroborated by men is nothing new. Hilariously, on several occasions I've had male colleagues disagree with my take on a situation, only to agree with it when it's spouted out by a man who overheard me say it in the hallway to someone else and adopted it as his own opinion, nearly word for word. In 2017, I had to get a mouth guard to sleep in because I was clenching my jaw so tightly at work.

Think about the way most sideline-to-studio reports or updates work. The (usually male) hosts throw to the (often female) sideline reporter. The sideline reporter gets thirty to ninety seconds to tell the hosts what she has learned. The hosts then thank the reporter, thereby corroborating what she said and verifying for the audience that it's true. I firmly believe that without that verification by the hosts, people would question what women say from the sidelines and update studios much more than they do.

L. A. Jennings, PhD, a feminist scholar and professor, as well as an MMA fighter and gym owner, thinks there's an additional reason women are not hired into roles that ask for their opinions. "I think it's not just a trust thing," she said. "For a lot of sports, there's this idea that, historically, sports was a masculine realm. Any woman that came into the sports world historically was seen as an interloper. 'Oh, she's trying to somehow enter this masculine world, she's going to ruin it with doilies and potpourri and suddenly [the men] are going to lose this space.' I think for a lot of men, the idea of women as analysts, of women having an opinion, and a valid opinion, is going to, somehow, take space away from all the men who already occupy the arena. So it makes sense why women are given these roles in sports media of being the ones who interview the coaches or players rather than analysts, because to do otherwise would necessitate men giving up a type of power that they've had forever, essentially."

Asking men to accept a woman in a role traditionally held by men is not for the faint of heart. From the first women who made their way into pro sports locker rooms (often with the help of the legal system) to the women like Jessica Mendoza and Doris Burke fighting their ways into the broadcasting booth (in heels, no less!), the more women I talked to for this book, the more I realized that women working in prominent roles in sports media share a very specific kind of anxiety; one that is intertwined with the issue of men not believing women. And when it's your job to be an expert or authority on a certain sport game, having 50 percent of the fan base immediately write you off as not credible is a big problem.

I used to arrive at work for three hours before my show started to prepare, and that's in addition to all the reading and compiling of information I did during the day before I even started my commute. Plenty of times, I would see male hosts arrive at the station twenty minutes before their show started, sit down behind a mic with no notes, and just start holding court on whatever the topic of the day was. Not me. I knew I had to have statistics and quotes to back up every position I took. Years after I left my career as a lawyer, I prepared for nearly every show like I was preparing to argue a motion in court. If I was challenged, I had to be able to point to empirical evidence. I realize this sounds really dumb when talking about, for example, why Jim Boylen was a terrible coach for the Chicago Bulls or why Kris Bryant should bat leadoff, but I learned early on that I had to bombard my listeners with information that supported my take.

"I always laughed at this kind of thing," Okmin told me on the topic of women overpreparing for sports jobs. "I have plenty of male peers that have messed something up. You say something wrong, you get a team wrong, you get a player wrong. And a man might get ripped on social media for a second, like 'Ha, that's so stupid. He called it this team instead of that team.' But they *said* something stupid. *They're* not stupid. And I still feel that after three decades in the business. You have to be so hypersensitive to what you say, a fact or an opinion, because if you're deemed wrong, you don't know what you're talking about. That's such a big difference: a man *says* something stupid, but we *are* stupid."

One particular day, I had made the mistake of calling Bulls player Denzel Valentine "Denzel Washington." Frankly, I blame Valentine's parents for this. I've spent my entire life saying "Denzel" followed by "Washington." I can't just switch it up on a dime! Regardless, it was my job to get it right, and I kept getting it wrong. Even as I was getting ready to say it, I'd be talking to myself. "Don't screw it up, Julie. It's Denzel VALENTINE." Then I'd get to the part where I'd say his name. While my brain was saying "DENZEL VALENTINE," my mouth would spit out "Denzel Washington." Honestly, it was funny. It was like my mouth rejected all but the one true Denzel.

Every time I spit out the wrong Denzel, though, the text line would go crazy. "This is why we shouldn't have women working in sports," and "Of course the woman can't tell the Denzels apart," blah blah blah. All day. They just kept coming. It wasn't funny that I couldn't say "Denzel Valentine"; it was that I was a woman who got my job on some kind of diversity program and didn't deserve to be there. Meanwhile, one of my male colleagues referred to NFL wide receiver Laquon Treadwell as "Laquon Treadmill" a couple of times that same week. But *that* was funny. That was a knowledge-able man just mixing up words. I don't remember anyone question-ing how he got his job.

ESPN's Mina Kimes, who spent time in the broadcast booth for Los Angeles Rams preseason games in 2019, and was a named an analyst for *NFL Live* in 2020, worries that the fear of making mis-takes keeps women in sports media from expanding into roles out-side their comfort zones. "I don't want to speak for all women, but I know that I have a tendency not to jump into things when I feel I'm not one hundred percent prepared," Kimes said. "That seems to be a fairly gender-specific element. So when you've got [manage-ment] not knowing there are female candidates to do these things, and women who are afraid to take risks for fear of outside criticism, I think it all adds up to a lack of representation." Kimes told me about the time she inadvertently called a player by the wrong name, then continued to obsess over her error until one of her male colleagues convinced her to forget it. "There's that constant fear of making one tiny error. And it's so specific to being a woman, I think, and it's very hard to overcome."

I'm already imagining women who have excelled in roles as sideline reporters, update anchors, and other reporting roles bristling at the idea that their jobs are somehow lesser than those dominated by men. The point of talking about the roles women have traditionally been consigned to in sports media is not to pass judgment on one job over another. As Okmin herself said, she works just as long and hard as her male colleagues in the broadcast booth. Certainly, there's an art to hustling for information and distilling it down into chunks fans can quickly digest. Okmin points out that she has to be able to handle herself in any situation during a game, including power outages, serious head and spinal cord injuries, paralyzed players, and coaches and players who are giving her no useful information when she's expected to provide it to the broadcast.

The real point, though, is that in a perfect world, women would be in roles of sideline reporters and update anchors because they chose to be, not because it's where women are expected to start out or because there is nowhere else for women to go. Nor should women have to prove their sports bona fides at every level along the way. As NBA reporter, host, and analyst Katy Winge said, "It's like women have to prove they can do every job all the way up the ladder to host or analyst. Whereas men are often hired directly into those roles with far less experience."

While there are more women working in roles as hosts and

analysts in sports media than at any time in history, the numbers themselves are still depressing. For example, according to the Women's Media Center report "The Status of Women in the U.S. Media 2019," only two women, Maggie Gray and Dawn Davenport (both of whom are white) made Talkers 2018 list of the "Heavy Hundred" of sports talks radio shows. And remember that APSE "Racial and Gender Report Card"? The one that gave sports desks an F for gender diversity? It turns out those numbers are even worse when you take ESPN out of the mix:

> Of the forty-four women who were columnists at this level, thirty-eight worked for ESPN. Of the forty-four women, four were African American, one was Latina, and two were Asian. All eleven women of color [some who fell outside the groups mentioned above] were employed by ESPN. If the ESPN columnists who are women were removed, the overall percentage of female columnists would drop from 19 percent to 3 percent.
>
> Of the forty-one men of color who were columnists at the largest newspapers and websites, thirty-two worked for ESPN. ESPN employed eighteen of the twenty-four African American male columnists, six of the eight Latino columnists, all three of the Asian columnists, and five of the six people categorized as "Other." If the ESPN male columnists who are people of color were removed, the percentage of male columnists of color would drop from 22 percent to 6 percent.

There are certainly major issues women face working at ESPN, as we'll discuss in another chapter, but there's no question that the Worldwide Leader in Sports is one of the few outlets going out of their way to curate a staff that is diverse in both race and gender.

When I suggested hiring more women to my boss, I was often met with the standard line: "We hire the best person for the job." That sounds great, in theory. (Other than the fact that it implies a tiny fraction of women are the best person for their jobs. . . .)

In reality, there are mountains of research and scholarly articles about "similar to me" bias, in which those in the position to do the hiring tend to hire candidates who are the most like themselves. And when most programming and station managers, sport editors, and editors in chief are overwhelmingly male, it's not difficult to see how women get frozen out not just of higher-profile roles, but of sports media altogether.

Add to that the fact that women in male-dominated workplaces are often left out of the whisper network, the interoffice gossip grid that always seems to know who's coming, who's going, and who's in the mix for job vacancies. I was definitely not part of it in my last radio job, where I often found out such bits of information from a friend who hadn't worked at my station for years. He always knew much more than I did.

I reject the premise that sports media has historically hired "the best person for the job." If that were the case, sports media would be far more diverse and far fewer people with famous broadcasting dads would have plumb jobs. The fact is that diversity doesn't just happen; it's something that outlets cultivate by reaching out to a variety of candidates, not just limiting hiring to the same white male candidates who are able to get their résumés into the boss's in-box because their buddy slipped them his email. Cultivating diversity also means allowing women the chance to make mistakes, learn, and grow in a supportive environment. And it means recognizing that an entire generation of women has grown up as daughters of Title IX, with sports playing as big a role in their lives as it has for many men.

CHAPTER 4

#BELIEVEWOMEN

Exploring Sports' Broken Relationship with Domestic Violence and Sexual Assault

et's take a look at a typical stretch of time in 2019. That fall, the Houston Astros fired an assistant general manager for taunting female reporters over domestic violence during the team clubhouse celebration after winning the pennant. Antonio Brown vowed never to play in the NFL again after he was released by the Patriots due to allegations of sexual assault and sexual harassment by multiple women. The Oakland Raiders' Trent Brown was accused of domestic violence by an ex-girlfriend in a civil suit but remains an active player in the NFL, the second Raider (Antonio Brown was the first) accused of violence against a woman in a single season.

That same year, a person claiming to be a grieving mother shared on Twitter that her daughter died by suicide after being raped by Michigan State football players. Pittsburgh Steelers quarterback Ben Roethlisberger enjoyed plenty of positive attention from his dedicated fans, despite the multiple allegations of sexual assault that have been brought against him. The Chicago Bulls fans chanted "MVP" at Derrick Rose upon his first game in Chicago in 2019, even though Rose could not define "consent" in a deposition during a 2016 lawsuit against him for orchestrating a gang rape of a woman he had formerly dated.

The Cubs decided not to tender a contract to Addison Russell in 2019 but also issued an inexplicable statement telling us all that his history of beating a woman was definitely *not* the deciding factor in cutting him lose. Art Briles, who ran Baylor University's football program during an unprecedented run of sexual assaults, was hired to coach a high school team. After admitting to helping cover up a slew of physical and sexual assaults by minor league baseball players, Gabe Kapler was hired to manage the San Francisco Giants.

Just another day when women working in sports media are repeatedly admonished, mostly by fans but often also by their bosses and colleagues, to "stick to sports."

This is the toxicity women in the world of sports media swim in every day. We are constantly weighing how much we can discuss allegations of an athlete's violence against women without turning off our male audience, while at the same time internally seething that we have to. We silently rage at seeing our male counterparts mention that an athlete has been accused of rape or domestic violence and then immediately move on to discussing what really matters to them: his performance on the field.

Women have long been the ones cataloging the sins of violent athletes and those who cover for them. *We* don't just mention allegations of violence. *We* talk about them at length, or try to. *We* explain to an audience why it's not fair to assume a victim is lying, or making a money grab, or trying to ruin an athlete's career because he dumped her for someone else. *We* have guests on our shows who talk about the nuance of domestic violence and sexual assault. Why women don't report rape. Why women don't (often can't) "just leave" violent men. And too often, we do this by laying bare our own past traumas. You think you don't know anyone who has been sexually assaulted? Well, now you do.

Because *we* are the ones who talk about the uncomfortable realities of violence against women by some of America's favorite athletes, something that no one actually wants to talk about; *we* are also the ones who experience the blowback. It comes in the form of online harassment, disapproval from colleagues and employers, and strained relations with professional sports teams, who, no matter what they say, definitely *do not* take violence against women seriously. And it's the relationships we have, we need, with teams that do more to censor women's voices on these issues than anything else.

What happened in Houston during the 2019 MLB playoffs is a perfect illustration.

In 2018, the Houston Astros traded for reliever Roberto Osuna. Osuna was considered damaged goods, following a seventy-five-game suspension for violating the league's domestic violence policy. Osuna had been arrested in May 2018 by Toronto police and charged with assaulting the mother of his three-year-old child, who was visiting Osuna from Mexico. The concierge of Osuna's residence was the one to call police, who said they saw "significant injuries" to the woman. Later, the woman returned to Mexico and declined to cooperate with police. The charges against Osuna were eventually dropped, but MLB's separate investigation found the allegations were credible enough to hand Osuna that lengthy suspension.

As in any commodity-driven industry, pro sports teams are obsessed with getting high-value players at low-value prices. With a seventy-five-game suspension and an irate Toronto fan base hanging over his head, Osuna was the definition of reduced rate. The Astros didn't hesitate to bring him to Houston, igniting a firestorm of debate among their fans. Osuna, failing to read the room, didn't help his own cause by accusing fans of unfairly judging him.

Still, the Osuna saga was news, and some women reporters weren't exactly excited about having to cover him. Not that this was a new issue. Take, for example, the Cubs trading for Aroldis Chapman after his thirty-game domestic violence suspension in 2016, or tendering a contract to Addison Russell (forty-game domestic violence suspension in 2019); or Antonio Brown's recent career—released by the Raiders after, but not because of, sexual assault allegations, he was signed and then released by the Patriots after a second allegation of sexual misconduct surfaced, *then* he was signed by the Tampa Bay Buccaneers in 2020 at the insistence of Tom Brady and his ego, allegations of rape be damned.

What you can say and who you can talk about in the world of sports media depends a lot on who you work for. If you're with a media outlet that only covers pro sports teams, you have a lot more freedom than, say, someone who works for an outlet like MLB.com or NFL Network, which are owned by and are extensions of the leagues themselves. If you work for NFL.com covering the Bucs, there's no way you're going to be allowed to write a twelve-hundred-word diatribe on allegations of sexual crimes by Antonio Brown, because you're basically working for the team.

Similarly, if you work for a media outlet that has a relationship with a pro sports team, because, for example, your radio station carries their games or they provide regular guests for your TV show, you're also restricted in what you can say. Teams are usually fine with analysts and hosts beating up their guys for what happens on the field, but they bristle at us talking about the players' private lives, even when they involve allegations of violence against women. "You're supposed to be on *our* side" seems to be their thought process.

The "us against them" attitude, in which the good "us" includes an athlete accused of raping or beating a woman, while the bad "them" includes reporters and analysts trying to do their job, is problematic for about a thousand different reasons. Unfortunately, it's a reality in the sports media landscape, and one that many of us are constantly trying to navigate. It's also the product of an era in which teams, via their own networks, YouTube channels, and social media feeds, largely control what fans see of the players on the teams they root for. Marketing and public relations firms make slick videos and ads that assure fans everything about the team they love is wholesome and aboveboard.

Meanwhile, those in the media are expected to stay quiet about what we know about players and coaches and organizations. It's part of the deal with the devil you make for working with a team. Or working for an employer who works for a team. And for the most part, I can live with it. I'm not someone who wants to out a guy for cheating on his wife or being widely considered the biggest asshole known to man, though I will admit to grinding my teeth a bit when I see team-produced product portraying a bad guy as a great one. By and large, I tend to smile and nod when a fan tells me how much they love a player I know for a fact is a terrible person. Why should I ruin their enjoyment of the sport? Let them have their fantasy.

Sexual assault and domestic violence, though, are different. We're talking about actual crimes being committed and people being physically hurt. Those events, and the way in which a team handles them, should be fair game for the media to investigate and discuss without fear of retribution from the team itself.

Back in Houston, there were plenty of media members, men and women, who were sharply critical of the Astros trading for Roberto Osuna. But like with so many of these cases, the teams seem to feel that once they hold their obligatory press conference affirming how seriously they take domestic violence / sexual assault / child abuse and assure everyone the player is on a tight leash, understands what behavior is expected of him, blah blah blah, the whole thing is supposed to be over. Media isn't supposed to bring it up again. That's it. The team is bringing in a guy MLB saw fit to suspend for domestic violence, we said the things we were supposed to say, now we're done.

According to the National Coalition Against Domestic Violence, one in four women and one in nine men will experience severe intimate partner violence in their lifetime. Per Rape, Abuse, and Incest National Network (RAINN), one in six women and one in thirty-three men have been the victim of an attempted or completed rape. Physical and sexual violence are a massive scourge on our country, and you can bet there are people working in the media, like everywhere else, who have been victims of violence themselves or know someone who has. And aside from that, there are plenty of intelligent people who are disgusted by abusers and rapists and resent having to write about how well they play sports without being able to weigh in on what they think of said abusers and rapists as human beings.

Kathy Redmond, who founded the National Coalition Against Violent Athletes after she was sexually assaulted by a football player while at the University of Nebraska, describes the conundrum of team access, especially for women. "Sports reporters essentially get paid by the access that they have to athletes and to coaches," she said. "And if you happen to raise the difficult questions that need to be asked that everybody's thinking, if you happen to raise those questions, your access is threatened."

It doesn't help that so many of those now involved in media relations in pro sports franchises come from a public relations background, where anything other than predetermined talking points are considered a threat to the organization, as opposed to those from editorial backgrounds, where negative views of the team may not be appreciated but are tolerated.

The Chicago Cubs media relations department, for example, employs one person known for calling around to all the local media outlets and complaining about what he deems "unfair" press coverage. Worse, he doesn't call the reporters with whom he has issues—he goes straight to their bosses, which is an implicit threat to the reporter's job security.

For example, in early 2019, after Addison Russell was tendered a contract by the Cubs in the off-season, he held a spring training press conference to address his domestic violence suspension, during which time he stumbled over his answers and took no responsibility for his actions but made sure he thanked every single reporter for their question. Back in Chicago, I listened to the presser on the radio, which was carried by my station.

Almost immediately after it ended, I began messaging with some media members who were in the room with Russell, asking if he came off as badly in person as he did over the airwaves. To a one, they expressed incredulity that the Cubs allowed the press conference to even happen, given how unprepared Russell seemed to be to answer for his actions. One media member compared it to the historically bad Patrick Kane press conference, which followed accusations that the NHL player had sexually assaulted a woman. Another called Russell's performance "a shitshow."

As someone who has also been outspoken about violence against women, particularly in sports, I knew my followers were waiting for me to put out a reaction, especially as I wasn't on the air at the time it happened. So I tweeted out exactly what I was told. That one reporter told me it was as bad as Patrick Kane's presser and that another called it "a shitshow." I went about my day and didn't think much more about it.

But that night, I got a call from my station's program director. He was clearly upset, telling me he had just spent the last hour and a half on the phone with the Cubs, who were livid about my tweet. They saw me as a media figure who worked for their flagship station, someone who was supposed to be on their side. I saw myself as a reporter and commentator who owed it to my audience to tell the truth. But I hated that my boss, who was always kind to me, had been dragged into it, and I was afraid that the Cubs had enough clout to cost me my job. I deleted the tweet.

Back to Houston, where several men and women were forced (by virtue of their roles as beat reporters) into covering Roberto Osuna after he arrived fresh off his suspension. Being put in the unenviable position of having to maintain access to players and the team while trying to be true to her own values, one reporter tweeted out the number to a domestic violence hotline when Osuna took the mound. She also wore a purple domestic violence awareness bracelet. These were essentially the two most unobtrusive things a reporter could do to push back against a team signing a player credibly accused of assault.

Even these minor protests were too much for Astro's assistant general manager Brandon Taubman. He complained about the reporter in multiple conversations over the course of the season. He seethed and simmered over her dissent from the unspoken "one and done" rule—she dared to reference Osuna's violent history after the requisite presser. And, following the Astros' pennant-clinching win, he saw his chance.

As the Astros celebrated in their clubhouse, Taubman, one of the many bros who came to an MLB front office from Wall Street, walked over to a group of women reporters covering the game. Stephanie Apstein of *Sports Illustrated* was the first to report what happened next. Getting right in the face of the reporter who had been the object of his ongoing wrath, Taubman began taunting the reporter. "I'm sooooo glad we got Osuna! I'm sooooo fucking glad we got Osuna!" he chanted, over and over. The incident was so alarming, another Astros employee apologized for Taubman's behavior.

The rest of the story has passed into legend. After Apstein's story broke, the Astros put out a remarkably tone-deaf statement, calling her reporting irresponsible and implying she made the whole thing up. That was followed by several male reporters verifying the story, at which point the Astros presumably realized they had a problem on their hands. You know, once the men called it out. Taubman put out a statement the next day, claiming it was exuberance at the win that he meant to express and apologized for "inappropriate language," as if women who spend a good deal of time talking to half-naked players in an MLB locker room were offended at hearing the word "fuck." He went on to tell the world what a progressive husband and father he is and closed with the standard non-apology: "I'm sorry if anyone was offended by my actions."

In the days following the incident, the Astros and their general manager, Jeff Luhnow, continued to double down on their "you guys have got it all wrong" story, and it wasn't until MLB got involved that the team was forced to fire Taubman and issue a formal apology to Apstein. Though before we give Luhnow too much credit, I should point out that he declined, days prior, to apologize to Apstein when she was sitting in the front row of his press conference. Never have women rooted so hard for a team as we did for the Nationals in that World Series.

The reporter Taubman targeted is a friend and colleague of mine, and she understandably doesn't want her name associated with this event. Every woman who has criticized a team she covers on these issues can imagine why. As much as she was minding her own business at the time Taubman decided to go after her, and as bad as the Astros' organization has looked throughout this entire saga, she's the one who will wind up paying the price if her name gets out there. No matter how terribly a team behaves, it's always the woman who calls them out who winds up labeled as "difficult" and a "feminazi." Imagine getting slapped with those labels for tweeting out the number to a domestic violence hotline. If anything, that's something we should all be doing more often in this field.

The long-term issue with the "one and done" unwritten rule is that it serves as a kind of "reset" for men accused of bad acts. Not that people don't deserve second chances—they do. But second chances should come after personal reflection, hard work, and an effort to make things right, not a half-assed press conference where you repeatedly thank reporters for their questions while refusing to admit you did anything wrong. Putting a moratorium on how long fans and media are allowed to bring up the fact that a player purposely injured an intimate partner only serves to normalize domestic abuse.

I've been looking for a word for the phenomenon whereby the entire media gets collective amnesia about an athlete's prior behavior, à la quarterback Ben Roethlisberger and the late Kobe Bryant. I was sort of musing about it on Twitter when the fantastic Dallas sportswriter Levi Weaver threw out "manitizing," like "sanitizing" but only available to men in certain situations. Leave it to a man to jump into my mentions—although not many of my reply guys can best me at wordplay, and Levi definitely did. Dammit.

But he was right. "Manitizing" is the process whereby a media, largely populated by men, unofficially decides that enough has been said about, say, the rape charges brought against Kobe Bryant or the multiple women who have accused Roethlisberger of rape, and they just stop mentioning it. Forever. In really special cases of manitizing, we get feature fluff pieces about how much the player has "matured" since he violated a woman's bodily autonomy. Bonus manitizing points if the guy got married after his alleged assault.

Here's a perfect example of manitizing at work. Back in February 2015, Gabe Kapler was serving as director of player development for the Los Angeles Dodgers. During that time, he was made aware of multiple incidents involving Dodgers' minor leaguers sexually and physically assaulting women. Kapler dealt with the incidents in-house, in one case trying to set up a dinner with a seventeen-year-old girl and two minor leaguers who had been drinking with her earlier in the week. One of the players had filmed the girl being beaten up by two other women and, instead of intervening or seeking help, uploaded the video to Snapchat. In an email to the girl's grandmother, Kapler said he saw it as a teachable moment for his players. Later, Kapler learned that one of them had sexually assaulted her.

Neither this incident nor other allegations of inappropriate and violent behavior by players in Kapler's charge were reported to the police or MLB, as required by MLB's joint domestic violence policy. And in case you're thinking that Kapler didn't know any better, he founded the now-defunct Gabe Kapler Foundation with his ex-wife in 2005. The goal of the organization? To raise awareness and educate the public about domestic violence.

These revelations about Kapler's time with the Dodgers didn't become public knowledge until 2019, while he was managing the Philadelphia Phillies. Kapler attempted to defend himself on his personal blog, admitting he got it wrong using the obligatory language: "I take violence against women, especially sexual violence, incredibly seriously." Kapler was fired by the Phillies after the 2019 season for baseball reasons (because it turns out he sucks at managing a baseball team almost as much as he sucks at handling abusive players), but it would be nice to think that his now-public absence of judgment while with the Dodgers played some role in his dismissal.

But once Kapler was on the job market, the manitization of his past went into full effect. Writer after writer summarized his baseball bona fides, with most completely omitting any mention of Kapler's terrible judgment in handling violence against women by men under his watch. The Chicago Cubs, still reeling on the public relations front from trading for Aroldis Chapman in 2016 and tendering a contract to Addison Russell in 2018, didn't hesitate in interviewing Kapler for their open manager position. In fact, the Cubs, who have learned how to get ahead of stories involving domestic violence and sexual assault (to be fair, they've had more practice than most other teams), didn't even bother to address Kapler's past. Multiple male analysts suggested that if Kapler didn't get a managerial role, he could head up some team's player development department, *the exact same role* in which he got into trouble with the Dodgers in the first place.

Once again, it was mainly the women calling attention to Kapler's history, tweeting out reporting about his handling of violence against women by his players. Ann Killion of the *San Francisco Chronicle*, who can always be counted on to do the right thing, was one of the first reporters to go right at Kapler, both in his introductory press conference and in print. On a podcast, veteran baseball reporter Susan Slusser questioned Kapler's decision-making and calling him an "odd hire," pointing out that the San Francisco Giants were still reeling from suspending CEO Larry Baer for publicly shoving his wife down that same year.

Over at the *Ringer*, Michael Baumann wrote one of the few articles demanding Kapler be held responsible for his actions. Otherwise, it was as if baseball media had tacitly agreed to not discuss anything other than Kapler's performance as the Phillies manager.

By the time he was hired as manager by the San Francisco Giants in November 2019, a groundswell of outrage had arisen in the Bay Area. The Giants tweet announcing Kapler as manager was met with a barrage of angry fans. When the Giants introduced Kapler to the media in mid-November, both he and Giants president Farhan Zaidi (*another* Dodgers front-office guy implicated in not reporting violent Dodgers minor leaguers alongside Kapler) were rightfully forced to spend most of the presser addressing their misdeeds in Los Angeles.

I can't help but wonder, if it hadn't been for women like Killion, who refused to back down from talking about Kapler's off-the-field problems, would the issue even have come up? The manitization of Gabe Kapler was strong.

Which brings me to Stephen A. Smith. It's not only athletes

women in the media carry the burden of calling out when it comes to sexist language or flippancy when talking about violence against women; it's also our colleagues. Back in 2014, ESPN's Smith—not exactly a bastion of progressiveness when it comes to gender issues—was discussing Ray Rice's two-game suspension for knocking his wife unconscious when he implied that women bear some responsibility for domestic abuse at the hands of men. Michelle Beadle, then the host of *SportsNation* on ESPN, bravely called out Smith on Twitter, saying, "So I was just forced to watch this morning's First Take. (A) I'll never feel clean again (B) I'm now aware that I can provoke my own beating." Beadle went on to share that she, too, had been in an abusive relationship, adding, "Violence isn't the victim's issue. It's the abuser's. To insinuate otherwise is irresponsible and disgusting. Walk. Away." Beadle's tweets got over 2,200 retweets, many of them from women; Smith was forced to apologize and suspended from *First Take* and his radio show for a week.

I've worked with my share of male colleagues who have used sexist language either on the air or on social media. Immediately, *I'm* the focus of the social media storm. "You call everyone else out, why not your colleague?" "Are you really going to be silent just because you work with him, you hypocrite?" But here's the thing: as the only woman employee at my station, I was more vulnerable than all the men who work there, even those who step into controversy on the regular. So why not put the onus on the other men I work with to call out sexism from their colleagues? Why was it always my job? I called out other people's colleagues because I could do so without risking my job. That just wasn't possible at my own station; I really needed my job, and those callouts were a real risk. It's almost as if they only cared about my reaction, not what was actually said. So maybe instead of calling the only woman at the station a hypocrite, all the guys tweeting at me could step up and say something.

Especially when women doing that work have paid dearly. Michelle Beadle was ridiculously brave in calling out someone as entrenched at ESPN as Smith was (and still is). In 2019, ESPN quietly removed Beadle from the airwaves and bought out her contract.

We're talking about a team's festering resentment against a woman who forces them to confront uncomfortable truths, or the way irresponsible members of the media go about erasing problematic pasts, but both of these issues are part of a much bigger systemic problem: pro sports and the juggernaut that covers them normalize violence against women.

It always baffles me that a country that has overwhelmingly supported "tough on crime" politicians uses such different standards when it comes to celebrities accused of violence against women. While many point to the video of Ray Rice punching and knocking out his wife, Janay, as the moment of reckoning for sports fans, it's important to note that fans and the NFL turned on Ray Rice precisely because there was incontrovertible evidence of his crime. And let's not forget that even after the video footage was leaked, the Baltimore Ravens held a press conference so that the victim, Janay Rice, could apologize for her role in being knocked unconscious by her husband. Which she did. Later, Janay would admit she apologized at the urging of the Ravens.

Too often, a story about a pro athlete being accused of sexual assault or domestic battery is met by a deluge of young men on social media reflexively defending their hero. Typically they do this by questioning the validity of the claims, with posts asking, "Where's the proof?" and "How do we know she's not lying?" and "Is there video tape of this?" Many fans, including women, turned on Ray Rice because they couldn't deny what they saw on video, but when no video exists, which is 99 percent of life, they happily go back to defending the athlete.

"We know these guys. Our empathy goes to these guys," said Kathy Redmond about pro athletes. "They can hit people. They can rape people. They can do whatever, but because we know them, we struggle with how they might be feeling going through this. We don't see their power network. We don't see the lawyers lined up behind them. We don't see the agents. We don't see the PR people. We don't see all of the entourage that they bring to the table and the amount of power that they have.

"We don't see [the abuse]. We see them, and then the victim is nobody that we know. We don't know her. We can't identify with her. We can't identify her. We've never heard from her, and for all we know, she's fine, you know?"

Anyone who has read Ronan Farrow's *Catch and Kill*, in which Farrow recounts breaking the story of Harvey Weinstein's history of sexual assaults, knows too well that a cottage industry exists to smear and discredit women who accuse powerful men of assault and abuse. And while most athletes accused of violence against women don't have the reach or resources that the head of a Hollywood studio does, athletes do have lawyers and agents and publicists, all ready to jump into action the minute their client is placed in a negative light. They have their marching orders the same way many reporters do. According to Redmond, players' agents or attorneys often hire a private detective, who digs up dirt on the victim and provides the dirt to the press.

When the NBA's Derrick Rose was sued in civil court in 2016 for orchestrating the gang rape of a woman with whom he'd had a relationship, the first thing his attorneys did was seek to disallow the woman to proceed with her lawsuit under the name "Jane Doe." And while it might seem only fair on its face that, because Rose's name was in the lawsuit, the victim's name should be as well, that "fair is fair" argument ignores the enormous disparity in resources between a player with an estimated net worth of $180 million and a young woman still living at home with her working-class parents. Rose's attorneys sought to paint the victim as a jealous gold digger and the allegations of gang rape as revenge for Rose's refusal to enter an exclusive relationship with her and to pay for sex toys she had purchased to use with him.

I was part of a group of reporters, all of us female, if I recall correctly, who took part in a conference call with Rose's victim ahead of the trial. Far from the money-grubbing Jezebel she had been portrayed as on sites like Twitter and some of the less-reputable sports blogs, she was quiet and timid and seemed to have a hard time expressing herself. She was quietly calling from the home where she lived with her non-English-speaking parents, hoping they wouldn't overhear her conversation. They still didn't know about the rape or the lawsuit.

Over the course of the next forty-five minutes, she told us how much she loved Rose, that, in him, she felt she had found a kindred spirit: a shy and sheltered person who sometimes struggled to communicate. She told us that she had engaged in sexual acts for Rose that she never would have done with anyone else, and that the only reason she brought up money to him was because he otherwise ignored her texts. She was adamant that group sex with Rose's friends was never anything she would have consented to and that she remembered almost nothing about the event itself, having blacked out on alcohol.

This was a far cry from how she was being portrayed on social media, where purported text messages were being taken out of context or downright photoshopped to cast doubt on her credibility. Meanwhile, Derrick Rose's deposition—in which he admitted he didn't know the definition of "consent," that the victim had previously refused his multiple requests for group sex, and that he felt that his text letting her know he was coming over to her apartment with his friends was proof of her consent—went largely unremarked upon by fans and the media. Rose's attorneys were admonished several times by the trial judge for "shaming and blaming" the victim.

But it worked.

Rose was found not liable by a jury, several of whom took selfies with him afterward. In his most recent return to the United Center in Chicago, where he played at the time of the assault, he was met with chants of "MVP! MVP!"

Of course, the playbook for how to handle violence against women committed by pro athletes had been written years earlier, in 2003, when Kobe Bryant was accused of raping a hotel employee in Colorado. Since Bryant's tragic death in a helicopter crash in 2020, his legend has only grown, and, as with Rose, bringing up the sexual assault allegations against him is now treated as sacrilege.

Maybe it's because it predated social media. Maybe it's because it predated #MeToo. Maybe it's because it's Kobe Bryant. For whatever reason, Bryant managed to disassociate himself with the ugly allegations against him in a way no other athlete, except for maybe Ben Roethlisberger, has. Even after his death, not a day goes by when I don't see multiple Kobe Bryant GIFs in my social media timeline. In the years before his death, he was interviewed for an ESPN for a project called *Dear Black Athlete*. He won an Oscar. He was a fixture courtside at Lakers games, often seen embracing current and former players.

Back in 2003, Kobe Bryant was on top of the world. With major endorsement deals with Nike and McDonald's, his face was everywhere. A legendarily fierce competitor on the court, he was handsome and fresh-faced enough to be marketable to both kids and adults.

On June 30, 2003, Bryant and his entourage checked into the Lodge & Spa at Cordillera in Edwards, Colorado. The next morning, a nineteen-year-old hotel employee would accuse him of violently choking and raping her as she desperately tried to escape his room.

When the victim submitted to the rape kit, the nurse conducting the exam found two significant lacerations to her vaginal area, and smaller lacerations—"too many to count," according to the police report. The nurse stated the injuries were consistent with penetrating genital trauma and not consistent with consensual sex. She also said the trauma likely took place in the last twenty-four hours. The victim had a bruise on her neck and her jaw. Bryant was discovered with the victim's blood on a T-shirt he was wearing, about waist-high. Consistent with having bent a woman over a chair and entered her from behind, as the victim claimed. She never wavered on her claim that she was raped. Bryant, at the time a married father with a seven-month-old daughter, never wavered on his claim that the sex was consensual. In an interview with the *Los Angeles Times*, Bryant said, "You guys know me. I shouldn't have to say anything."

Over the course of the months leading up to the trial, the true name of the victim, who had been proceeding in court under the name "Jane Doe," was mistakenly released by a court employee and further disseminated to the media and in internet message boards. Her mental health was questioned by Bryant's defense team, following a roommate's revelations that the victim had previously attempted suicide on two occasions. Her sex life, sadly but obviously, was fodder for both the defense and online forums.

The fact that she had reportedly had sex with another man in the days prior to her meeting Bryant was twisted into the allegation that she had sex with another man in the hours following her claims of rape. A man in Iowa threatened to sexually assault her with a hanger before killing her. Her life was laid bare before the entire world. Kobe Bryant had the power of the NBA, the Lakers, his agent, his publicist, his high-profile attorney, and his fans behind him. His victim had the government employees of the Eagle County District Attorney.

In the end, the victim decided the public's laser focus on discrediting her was too much. She informed the court she would not testify against Bryant. Instead, she filed a civil suit against him (the cries of her rape allegations being a "money grab" had begun much earlier, long before she sought anything but Bryant's prosecution), and the parties eventually reached a confidential settlement, which included an apology from Bryant. In his public mea culpa, Bryant said, in part, "I . . . want to make it clear that I do not question the motives of this young woman. No money has been paid to this woman. She has agreed that this statement will not be used against me in the civil case. Although I truly believe this encounter between us was consensual, I recognize now that she did not and does not view this incident the same way I did. After months of reviewing discovery, listening to her attorney, and even her testimony in person, I now understand how she feels that she did not consent to the encounter."

It's as close to an admission of rape as we've ever received from a pro athlete, and yet it's largely forgotten. In the years that have followed, media outlets, the NBA, and fans have set about manitizing Kobe Bryant's past. In fact, an entire generation of NBA fans and Kobe stans are convinced that the rape allegations against Bryant were "gold digging" from the beginning and that he was proven innocent in court.

To the first point, civil damages are how we settle literally every other grievous bodily harm in our society. Car accident? Civil lawsuit. Guy punches you in the face and breaks your nose? Civil lawsuit. Yet sexual assault and domestic violence victims, who experience some of the most egregious harms possible, are routinely considered "gold diggers" for making use of the system we've set up in this country to make people whole. And to the second point, a significant portion of Americans need to understand that when a case does not proceed to trial, there is no finding of guilt or innocence. There is simply nothing. Nothing is not the same as a legal exoneration, particularly when the "nothing" is requested by the victim.

If you don't believe me, throw out something about the rape case on Twitter and check out the replies. The Bryant case even changed the way we talk about sexual assault overall. In every other crime, we use the word "victim" from the moment a crime is alleged. When it comes to sexual assault and domestic violence, we're chastised for not saying "accuser."

Today, Kobe Bryant is still celebrated by the masses as one of the NBA's all-time greats; the allegations that he once grabbed a young woman by the neck, choked her, bent her over a chair, and raped her are long forgotten. So is the fact that the authorities who responded to the case and the lawyers who prosecuted it found her a credible witness. These days, Kobe Bryant is feted for showing up at the 2016 USA Gymnastic Olympic Trials, for an Oscar-winning cartoon about the love of basketball, for everything he did to encourage his daughter Gianna's love for the game. His face and "Mamba Mentality" appeared at the end of a video promoting, of all things, the WNBA. He even coached his daughter's basketball team.

Only a year after the allegations against Bryant surfaced, the Lakers gave him a $136 million contract. Two years after the allegations, Nike, who had paused promoting Bryant but, unlike Nutella and McDonald's, had not cut ties with him, began using his image in connection with the brand again. These days, the incident in Colorado is known more for the $4 million purple diamond Bryant gave his wife, Vanessa, as an apology for what he claimed was merely infidelity.

If you want an idea of how thoroughly the rape allegations against Bryant had exited the public zeitgeist, prior to Bryant's death in 2020, entering "Kobe Bryant se" into Google suggested the following searches before it got to "Kobe Bryant sexual assault":

Kobe Bryant seasons played
Kobe Bryant season stats

Kobe Bryant series

Kobe Bryant Serena Williams

Kobe Bryant second year stats

Kobe Bryant security

Kobe Bryant secret camp

Kobe Bryant see you again

Kobe Bryant season MVP

Kobe Bryant season 17 stats

In 2018, Kobe Bryant was removed as a jury member from the Animation is Film Festival in Los Angeles after women protested his involvement.

Maybe someone remembers after all.

Following Bryant's death, I debated whether I should remove him from this chapter entirely. I was sitting at the library one day in January 2020 working on this chapter when a TMZ story flashed across Twitter: KOBE BRYANT KILLED IN HELICOPTER CRASH.

I felt a jolt go through me, the kind you feel when you are well and truly shocked. I stared at the screen for a minute, then started looking at other outlets. No one else was reporting it. Maybe it was a hoax. Maybe it wasn't true.

A few hours later, it became clear that it was true.

In the coming days, I wondered if I should rewrite this entire chapter. After all, how could I use Kobe Bryant's sexual assault trial to illustrate the way sports handles violence against women now, when everyone was so grief-stricken? Was it even fair to do so?

In the days and weeks after, though, I became more and more

convinced that it was important to talk about the rape allegations against Bryant not just because of the way they were handled in his life but because of the way they were handled in his death, which is to say not at all.

At the time Bryant was accused, women who tried to bring up the subject were admonished to "wait for all the facts to come out," and told, "Don't convict a man without proof." Years ago, after the charges were dismissed, we were told to move on and to "stop trying to convict him of something he was found not guilty of" (he wasn't). In the years that followed, any mention of the allegations against Bryant were met with a "Why are you trying to bring up the past?" In the wake of Bryant's death, it was "Why do you have to bring it up now? Why are you trying to slander a dead man?"

For a large portion of America, it seemed there was never a time when it was appropriate to talk about the allegations against Bryant. I was one of the women who, in the days following his death, was on the receiving end of rape, assault, and death threats, as well as a disapproving employer, for acknowledging that for many of us, Bryant's legacy included not only basketball but also a playbook for slut-shaming and intimidating a victim into dropping rape charges.

Over at the *Washington Post*, reporter Felicia Sonmez, a rape survivor herself, was suspended for tweeting out a link to a *Daily Beast* article on the alleged sexual assault, without any commentary of her own, in the hours following Bryant's death. Any woman who admitted to being anything other than prostrate with grief was shouted down on social media, often with threats of violence. When I turned down the chance to write about Bryant for NBC News, explaining that I was in the middle of multiple threats over an innocuous tweet about Bryant's death, the editor who had reached out to me told me the reason she asked me was because the *last* woman who had written about Bryant for them was also in the midst of a full-on social media assault by Kobe fans.

Driving into work the night following Bryant's death, I tried to figure out what to say. I wondered if there was any room for nuance in the way we talked about Kobe Bryant's life. I wondered if I could talk about my feelings as a sexual assault survivor. I hoped I could be honest with my audience and admit that I didn't know how to handle the situation. As the Chicago skyline came into view in front of me, I knew in an instant none of those things were possible. Many of the buildings glittered purple before me, lit up in a tribute to Kobe Bryant.

I wondered if any of the people responsible for lighting up those buildings purple, or for any of the full-page newspaper tributes to Kobe Bryant, or for the glowing retrospectives on what he meant to men that dominated the radio and television waves, knew anyone who had survived sexual assault. Or if they cared. I was far from the only woman struggling with the coverage of Bryant's death. Privately, women working in sports media messaged back and forth. How could so many of these guys, who we trusted as friends and allies, describe Bryant's legacy as "complicated" and go back to talking hoops? Was there anyone out there who would stand up for us?

The question I found myself asking silently inside my head, even when listening to my guy friends extoll Bryant's virtues, was "Do you not believe the victim? Or do you just not care?" In those weeks following Bryant's death, I found out how many of my guy friends were great at compartmentalizing their feelings. Sure, he may have raped a woman, but what a great player!

Soraya Nadia McDonald of ESPN's *The Undefeated* is a rape

survivor herself, and she, too, was uncomfortable with the way the media glossed over the 2003 sexual assault allegations.

"This goes back to the way [the media] covered those allegations when they first came out. I would say that not much has changed in sports media since then," she told me. And while the allegations against Bryant were less than twenty years old, the conversation around sexual assault has changed in our society. While I have plenty of issues with *Law & Order: Special Victims Unit*, I'm at least grateful that twenty-one seasons of Olivia Benson kicking sex offender ass has moved the conversation from "she's totally lying" to "she *might* be lying." Let's all be thankful for small victories.

"Part of what's really frustrating is the way the news media was complicit in making the victim's life worse," McDonald told me. "That had a really powerful effect on the way people thought about that case and thought about rape allegations made against professional athletes. Men and women were just convinced that we were basically just out to tear down Kobe Bryant and his legacy. Part of that is because the media did such a piss-poor job in the way that it covered this rape accusation when it happened."

Like many of us who had survived sexual assault and had to cover Bryant's death in order to do our jobs, McDonald struggled. "I had a rough two-and-a-half, three weeks where I don't think I realized quite how affected I was. And there was this collective movement to shout down anyone who brought [the rape allegations] up. It was awful. I was like, 'Oh wow, you just do not care.' There was no recognition that we might see things differently through the lens of a survivor. There was no room for anyone to think about things that way.

"Even when you had a sexual assault survivor talking about it publicly, she just ends up getting told by her bosses that she is making the institution look bad," she says of Sonmez. Then McDonald put her finger on the real problem. "Allegations of sexual assault and domestic violence against athletes bubble up, and then we just kind of forget about them. Nobody says anything about Ben Roethlisberger anymore. It's really frustrating. It's irritating."

It is frustrating, as is the number of women who also publicly throw their weight and support behind athletes with a history of violence against women. And while I do believe in second chances, second chances must be earned by addressing the problem, head-on, and working to alleviate it. For some fans, what good Kobe Bryant did after he left Colorado, of which there undeniably was quite a bit, was enough to make up for what he was accused of doing while there. I saw many women paying tribute to Kobe Bryant for the time he spent promoting women's sports, including the WNBA, where his late daughter, Gianna, hoped to play one day. That's a great thing; a laudable thing. But one doesn't make up for a sexual assault by throwing their weight behind women's sports. As far as I can tell, after he issued his apology to his victim, Bryant never spoke publicly about sexual assault again. Not a simple #Believe Women on Twitter, not in the context of how he talked to his daughters about consent, not in all the time he spent coaching and mentoring young women. And despite what people on social media say, no rape survivor was screaming for Bryant's head after his death. We just wanted to see his legacy described in more detail than "complicated," which has become media code for "yeah, we know there's bad stuff here, but we're not going into it."

I asked Nicole Bedera, a PhD candidate at the University of Michigan who studies sexual violence, masculinity, and gender equality, about the dissonance surrounding women and male allies who continue to support violent athletes. "At this point, nearly everyone knows that they have survivors in their life—whether the survivor is someone you know personally or a beloved celebrity. It's much more uncomfortable to realize that we also all have perpetrators in our lives," she told me. "Most people think that rapists are a few bad apples who perpetrate lots and lots of assaults. In reality, sexual violence is more mundane than that."

Bedera points out that one in two male college athletes admits to committing some form of sexual violence before graduation. "Many of the athletes we cherish are also rapists, but that's an uncomfortable reality when the rapist is someone you consider to be an idol or a role model," she said. "The reality is that we still love them and want to continue to love them, so we shame the people who speak up."

Of course, the issue is even more complicated when the beloved athlete is a Black man. "There are so few Black men who are respected role models the way Kobe Bryant was. It's hard to lose one—or even to find a way to grapple with that complicated legacy. Not to mention, there's a stereotype that Black men are sexually aggressive, and recognizing that Kobe Bryant committed a rape—and essentially confessed to doing so—feels like reinforcing that stereotype," she said. And while I'm not the person to write about it, it's worth mentioning that Black women are too often put in the position of having to choose between their race and their gender when it comes to speaking out about issues like violence against women. Regrettably, I know that I haven't been as sensitive to that tension in the past as I try to be now that I know better.

I don't want to give the impression that all men refused to look Bryant's true legacy in the face. While they were few and far between, there were men who talked about Bryant's death with sensitivity and understanding. One of them was David Dennis Jr. at *The Undefeated*, who wrote:

> We cannot let our love and defense of Bryant turn into the same perpetuation of rape culture that made Colorado, where the alleged sexual assault occurred, acceptable for so many in the first place. We can't go back to the same dangerous "she dropped the charges so he's innocent" tropes that have let far too many guilty men go free. We have to be more nuanced and intentional than that. Because, let's be clear, the biggest victims of rape culture in the end will always be black women. Every time. So it's our responsibility as men to stop it for their sakes. Even if that feels uncomfortable and painful. If we believe Bryant did enough to make things right, then we need to talk about the true steps of reckoning he took and how that can look for more men.

Now if we can just get the rest of the men in sports media on board.

Of course, the way in which pro sports leagues handle, and the way in which the media portrays, violence against women has contributed significantly to a large chunk of American sports fans viewing violence against women as no big deal; something you have to accept with pro athletes, like the inevitable injuries and retirements.

Baseball writer Jonah Keri, once the darling of stat heads and baseball purists alike, was arrested three times in 2019 on charges relating to domestic violence and violation of a protective order.

Skip Bayless, who has one of the biggest platforms in media, posted a video of himself angrily throwing an Ezekiel Elliott jersey into the trash after a Cowboys loss, something he had apparently not seen fit to do when Elliott was suspended for six games by the NFL for "multiple instances of physical violence" against a former girlfriend. Bayless later retrieved the jersey after Elliott rushed for 117 yards against the Rams.

In the same season that NFL fans had heard Kansas City Chief's wide receiver Tyreek Hill tell the mother of his child, "You need to be terrified of me too, bitch" in a recorded phone conversation, *Sunday Night Football* portrayed Hill as an elf to Andy Reid's Santa Claus in a pre-Christmas graphic. The phone conversation, over whether Hill had broken his young son's arm, was with the same woman Hill was convicted of punching and choking while she was pregnant with his son in 2015.

When the Cubs traded for Aroldis Chapman in 2016, multiple media outlets wrote pieces about the deal without ever mentioning his recent suspension for choking his girlfriend and waving a gun around.

Sadly, it's not like the largely male-run sports media juggernaut is alone in normalizing abuse. I've long said that team owners and front-office honchos need domestic violence and sexual assault education as much as, and maybe more, than the players do.

In March 2019, San Francisco Giants CEO Larry Baer was caught on video knocking over his wife in the process of taking away a phone from her. Chicago Bears president George McCaskey once justified signing defensive end Ray McDonald, who was charged with multiple counts of domestic violence and sexual assault, by saying that rape victims were "biased" against their attackers. Dallas Cowboys owner Jerry Jones continued to defend Greg Hardy, even after horrific photos of the aftermath of a beating at his hands were released. The photos of Hardy's victim, first published by *Deadspin*, were so brutal that one of the responding officers described her as looking like she'd been in a car accident. Jones later praised Hardy as "a real leader."

The New Orleans Saints, ever looking to stick a finger in NFL commissioner Roger Goodell's eye, publicly kicked around the idea of signing Antonio Brown, who was cut by both the Raiders and the Patriots, the latter after multiple allegations of sexual assault and harassment were lodged against him. I'm happy to report that a good number of Saints fans were upset by the prospect of Brown wearing black and gold, but I regret having to point out that it was because they felt Brown's tweets on his way out of the league were "disrespectful" to his former teams. In fact, *ProFootballTalk*, a popular site with a history of questioning victims of popular athletes, wrote that the Saints had "nothing to lose" by signing Brown. ESPN's Adam Schefter reported that the Saints were "doing their due diligence" on Brown. No word on if that due diligence involved speaking to any of the three women who had accused Brown of sexual assault, sexual harassment, or domestic violence.

So how can pro sports better handle allegations of domestic violence against their employees, from players to presidents?

First, I can't stress how helpful it is for a league to actually *have* a policy. While MLB and the NBA have specific protocols to address both sexual assault and domestic violence, the NFL punishes domestic violence under a catch-all code of conduct, and the NHL has no official policy at all. It's tough for a league to argue that it takes violence against women seriously when it can't even take the time to spell out what the specific repercussions might be for beating or raping a woman or child. And keep in mind that every major league but the NHL, including Major League Soccer and the WNBA, has an official policy to test for varying drugs.

Pro sports: where "just say no" takes priority over "#NoMore."

Of the pro sports leagues that do have an explicit policy regarding domestic violence and sexual assault, MLB probably does the best job of handing allegations against players, in that they have a unit that independently investigates allegations, comprised of former police officers, investigators, and others with a background in violent crimes. MLB has been willing to suspend players absent formal criminal proceedings, which is key in handling such cases. According to RAINN, only five sexual assaults out of every one thousand committed will result in a felony conviction. According to one report, only 50 percent of domestic violence incidents are ever reported to the police. To their credit, MLB has placed less of an emphasis on a prosecution itself, which can be derailed for any number of reasons having nothing to do with guilt or innocence, and made an effort to assess the evidence against a player independent of any decisions made by law enforcement. MLB also requires players who violate their domestic violence and sexual assault policy to be evaluated by a professional, who then recommends what type of counseling they need to undergo, if any.

But just because MLB does the job of handling allegations of violence by athletes better than the other three major pro sports doesn't mean there isn't a lot of room for improvement. For example, the preferred method of counseling for men who abuse women is many months of group therapy where abusers, who are notorious for their ability to manipulate people and come off as "nice" guys, can call each other out on their bullshit. But how does a player continue to participate in group therapy once his suspension is over and he's back on the road?

What's more, given Americans' ability to throw any sense of moral decency out the window when a celebrity is involved, how does having a pro athlete change the dynamic of group therapy? If fans and teammates aren't willing to publicly criticize a player for being violent and abusive, can we expect regular group attendees to treat him differently? Keep in mind how Derrick Rose's jury, who stated in jury selection that they wouldn't be influenced by Rose's celebrity, lined up to take photos with him after the trial.

And then there's the length of the suspensions. The longest one MLB has ever handed out was one hundred days to the Padres' José Torres, and the shortest was fifteen games, to both the New York Mets' Jeurys Familia and the Boston Red Sox's Steven Wright. Michael Feinerman, programs director at the Center for Advancing Domestic Peace, works to develop counseling programs for abusers. Feinerman told me that he doesn't believe much can be accomplished in that time frame. "Change takes time," Feinerman pointed out. "We often find that the six months that a person is in our program is hardly enough time to begin this process, and research tells us that it may be a few years before new behavior is fully integrated. It's hard for us to believe that a three-to-six-week series is likely to be effective in producing lasting (or even immediate) change."

While those who work in the domestic violence field debate whether the purpose of MLB's policy is PR-driven or reflective of a real desire to move the needle on domestic violence, there's no denying that MLB is ahead of the NFL, whose violence-based suspensions are solely punitive. Players are off the field and losing money, but there's no attempt to rehabilitate anyone.

Though they fly under the radar with this kind of stuff, the NHL is arguably the worst league around when it comes to caring about violence against women. When Colorado Avalanche goalie Semyon Varlamov was arrested for beating up his girlfriend in 2013, the league took no action after his criminal case was dismissed due to a lack of cooperation from the victim. In fact, Varlamov was back in goal for the Avs two days after his arrest.

When Patrick Kane was under investigation for sexual assault in 2015, the Chicago Blackhawks not only didn't take him off the ice while the investigation was pending, they went out of their way to push him forward, inexplicably putting him front and center at every media and publicity event while men on social media were harassing his alleged victim into having to move to a new state. The team didn't appear to prep Kane's teammates on diplomacy and sensitivity, either, leading to several statements from Blackhawks who said they supported Kane. This carelessness with words was interpreted by fans and media as their heroes calling the victim a liar and giving their fan base, who had uncovered the name of the victim and circulated it online, permission to keep harassing her. As Chicago sports blogger Jason Parini pointed out on Twitter, the NHL has a much more defined rule for violence *on* the ice than off it.

NHL commissioner Gary Bettman has said the league prefers to focus on education and counseling, but it's still not clear that the league has a formal structure in place to do so. In 2016, the league began sexual assault and domestic violence training. In 2019, the NHL banned player Slava Voynov for the 2019–2020 season for past incidents of violence against his wife. In that sense, the league may be trying to catch up to others when it comes to making an example of players who commit violence against their partners, but the lack of policy still means a lack of consistency and punishments left to the whims of Bettman.

Formal domestic violence and sexual assault policies created by sports leagues leave a lot to be desired, and we could talk all day about the need for policies that support victims better or are more racially balanced in application. But if there is one thing leagues could do across the board to give their polices more teeth, it's to add a mandatory postseason ban.

Let's go back to Roberto Osuna. He was suspended by MLB on June 22, 2018, retroactive to May 8, the day he was arrested. With the July 31 MLB trade deadline less than a month away, the Toronto Blue Jays made the decision that, despite Osuna's 3.38 ERA and 2017 all-star season, he was damaged goods and not worth risking the goodwill of the fan base for. They traded him to Houston on July 30, 2018, for a package of pitchers far below what he probably would have commanded sans suspension.

From Houston's standpoint, once they got past the fan backlash for trading for an abuser (similar to what the Cubs front office had to deal with in 2016 for trading for Aroldis Chapman), it was a hell of a deal. For a mediocre reliever and two prospects, they wound up with an elite closer who would go on to pitch for them in two straight postseasons. If a team doesn't care about integrity (and it's pretty clear from the Astros' cheating scandal that they don't), this deal is a no-brainer.

And therein lies the problem with not banning suspended players for the postseason. Remember, in Osuna's case, all his domestic violence suspension did was make him an undervalued commodity for Houston—worth far more than his asking price. And the lack of teams trying to acquire him for fear of upsetting their fan bases only made him easier to acquire. And, as we saw with Aroldis

Chapman playing a major role in getting the Cubs to the World Series in 2016, if a player wins enough big games, fans are willing to forgive anything.

And this is where sportswriters and broadcasters with big platforms come in. No one is asking for an asterisk every time a player with a violent history is mentioned, as guys on social media love to claim. "What? Do you have to bring it up *every* time we talk about the guy?" No, but sports media does have an obligation to bring it up when it's relevant. In 2016, after the Cubs acquired Aroldis Chapman, catcher Miguel Montero referred to him in an interview as "not a bad guy." Manager Joe Maddon referred to him as "Chappy." In his book, *Teammate* (which I bought just so I could call him out on this), Cubs skipper David Ross says of Chapman: "Everyone knew he was a great guy." Well, guess what? There's a pretty detailed police report and MLB investigation out there showing that Chapman is *not* a great guy. Guess who was the one to bring this stuff up repeatedly on her station?

Surprise! It was me.

I don't know if it's some kind of weird male loyalty to the alpha male or fear of not being part of the cool kids or what, but I don't remember a single reporter asking Maddon why he gave a diminutive nickname to a guy coming off a domestic violence suspension. When Ross was hired to manage the Cubs in 2019, no one asked him about Chapman "being a great guy" or his views on domestic violence. If we ever want to get better on this topic, sports media cannot be complicit in letting guys get away with saying things like this.

We have to do better.

CHAPTER 5

DON'T @ ME

Adventures in Online Harassment

t took me a few seconds to realize what I was looking it. The picture was in black and white. A group of seated men held a bound naked woman across their laps. She was blindfolded. Her throat was slit. They were holding her in an awkward position because they were draining her blood into a bucket. The looks on their faces were sympathetic, paternal. Like a parent who is reluctantly forced to punish a naughty child. *Look at what you forced us to do.*

It was a random Tuesday. It was impossible to tell if the picture was real. It looked real.

I still have nightmares about it.

One thing about online harassment is that you never know when it's going to hit. Immediately before sitting down to write this chapter, I received two direct messages on Twitter. One was a strange man calling me a fat whale and suggesting I'd soon die of diabetes. The other was from another man I don't know calling me "the most vile piece of shit I've ever seen."

The other thing about online harassment is that when it's happening to you, it's all you can talk about and think about. You feel like you're standing, naked and exposed, in the center of a circle of people who are all yelling and screaming insults at you. But the rest of the world doesn't notice.

It's also deeply isolating. No one really wants you to talk about it, at least not to the extent that you feel you *need* to talk about it. Well-meaning friends and coworkers will advise you to "just ignore it!" But you can't ignore it, not really. Not when all you see are people calling you names, threatening you, and trying to find out where your kids go to school and where you live and who your husband is, so they can harass them, too. Not when someone shares that they hope your dog gets hit by a car. Not when someone puts up a fifteen-minute video encouraging others to "go to war" with you because they didn't like your opinion about a retiring sportscaster. Not when you're minding your own business and working on editing your book when some rando asshole New York Jets fan from Towson University sends you an Instagram message calling you a "fat cow" and telling you "u just mad because no guys would ever wanna be with u." Sorry if that last one was oddly specific.

My first experience with mass trolling was in 2013. I had recently published a piece that attempted to dispel some of the myths about the behavior of rape victims by sharing, for the first time, my own rape story. I'd written it in response to all the slut-shaming comments I'd seem about the sexual assault victim of then Florida State quarterback Jameis Winston. A segment of FSU fans, educated neither in the dynamics of sexual violence nor in the psychology of trauma, had taken to Twitter to point out that his accuser *had* to be lying, because she didn't report the rape immediately and because she texted Winston after the attack.

In the piece, I wrote about how it took me months, maybe years, to consider what happened to me "rape," even though an army officer, much bigger and stronger than I was, held me down and overpowered me. Even though I kept saying no. Even though I was sore for days afterward. It happened during spring break of my senior year of college. The next night, I saw my rapist again at a bar. I made a beeline for him and chatted with him about college basketball. I couldn't tell you to this day why I did that. Maybe because I needed to convince myself it wasn't rape.

The day the piece ran, I was introduced to my first mass troll attack. As quickly as the piece went up, I had dozens of complete strangers threatening to kill me, accusing me of making up my own rape, and describing to me, in detail, what they'd like to do to me should our paths ever cross. I was so shocked that I made my account private and stayed away from Twitter for days. Eventually, it blew over.

The second time I was attacked by a troll army was far, far worse.

t was August 2015 when Chicago Blackhawks star Patrick Kane was accused of sexual assault. I had started working at my radio station, the biggest sports station in Chicago, only a few months before. Because I'd both been a criminal defense attorney and worked with victims of sexual assault and domestic violence, I was in a unique position to explain to our listeners how the investigation would proceed and what each step meant. And because I'd already developed a reputation of writing about violent athletes, several people close to the investigation reached out to me privately to talk anonymously and sometimes off the record.

At the time, I was working as an update anchor for my station, which meant I was mostly on the air in a reporting role, but as the story progressed, several of the shows had me on to provide analysis of the evidence and explain what every new bit of information could mean for Patrick Kane and the Blackhawks. A few days after the story broke, I wrote a piece for our website titled "How NOT To Talk About the Patrick Kane Case," calling out some of the "fans" who had taken to social media to share photos of the victim talking to Kane at a bar earlier in the evening and to speculate that she invented the rape as a "money grab," even though she never sought a financial settlement from Kane. We were told by our station's management to be extremely careful not to weigh in on Kane's guilt or innocence publicly. I tried to analyze the case straight down the middle but found myself spending a lot of time online and on the air debunking myths about rape victims and women in general.

During the time, I was talking constantly with those sources involved in the investigation. They were anonymous, vetted by our digital editor and by the higher-ups at CBS Radio, but their identities were withheld from the public. When I reported what I was told by multiple sources, I was met with responses like "Reveal your sources or shut up!" and "Unless you tell us where you're getting this info from, I'll assume you're making it up." Apparently, a significant portion of Blackhawks fans have no understanding of journalism and/or have never seen *All the President's Men*.

And then the case against Kane fell apart. I have very definite feelings on how and why that happened. I stand by every iota of reporting I did during that time. I still believe all of it to be true. I never once weighed in on Kane's guilt or innocence. I would have been fired if I had stated my opinion one way or the other.

The day we got word that a family member of the victim had interfered with the investigation and that the case would not move forward, the trolls descended on me like a nuclear bomb. More than one man threatened to come to Chicago to kill me. Another suggested the only just punishment for me was to be raped with a hockey stick. Another said he hoped I would be raped "again." Someone else sent me the worst message I have ever received. It was that naked woman, bound and blindfolded and bleeding. I still haven't recovered from that one.

And then there was a much more direct threat. In the midst of all the notifications I was getting about all the ways Blackhawks fans wanted to maim and kill me, someone sent me a picture of the entrance to the building where I worked. It wasn't the main building entrance; it was a small entrance around the back: the way I got into the building every day.

That was the first time I understood what it meant to have your blood run cold. Remembering that moment, I can feel my blood going cold again. This was before I got into the habit of taking screenshots of all the threats. The first thing I did was pick up the phone and start shouting in a panic at my husband, who was in the middle of a conference call and was completely unaware of what was happening. Next, I called my boss. It was near the end of the week. We agreed it was safest for me to stay home until the following Monday.

Over the course of that weekend, the threats continued to roll in. I was afraid to go outside, afraid to be online. The camera on my laptop kept turning on by itself. I covered it up with tape. Word had gotten out, and a dozen media outlets contacted me for an inter-view. I was too afraid to talk to anyone.

I stayed in bed almost the entire weekend.

When Monday rolled around, I took a deep breath, donned the biggest pair of sunglasses I could find, and stuffed all my hair, which is recognizable, into a hoodie. I kept my head down the en-tire long train ride into the city and on the bus to my office. As I walked along the side of my building to a different entrance than the one I used, I caught a glimpse of myself reflected in the glass. Head down, shoulders hunched, looking like the Unabomber. I stopped and stared, disgusted with myself. This was *not* me. I was cowering and hiding because of a bunch of jerks on Twitter who were so worked up over a player they had never met that they were threatening to hurt me? SCREW THAT. I ripped off my hood, took off my sunglasses. I held my head high as I rode the escalator to the second level of the lobby. In the coming months and years, I would protect my Twitter and Facebook accounts many times, but I would never hide again.

My story of online harassment is far from unique. The day the Patrick Kane investigation ended was the day my life changed. More than five years later, it's still not normal. But I'm far from the only woman working in sports (or media in general) dealing with this sort of harassment.

In the months after that incident, I wrote a piece that revealed how much online abuse women in sports media have to wade through on a daily basis. I reached out to several women in the in-dustry, and, almost to a one, they asked me if I wanted their entire file of abusive screenshots or if I just wanted a few examples. Every time I get a new laptop, the first thing I do is move the massive file of screenshots threatening me with rape, death, and worse to the new computer. On the off chance that something happens to me, I want the police to have somewhere to start looking, even though they've been disinterested in helping me while I'm alive. What I remember most about that story going up was that someone at *Sports Illustrated* insisted that they tweet it out first, so as to use their platform to get more eyes on the piece. And while I was a little irked that I wasn't the first to put my own story out to the public, I was grateful for all those with bigger platforms than me who helped the story go semi-viral. At least in the sports media industry.

Six months after the *SI* story, I stood in an artist's warehouse in Ukrainian Village with a bunch of guys I've never met. A few weeks earlier, one of them had contacted me about filming a public service announcement on the harassment of women in sports media. They reached out after reading the piece I had written on the topic, and they just happened to catch me at the end of a really terrible day online. Because I'm nothing if not impulsive, I responded to his cold email with something super professional, along the lines of "Fuck it, why not?"

So there I was in a studio, still slightly damp from rushing over after work, in an unflattering sweater that I, in that moment, had no idea would (1) look horrible on camera and (2) be seen by something like fifteen million people. Brad Burke, one of the producers, had asked me if I wanted them to arrange for professional makeup. I said no. Life lesson: Always, *always* say yes to the professional makeup.

The concept was simple. We'd start off the video like Jimmy Kimmel's popular "Mean Tweets" segment, having random guys read mean tweets to me, the camera capturing my reaction. The first couple of tweets are funny, but they slowly get darker and more threatening. As we reach the last few tweets, the viewer is hearing the men read some of the more vile messages I've received. Only they weren't the *most* vile. We had to make sure YouTube would let us keep the video up, so we decided to go with the R-rated tweets instead of the worst of the worst, X-rated tweets. By the time my day of filming was over, I'd heard guys calling me fat and ugly and praying for my rape so many times they didn't register anymore. But the discomfort of the guys reading the tweets across from me was palpable. Some of them couldn't look at me and read the tweets at the same time. And they hadn't even written them—these were wholly innocent guys who volunteered for a fun *"Kimmel-type"* segment and wound up sweating and trembling and apologizing over messages someone else wrote.

With that, #MoreThanMean was born.

We knew from the start that the video couldn't be just me. That would make it a "Julie DiCaro" problem and not a universal problem for women in media. We asked women sportswriters and broadcasters all over Chicago to be part of it, but nearly every single one turned us down. They either didn't want to paint a target on their back for the trolls, or they were wary of getting the side-eye from their employer over it. In early 2016, online harassment in media was still something no one really wanted to talk about. In the end, every single woman we asked said no.

Except one. ESPN's Sarah Spain was game, and I knew she had been dealing with the same kind of harassment I had because I saw it regularly on Twitter. A week or so after I recorded my video, Sarah filmed her segment with the same crew.

And then, I just sort of forgot about it. I had no idea what the final product would look like, but I figured these guys would put out the video, maybe some people in the industry would see it, and I'd help out with a retweet.

That is not what happened.

The day the video was released, April 25, 2016, I was home sick from work. I'd taken a nap around the time the video went up. I woke up two hours later to something like 750 notifications on my phone. #MoreThanMean was the top trend on Twitter. That night, my parents found out about the video because they saw it on *CBS Evening News*. Sarah and I were doing interviews via FaceTime and Skype on the way from one on-camera interview to another. The initial round of interviews slowed down after a few days, but I didn't stop doing interviews or speaking about the video for a year. Even now, I regularly speak to high schools and colleges about online harassment.

At the height of the video's popularity, we saw it discussed on shows like *The View*, *Outside the Lines*, *The Talk*, *His & Hers*, and CNN International. Celebrities from Erin Andrews to WNBA superstar Elena Delle Donne tweeted about #MoreThanMean. Even celebrities like Kris Jenner, Terry Crews, and Jared Leto shared the video and tweeted out their reactions. Overnight, it was everywhere.

I haven't worn that horrible sweater since.

Sarah and I were asked frequently why we thought the video struck such a chord with people. Unfortunately, we'd both come to the same conclusion: it was the discomfort of the *men* in the video that made it stand out and resonate with people.

I can't tell you how often, in the days following #MoreThanMean, I was asked if the *guys* in the video were okay, or if we'd apologized to them for . . . I'm unsure for what. Including them in a viral video they volunteered for?

It was stark reminder to Sarah and me that people might shake their heads and click their tongues when women show despair or sadness, but it's an upset man that people really can't take. If the mean tweets had been read to us by an off-screen voice, if you couldn't see how hard it was for the men to get through reading the tweets, if it had been women reading the tweets to us, would the video have had the same impact? I don't believe it would have.

Let me be clear: all of us involved in the video, which won a Peabody Award in 2017, are bound together by a common experience we will never forgot. The men who came up with the idea for and produced the video, Brad Burke, Adam Woullard, Chad Cooper, Gareth Hughes, and Joe Reed, had made the video to shed light on how hard online harassment is for women. Why so many people focused on the men's reactions is something I'm still trying to wrap my head around. And don't worry, all those guys are completely fine.

Before I started writing this chapter, I put out a call on Twitter for women in sports media to tell me their stories of online harassment, just like I had back in 2016 when writing for *The Cauldron* at *SI*. It was immediately met by a very thoughtful response from a complete stranger whom I have never met and don't follow and who has New York Giants quarterback Daniel Jones as his avatar, who decided to say this:

Aww someone needs attention I guess it's ok if it takes away your attention from the donuts.

Just in case I didn't get his extremely subtle point, he followed it up with a pig emoji.

This kind of response is par for the course for many women who work in media, and especially for women in sports media, which has traditionally been the domain of men. A quick perusal of my phone, which contains many screenshots of harassing tweets and messages, reveals similarly charming messages. Here's a quick sampling: one gentleman called me a "nasty pig who sees younger, prettier women being successful and can't stand it," and another user sent me a message that said, "fuck you feminist bitch, go to the kitchen and make me a sandwich. Suck my peen . . . bitch." And they're not just on Twitter! Take, for example, another portrait in courage from the anonymous user who emailed me to say "you are a cunt and a fat whale. You are a feminazi, too," and "Lay off the Twinkies feminazi." Thank you so much for your thoughtful and constructive criticism of (checks notes) . . . me.

A 2014 Canadian study revealed what anyone who has ever dealt with a troll already knows: they exhibit the same personality traits as narcissists, psychopaths, and sadists. Their "troll" personalities, which are sometimes separate from their personal profiles, exist solely for the purpose of upsetting, disturbing, and humiliating their targets. Further research has shown that trolls absolutely understand the distress their behavior causes; they just don't care. One study showed that trolls were far more likely than the average person to find humor and amusement in others' pain and minimize blame on the perpetrator who caused it.

We'd like to think that people who legitimately enjoy inflicting emotional pain on others, usually complete strangers, are few and far between. Believing that trolls are just a few bad apples certainly makes it easier to get out of bed every morning and face the day. But in a 2018 report, Amnesty International found that 23 percent of women polled had been harassed at least once online, 59 percent of the time by a total stranger.

Kristen Ledlow, a host and reporter for NBA TV and TNT, was one of the first to volunteer to talk about her experiences with social media.

"I actually remember reading the first really awful thing about myself when I was twenty-two and I was working the local news, and it bothered me so greatly that this person that I didn't know could hide behind anonymity and not just criticize my work, but attack me as a woman and get away with it," Ledlow said. "I decided very early on that any and all of what I would share [on my social media accounts] would be what was already made available to the public. It would be about my very public job in the public eye. And anything that was beyond that for me was going to be considered private and off-limits."

At first glance this seems like a rational and savvy idea from a young Kristen Ledlow. And it might have even worked, if trolls didn't have an uncanny ability to find something to criticize in every single thing their targets do. Full-body shot on camera? *You look fat.* Blond hair? *You're an airhead.* Doing your job talking to a player? *You probably want to sleep with him.* Get a hard-earned promotion? *You're a diversity hire and/or are sleeping with your boss. Probably both.*

So why not just get off Twitter? This is what people who don't work in media love to suggest to those of us who do. Just get offline. This idea has two main problems: first, dedicated trolls will follow us across platforms to continue their harassment, and second, it's impossible to be good at your job in sports media and *not* be on social media.

Ledlow said, "A few years ago it got to the point with the kinds of things that I had to read on a regular basis about myself and to myself, that I decided that I wanted to be done with it altogether. It was a season of not just basketball but of my own life where I had just come from being the victim of a gunpoint robbery at my home. Someone who knew who I was, who knew where I lived. And that's of course being the ultimate invasion of privacy. I felt just this animal need to protect what was mine to protect my very soul."

I don't know a single woman in sports media who feels good about the balance they have between social media and their personal lives. There is simply no way to give the public what they want (and often, when it comes to women in sports, what they want are pictures) and maintain total protection of your privacy. I'm cagey about what town I live in on social media, because I don't want anyone to know exactly where I am or figure out where my kids go to school. Sometimes I mention my town, sometimes the town next door, sometimes I vaguely reference the "western Chicago suburbs." But a couple of years ago, when attempting to help then *Sports Illustrated* MLB editor Emma Span promote their annual MLB preview issue, I tweeted out a pic of the magazine that had just arrived in my mailbox. My address was clearly visible. I took it down as soon as people alerted me and it was only up for maybe five minutes. But it was long enough. Now when I go back to being vague about where I live, trolls immediately respond with the name of my town. So much for privacy.

"I stopped for months even logging on to social media because of the kinds of things that were so regularly said to me," Ledlow told me. "But also so easily sent to me because of the way that social media platforms are set up. They can so often hide behind anonymity, send a message directly to me so there's no answering to it in front of anyone else. And the kinds of things that I was reading was actually feeding into, at that point, a depression that stemmed from this invasion of privacy that I could no longer take, I could no longer accept. And so it was months. But unfortunately, what I realized in those months is thousands and thousands of people stopped following me and stopped following my work."

Lest you think Ledlow is simply being vain or bragging about her follower count, you should know that growing social media followings is an integral part of working in sports media, and one that writers and broadcasters are often required by their employers to do. Sure, there are a few old crusty sportswriters who refuse to use social media, but for a younger generation, your follower count can get you in the door for more and more prominent jobs.

"I'm recognizing that while I have this desire to protect my privacy and protect those around me who didn't sign up for any of this, I also have a responsibility to the work at hand to promote my work and to continue to grow my platform and to continue to point people to the content that we're creating," Ledlow said. "And so it was a short-lived social media hiatus in the scheme of ten years, three or four months, a very short-lived social media hiatus. People have to listen to this radio show in order for me to get to do the radio show. People have to buy and read this book in order for me to get to write another book. It's not as simple as just ignore it or block it or just don't get on social media for a while."

Ledlow's story is so familiar to those of us who have dealt with online harassment as part of our jobs. Most days, going to work entails having to wade through a bunch of ugly comments on our social media in order to get the information we need for our jobs or to interact with sports fans, which is also an important part of our work.

Which brings me to my all-time favorite bit of terrible social media advice: don't feed the trolls.

No one who has ever dealt with online trolls has ever said this seriously to someone dealing with mass, ongoing harassment. Most of the time, this particular bit of advice comes from Steve with twenty-five Twitter followers or someone's mom on Facebook. So let's talk about trolls.

First, I recognize that this advice is well-meaning, in the same way telling small children being bullied that their parents can't fight their battles for them is well-meaning. It's really off base and ignores the reality about bullies and how they operate, but it's meant to help. I think. It's also possible it's meant to tell harassment victims to shut up and stop whining. It's problematic and unfair to tell victims that they have to deal with people insulting them all day, every day, without fighting back. We wouldn't say that to someone being verbally harassed on the street, and we wouldn't say it to a child being picked on at school.

Telling people to ignore the trolls assumes that all trolls are the same and have the same objectives. It's true that some trolls just want attention and, if you ignore them, they'll move on to bother someone else. But other trolls will ratchet up their behavior until they get the reaction they want from you. Block them and they create ten new accounts. Mute them and they keep going. The lies and insults they send your way will keep increasing in volume and intensity. Some trolls want to ruin your reputation. Some trolls want to make you cry. Remember that when we're dealing with dedicated trolls, we're often dealing with psychopaths, sociopaths, and extreme narcissists. Remember the asshole Jets fan from Towson University? He's a great example. He had made a few (really poor-quality) videos about me in the past. Seriously, dude, don't quit your day job. When those videos didn't get my attention, he started tagging me in them. When that didn't work, he started sending me messages. Some trolls will not be ignored.

National sports talk radio host Amy Lawrence has had enough of people telling her to ignore the trolls. "Not everyone who hangs out a DON'T FEED THE TROLLS sign is suggesting women shouldn't fight back or stand up for themselves," she told me. "But when I *do* respond to those who harass, chastise, or insult me through social media, there is a common response. Others inevitably jump in to suggest I'm being too sensitive, too defensive, or too harsh. Forget the fact that I'm reacting to a post or message initiated by a troll or critic; women who stand up for themselves online are judged more vigorously than men."

Of course, those who admonish victims of online harassment to ignore the trolls don't bother to jump in and defend our honor, not that we need or expect it. But it would be nice if onlookers who seem so invested in our reaction would care as much about the instigators as they do the targets. "Often we are perceived as less feminine if we 'fight back,'" Lawrence said. "I try to use humor to defuse and disarm pundits on Facebook and Twitter, and I find myself using a smiley face or 'ha' in my replies so fewer people will think negatively of me."

For help in understanding trolls, I called up Anita Sarkeesian of Feminist Frequency, a popular speaker and YouTuber. She's also someone who has dealt with some horrific trolling and speaks about it regularly.

"Trolls believe they are the heroes of their own stories,"

Sarkeesian said. "So in order for them to be the hero of their story, *you* have to be the villain."

This is the best explanation I've ever gotten for why certain trolls fixate on a victim who essentially becomes their "hobby." I have a small-but-steadily-growing group of trolls who are now in year five of tweeting about me for multiple hours each day. I've seen them analyzing my tweeting patterns to try to figure out why I was online less during certain times of the day. Discussing where I live and where my kids likely go to school. Searching legal databases looking for dirt on me. Trolling me is what they do for fun. Imagine having that much free time and using it to harass a perfect stranger. Get a real hobby. Work out. Take up ceramics. Learn to play bunco. Contribute to society in some meaningful way.

When #MoreThanMean was nominated for a Peabody Award, and I raised more than $2,000 via GoFundMe to attend the ceremony in New York, they accused me of stealing the money. No matter that tickets for the awards show were $1,500 even for winners, plus flight, hotel, and $400 for the actual award (which I still haven't been able to bring myself to buy), or that I was working more nights and sleeping in late. Every single thing I do has a selfish or nefarious purpose, and they are there to . . . what? Keep me honest? Ruin my reputation? Make me cry? I'm still not sure.

And it's shameful that the platforms these ghouls use allow them to operate unbothered. One of the ways in which social media platforms like Twitter, Facebook, and Instagram have really let harassment victims down is how they evaluate and punish harassment. Absent an explicit threat to your physical safety, most reports get dismissed as not in violation of community guidelines. But what these platforms miss is the very real threat presented by cyberstalking. I have reported accounts to Twitter and said, "Look. This guy has tweeted over one thousand times in the last six months, and every single tweet is about me." I've sent reports telling multiple platforms, "This person has shared out over 150 posts about me that are demonstrably false and are fabricated to impact my reputation." I've reported, "This person put up a video going on a fifteen-minute rant about me and telling everyone he is 'going to war' with me, and I am afraid for my safety."

Crickets. Doesn't violate community guidelines.

Ledlow says she has dealt with similar situations on Twitter and Instagram: "While I was covering one specific NBA playoff series in the same city over and over, I had someone that by all legal terms should have been considered a stalker. But because the rules governing the online bodies are still far behind rules governing our literal bodies, it's difficult to prove (A) who that person is, [and] (B) that they're actually a threat to your safety."

Luckily for Ledlow, she had a group of internet sleuths on her side in the form of some coworkers. I have some Twitter followers I will never know in person who, out of the kindness of their hearts, helped me track down some of my worst trolls, for no reason other than to tell them that I know who they are. They can't skulk around in the shadows anymore. I see them. When this first started happening to me, I would have kept their identities to myself; maybe send them a connection request on LinkedIn, just so they know that *I* know who they are. These days, I'm so fed up I put everyone on blast.

"There were several people from my network that were able to figure out who it was and where he lived," Ledlow said about a troll her followers helped identify. "And that in fact he did live in the city that I was regularly working in. And every single day [he] was making at least a dozen accounts—we ended up counting about 144 accounts—that this person made using my name. It was @Kristen LedlowIsAWhore, @KristenLedlowIsASlut, @KristenLedlowIs, on, and on, and on, and on, and on."

So what's the problem? Just block the guy, right?

First, I can't even begin to count how many days I have lost hours and hours blocking everyone who is trolling me, every new account they made, every person who follows them, and every person who has liked, retweeted, or commented approvingly on their trolling. A whole lot of hours. Back when I was an update anchor at my former station, I had about thirty minutes in between each update. There were days when I spent my entire shift blocking trolls during every thirty-minute break. There are multiple "parody" accounts of me, according to Twitter. There were at least a dozen at one time. There's @JuliesPeabody, @JulieCantWrite, @JulieDSho, @NullBromley (who has an image of me as his avatar and goes by "Julie DiCaro: Fanatic"), @dicaro_julie, and on and on and on.

Most important, though, if someone who is stalking you constantly across social media lives in a city you are headed to, wouldn't you want to know? Sure, social media platforms have given us the ability to see posts only from people we follow, or to block out certain obnoxious comments. That's great from a mental health standpoint. But women working in sports media live in the tension between their mental health in avoiding these messages and their physical safety by maintaining constant vigilance.

"If I don't block," Ledlow said, "he's going to start talking more boldly from behind this one specific screen name, this one specific username. So I've got to make a decision every day. Am I going to protect my mental health and what feels like my very right to show up as a woman working in sports? Or am I going to read this necessary information about a man who was so bothered by my very existence in the city he's living in that perhaps I need to be aware of where he's going to be?"

This tension that women in media are forced to live in results in a lot of self-censorship, meaning women simply censor their own thoughts and opinions online out of fear of harassment and reprisals.

All of this is made even worse by a letdown more personal than nebulous community guidelines: a total lack of institutional support offline.

The entire time I was getting death threats from Patrick Kane fans, it wasn't lost on me that the Blackhawks could have ended it instantly by telling fans to stop harassing reporters covering the story. Or Kane could have. I was far from the only one being constantly threatened and harassed, and the Blackhawks have prided themselves on their social media presence and engagement with fans. It wasn't like they didn't know it was happening. And it would have been so simple: a single tweet. "We know this is an emotional time for everyone, but please don't threaten media members doing their best to cover the team."

And yet . . . silence.

In the days following the debut of the #MoreThanMean video, I was struck by the difference in the reaction from Sarah Spain's employer, ESPN, and my own then-employer, CBS Radio. Sarah got a call from John Skipper, then the head of ESPN, pledging to do whatever he could to help stamp out the harassment his employees were dealing with. And while my boss has always done his best to support me emotionally, I don't think his boss, the head of CBS Radio, had any idea I existed. In fact, I know he didn't because he once introduced me at an event as "Cara." CBS Radio probably had one-tenth the number of employees that ESPN does.

ESPN threw its arms around the video and message, helping promote it and discussing it on multiple shows. Looking back, Spain told me, "ESPN was happy to support and spread the word about the video, inviting me and others on shows to talk about it and helping track all the media mentions, appearances, and reactions to the piece for me. Coworkers were pretty universally supportive, and I especially appreciated the men who told critics that while no one is safe from internet trolling, the experience is far different for women. ESPN went even further following #MoreThanMean, sending out info to the company for anyone who might want security or support."

Meanwhile, most of my work colleagues never even mentioned the video to me, even when I had camera crews at the station interviewing me about it during breaks. Though a few shows on my station did mention it, they never asked me to weigh in on the topic, even though at least one time I was sitting in the update studio, listening to them opine about the video I had been part of. One show even had another woman on to talk about it. Years later, I still have a hard time wrapping my head around that one.

At both the Peabody and Gracie Awards, CBS Radio and ESPN took out full-page ads in the program congratulating their employees who had won awards. Sarah was included in both ESPN ads; I was included in neither CBS Radio ad. ESPN seemed to have taken the video and the message behind it to heart. CBS Radio seemed embarrassed to be associated with it.

Kristen Ledlow agrees that too many media outlets and the men who work for them don't understand the dynamics behind online trolling and don't go far enough to support their employees, who could be struggling with major mental health issues as a result. "I think they still don't understand either at an institutional level, or, as male colleagues, the depth of how difficult it is. Because if it's not your fight, it's a little easier to ignore how hard someone alongside you is fighting."

Being left to fend for ourselves also impacts our ability to do our jobs well. I've been struck speechless more than once by particularly violent and misogynist messages that come in on the station text line, and silence doesn't usually make for great radio. Then the silence elicits more horrible texts, proclaiming me terrible at my job while I try to pull myself together and get back on track. Try getting into the nuance of the Chicago Bears' kicking competition when guys are calling you a "cunt" and a "whore" on a giant computer screen right in front of your face.

I wasn't alone, even in that really specific type of pain. "When I was working as a local sports personality in Atlanta on morning sports radio, I remember watching the text line and being in the middle of a sentence and feeling like I had to swallow tears and still make an impactful point," Ledlow said.

Of course, no one is suggesting that men in sports media don't also get trolled and harassed. But women experience online harassment differently. The Speech Project at the Women's Media Center found that "gender-based harassment is marked by the intent of the harasser to denigrate the target on the basis of sex. It is characterized by sexist vitriol and, frequently, the expression of violence. When men face online harassment and abuse, it is first and foremost designed to embarrass or shame them. When women are targeted, the abuse is more likely to be gendered, sustained, sexualized and linked to off-line violence."

I've gone to my employer several times about particularly problematic trolls, guys (and some women!) who are especially obsessed with me. I've witnessed them doing public-records searches about me, trying to find out where my children attended school, and tracking my social media use throughout the day, to say nothing of the threat that had me sneaking into work that one day. But my employer, unlike ESPN, seemed baffled by how they were supposed to help employees fend off external harassment. Though my boss listened to me cry in his office far more than his fair share of times and frequently sent my concerns up the chain of command, the response from the powers that be was never anything more than a sympathetic chuck on the chin.

In an age when so many companies are encouraging their staffs to get healthy, physically and mentally, with every program from discounted gym memberships to free mental health counseling, it's bewildering that there is such a blind spot for the toll on women dealing with continual online harassment. Even more, how can media outlets not understand the constant mental exhaustion of being angry all the time?

According to Dr. Cynthia Thaik, chronic intermittent anger has been linked to migraines, drug and alcohol addiction, depression, increased heart attack risk, higher blood pressure, and strokes. A state of continual anger can also cause increased anxiety and insomnia and can even impair one's immune system to the point of lessening its ability to fend off disease or cancer.

In Cynthia Lowen's documentary about online harassment, *Netizens*, Anita Sarkeesian speaks for many women dealing with ongoing harassment in a speech about what she couldn't say. "What I couldn't say is 'fuck you,' to the thousands of men who turned their misogyny into a game in which gendered slurs, death, and rape threats are weapons used to try to take down the big bad villain, which in this case, is me," she said. "I'm angry that I'm expected to accept online harassment as the price of being a woman with an opinion. My life, my words, and my actions are put under a magnifying glass. Every day I see my words scrutinized, twisted, and distorted by thousands of men hell-bent on destroying and silencing me."

I get asked all the time how I "deal so well" with all the hate, and my response is always that I'm not sure I do. I have good days and bad days. Days when it rolls off me like water off a duck's back, and days when I internalize everything and collapse into a heap of self-loathing. I am too fat, too ugly, too outspoken to do what I'm trying to do. If I only looked different, spoke different, didn't always feel the need to stick my nose into everything and offer up my two cents, this wouldn't be happening to me. I deserve it.

In *Netizens*, Sarkeesian sums it up plainly: "The thing about being attacked for four years is that it takes away your humanity. You don't get to feel to the extent of the human range of emotions because you can't, or you'd be floored all the time. You have to be hypervigilant, and you can't make jokes, and you can't be human, and you can't exist in the world like everyone else."

It's changed Ledlow's life, too. "It's not only impacted me, it's impacted my family," she said. "My husband asks time and time again that I don't tag him in anything that I post solely because he didn't sign up for it. He didn't sign up for the kind of harassment that I often receive. It's impacted my own immediate family as well in that neither my mom nor my dad are on any social media anymore because of how difficult it was for them during games, during big events, to see what they had to see on social media about their kid. And so it's more impactful than just to the person that it's being aimed at."

Sarah Spain, too, struggles with the daily roller coaster of emotions harassment brings with it. "Mostly I'll notice that I was in a perfectly fine mood and then suddenly be agitated and frustrated," she said. "I'll realize that my mood shift came after diving into social media and engaging. For the most part I try not to let it affect my job, but I'll occasionally want to talk about a controversial topic on my radio shows or in my social feeds, and I won't because I won't have the energy to respond to all the hateful messages."

Harassment is, in the end, about silencing women, which is why we get much more of it when we take a stand on certain issues than when we read sports scores. Sports scores are objective, lack any real thought, don't make men uncomfortable. In the same way that exiling all women to the sidelines in sports reporting is an act of silencing them, trolls seek to keep us from talking, or at least train us to say only the things they deem acceptable. Women are allowed to exist in a sports-only space, for the most part, as long as we're young enough and hot enough and appeal to men. While I was interviewing women for this book, there was a stark difference between the women who generally limit their sports presence to X's and O's and the women who say things people may not want to hear. Our experiences with harassment are very different. At the end of the day, the entire goal of harassment, to the extent that it even *has* a goal beyond giving men opportunities to scream what they feel into the void, is to teach us to self-censor. And it works. More and more, I notice myself not weighing in on a tough topic because I just don't have it in me that day to deal with the blowback.

ESPN's Mina Kimes told me she sometimes finds herself censoring what she talks about on social media, knowing that engaging in "controversial" topics, like domestic violence in sports, will elicit serious blowback. "I constantly question how much time and energy I should devote to this stuff," she said. "There's so much positivity [online] and excited engagement and there's so much good, but the negative can really ruin your day and make it hard to do your job. And I don't think anyone's quite figured out the right answer how to deal with this."

If you keep your head down and don't draw attention to yourself, you might survive in sports media. But if you weigh in on controversial topics—like sexism in sports, violence against women, racism, Islamophobia, homophobia—you light up like a beacon, and they all come for you. In a 2014 article at *The Awl*, John Herrman stated the obvious:

> *A great number of men, online and off, understand feminism as aggression—they feel as though the perception of their actions as threats is itself a threat. In other words, they too believe that unsolicited public attention is inherently aggressive, but only when that attention takes the form of criticism, and only when it comes from women. They live this belief on the streets, where they are nearly unaccountable, and argue it online, where they are totally unaccountable. And they are everywhere!*

If we're ever going to get a handle on online harassment as it relates to women in sports, it's essential that media outlets get involved in protecting their employees. In a 2020 report on the subject, the Women's Media Center found that for women, people of color, and members of the LGBTQ+ community, among others, online harassment is more frequent and more intense. Yet most media outlets lack both the education and the will to help their reporters handle the abuse. I've experienced this firsthand, working for two corporations, CBS Radio and then Entercom, who really don't think it's their job to protect their employees from this kind of thing. Moreover, according to the WMC report, women register "higher emotional resonance" when it comes to online abuse. In short, we feel it more than men do, which goes a long way toward explaining why my male friends are often so bewildered at my inability to "just ignore" a guy calling me a "fat whore whale," or whatever. Unfortunately for us, higher emotional resonance also means that women are more likely to self-censor in order to avoid more abuse.

Earlier, I talked about the lengths ESPN has gone to to help their employees navigate online abuse in the wake of the #More ThanMean video. In the Women's Media Center report, Soraya Nadia McDonald, a culture critic at ESPN's *The Undefeated*, said, "At ESPN, one of the first things we are told in orientation is about security measures. They have the resources to provide security, legal backup, and more."

While no one may have figured out the right answer, totally, ESPN seems miles ahead of the pack when it comes to having their employees' backs against external harassment.

In the spring of 2020, shortly before I lost my job (and I'll always wonder if this meeting had something to do with it; that I was just too big of a headache), I had a meeting with a regional HR representation for Entercom, the company that owned the radio station I worked for. For the week prior, Barstool Sports followers (more on them in the next chapter) had been calling into my show nonstop and spamming our text line constantly, making it impossible for me to take calls or texts from my listeners. I ignored it the best I could, but after a week of it, I'd had enough.

I'd spoken about online harassment with our previous HR representative for CBS Radio, but I had spent most of the time trying to explain Twitter (he wasn't on it) and the dynamics of online trolling to him. He promised to look into it but never offered any kind of substantive help or support. I was hopeful that now, working for a much larger outlet, I'd have better luck getting some competent backup.

Unfortunately, I found myself having a nearly identical conversation with the new HR rep. She suggested that I "stop pouring gasoline on the fire" to get men to stop harassing me. I told her about what ESPN does for their employees, which I don't think she believed. She ended by giving me a lecture about remembering that I "wear the Entercom logo at all times."

I got the message loud and clear. I was responsible for the harassment I suffered. Not only would the company not lift a finger to help me, they saw my ordeal with online harassment as an inconvenience that made the company look bad.

In hindsight, I should have known I was screwed when the new market manager, a woman, kept joking in a meet-and-greet about how bad the trolls were in sports radio. She relished telling us some story about her husband buying her a troll doll or Christmas ornament or something (I was too dismayed to pay close attention), because now she'd have to deal with trolls! Get it? I left that meeting feeling sick to my stomach, knowing I was dealing with yet another upper-management group that didn't care to understand the toll trolls can take on their employees.

I probably should have known better. As the old adage goes, HR isn't there to protect you, HR is there to protect the company. But it's still baffling to me that in a time when online harassment is so pervasive and has such an effect on the media's ability to do its job, HR departments across the landscape continue to be populated by people who seem to know very little about the dynamics of abuse, or social media for that matter. What's more, many companies have vague social media "policies" that allow them to discipline employees at any time for what they say online, while refusing to help employees combat the abuse they endure on those same accounts. Basically, if Entercom didn't like something I said on Twitter, they could discipline me for it and demand I take it down (which they had done, thanks to the Chicago Cubs). But when I needed help with random men threatening to kill and rape me, their position was "Hey, good luck with aaaalllll that."

For years, and especially since #MoreThanMean, people have asked me, with desperate hope in their eyes, if online harassment is "getting better." And they really, really want me to say yes. But the truth is, it's changing but not getting better. I can keep from seeing most of the harassment, if I have my filters set properly, but as Sarkeesian noted in *Netizens*, "It's not getting better—it's still terrible; it's still harassment every day, and just because you're not seeing it doesn't mean it's not happening. And just because you might be burnt out on it . . . so are we."

I had a similar experience following Kobe Bryant's death. While sitting in shock at the library when the news of his death hit, I tweeted that I didn't "know how to feel" about the tragedy and said I was thinking of Bryant's wife and daughters. This was well before we knew that Bryant's thirteen-year-old daughter, Gianna, had also died in the crash, along with several of her teammates and their parents. I was being completely honest—I didn't know how to reconcile my feelings about the way Kobe Bryant and his lawyers handled the sexual assault allegations against him in 2003 (and afterward) with what he clearly meant to so many people. I was shocked and horrified at the way he died, just like the rest of America.

But the cadre of trolls who count harassing me among their hobbies seized on the moment. Flooding my boss and station with demands that I be fired immediately. They turned the narrative into "She doesn't know how to feel about a thirteen-year-old girl dying! She's a monster!" Later, it became "She said she's glad Kobe is dead!" Of course, I never felt this, nor did I ever say it. But when others repeat a lie enough times, people start to believe it.

Management at the station called me, clearly frazzled by the influx of messages demanding my head. I tried to explain that this was the same group of trolls as always, twisting the story once again to get me in trouble at work. One upper-level manager told me I "should have waited" before sending out my tweet. They eventually got over it, but trolls continued to abuse me online for weeks. When several big-time outlets asked me to write about Kobe's death from the standpoint of a sexual assault survivor, I turned them down. I felt there was plenty to say, but not from me. I just didn't have the energy or the strength to go through another round with the trolls. Not too long after this, my position was eliminated, ostensibly because of COVID, but maybe my bosses never did get over it.

The trolls wanted to silence me. It worked.

If you work in sports media, or in any other field, and you've been the victim of mass troll attacks that have affected your standing with your employer, know that you aren't alone. I know several women working in media who have been labeled "lightning rods" because of the troll armies that created multiple accounts to get around being blocked, waited for any opening they could exploit, and then made life miserable for their targets by making life tough on their employers. And while I was sympathetic to my boss getting spammed by trolls because of me, it was also a seventy-two-hour window into what I deal with on a regular basis.

So, because Twitter and Facebook and all the other social media platforms have refused to deal with trolls and the harassment taking place via their platforms, how do we make sure people in general, and women in particular, have some protection at work? First, it's incumbent on every employer with public-facing employees to be educated about the dynamics of online harassment. It's inexcusable that I had to deal with two HR directors in a row who weren't on social media, basically throwing up their hands and telling me there was nothing they could do. If there was a guy following me everywhere I went and standing outside my building yelling every day, my company would handle it. When it's five hundred guys on Twitter, I'm on my own.

Second, more media companies need to look to the protections ESPN gives its staff as a model for keeping their own employees safe. Those protections need to be incorporated into a two-way social media policy. Most companies have a catch-all policy that says how they expect their workers to comport themselves on social media. You probably have one at your job right now. But what can employees expect from their bosses when the online harassment begins? Will you help protect me? Will you back me up if I go to law enforcement? Will you provide security for me if I need it? What will you do if you find one of your employees is using social media to troll people? Will you use your relationship with platforms like Twitter to advocate for me? Can I take a mental health day if I'm in the middle of a storm of abuse?

These are all reasonable requests for employees who are expected to take part in social media regularly as part of their job. Unfortunately, for the most part, media companies have been more concerned about being embarrassed by their workers making a misstep than about the very real possibility of mental or physical harm coming to one of them as a result of online harassment. Media companies must learn to back their employees, and it's high time we started demanding it.

CHAPTER 6

KICKING OUT THE BARSTOOL

Taking on the Industry Leader in Toxic Masculinity

'm going to regret writing this chapter.

It's not just me, though. Everyone who writes about Barstool Sports in a negative way winds up regretting it in one way or another. By the time you start reading this book, I'll have locked down every social media account and will have hired an expert to help scrub all private info about me from the web.

By the time Barstool came into my life, I'd already experienced online harassment on a massive scale. Death threats, rape threats, attempts to get me fired from my job. It was good that I'd been through the beginning and intermediate online harassment experiences, because Barstool definitely engages in advanced-level trolling. Many of the experiences in the previous chapter came from guys whose Twitter profiles reveal they're in their late teens or twenties, centered in the Northeast, curiously, and often have Tom

Brady as their avatar. Oh, and the vast majority of them interact with Barstool Sports regularly.

If you've never been to Barstool's website, you probably think of them as the guys that retweet funny videos on social media. If you've never been on the receiving end of one of the mass troll armies of "Stoolies," you might think of them as some of the guys from the popular podcast *Pardon My Take*. If you've really been paying attention, you might remember them as the guys who had a deal with ESPN for a regular show, only to have it almost immediately canceled after several ESPN employees objected. If you've never encountered Barstool Sports in any meaningful way, congratulations—and you might want to stop reading now, lest you have to sanitize your brain after this chapter.

Let's be clear: for dozens, maybe hundreds, of women working in sports, Barstool Sports is an insidious online community of men (and, sadly, some women) who get their kicks via misogyny and racism, and then attack, en masse, when someone points out their toxicity.

How bad is Barstool? I've adopted a practice I picked up from several other women who have been attacked by Stoolies. I call it the Voldemort Protocol. It was developed and honed to spare me the wrath of Blackhawks fans during the Patrick Kane unpleasantness (mentioned in chapter 5), and perfected as the result of multiple run-ins with Stoolies. These are the rules (*Law & Order* "chung chung!" sound):

1) Never, ever include the word "Barstool" on any public forum;
2) Block anyone who interacts with any of the Barstool accounts;
3) Block anyone who retweets Barstool accounts;
4) Block anyone who follows Barstool accounts.

At first glance, this probably seems ridiculous. How can an on-line entity be so scary that women won't even use the proper name of the site? I, too, was once like you. Then Barstool Sports entered my life. And I'm not alone. The internet hasn't been the same since.

To understand why, you have to understand what Barstool Sports is and where it came from.

Barstool Sports was originally established in 2003, and it mostly existed as a little-known sports and betting blog for its first few years. But it entered the national scene in 2011 with a blog post ti-tled "Check Out the Howitzer on Brady's Kid." Barstool originated in Boston; the Brady in question was Tom Brady, and the "howitzer" was a toddler's penis. At the time, Brady's son Benjamin was not even two years old. The post was headlined with color pictures of Benjamin, naked and frolicking with his family on the beach. The photos had obviously been taken without the consent of the family. The post, written by the founder and leader of Barstool Sports, Dave Portnoy, who goes by the handle @stoolpresidente on Twit-ter, included this text: "Just swinging low like a boss. That's what MVP QB's do. They impregnate chicks and give birth to big dicked kids. PS—The mom's ass ain't bad either." The last line references another picture, which included supermodel Gisele Bündchen in a bikini with her children.

Granted, this might seem tame by the standards of the cesspool that is the internet in 2021 but trust me, this was considered appall-ing behavior in 2011. Even Howard Stern thought the post went too far, calling it "kiddie porn" and telling Portnoy on *The Howard Stern Show*, "I don't think you should put [up] a picture of a two-year-old male."

Imagine starting out by having Howard Stern tell you you've gone too far, and then going further than that.

Over the course of the next several years, a disturbing pattern began to emerge at Barstool. In 2010, a year before the "Babygate" controversy, Portnoy had written "[E]ven though I never condone rape if you're a size 6 and you're wearing skinny jeans you kind of deserve to be raped right?" In a 2011 Portnoy post titled "Kobe Better Not Have Raped Alex Morgan," Portnoy wrote, "Like it's one thing to stick your dick in random chick's assholes and then buy them off, but it's a different game altogether when they are famous."

Both of those blog posts have now been scrubbed from the internet, along with a Portnoy post from 2012 in which he defended Barstool's college tour of "blackout parties" by saying, "Just to make friends with the feminists I'd like to reiterate that we don't condone rape of any kind at our Blackout Parties in mid-January. However if a chick passes out that's a grey area though."

Also gone from the internet is a post from 2010 about veteran sports reporter Tracy Wolfson with the headline "Slut Reporter Drinks Cam Newton's Jizz"; a 2014 Portnoy article about his desire to "bring back" the word "cunt" to everyday parlance; and a piece in which another Barstool employee slut-shamed a missing college student who was later found murdered.

What *hasn't* been systemically scrubbed from Barstool's site tells you more about the guys who run it than what has been removed. A sampling of those posts, which you can likely pull up and read right now, include a 2017 post saying that a baby with the rare condition of hydrocephalus is "a Martian" and the best thing to do was to "kill it"; many, many episodes of a photo series titled "Guess That Ass"; and multiple posts relating to "CuckCycle," the catchphrase Portnoy invented for harassing his ex-girlfriend after she allegedly cheated on him with her SoulCycle instructor. An attention seeker in any situation, Portnoy proudly posted screenshots of the memo SoulCycle had to send out to its employees after the company was bombarded with threats from Stoolies.

I could sit here regaling you with stories of all the horrible things Barstool has said and done on its website (they called Rihanna "fat"!), but all that stuff isn't really the problem. Or at least it's not the biggest problem.

The problem are the Stoolies.

"Stoolies" are what guys (and they almost always are guys) who are seriously into Barstool's culture call themselves. They are the ones who actually read the site and hang out in the comment sections because they like the misogyny and racism. These are guys who live and breathe Barstool and who have elevated coordinated online trolling to an art form before "Bernie Bros" were even a sparkle in Twitter's eye. Early on, women who pointed out the rampant denigration of women that seemed to be Barstool's bread and butter, and that Barstool's blackout parties seemed to excuse if not promote sexual assault, were quickly dismissed as "crazy bitches" and "ugly dykes who hate pretty girls."

I had been relatively outspoken about my objection to the rampant misogyny emanating from Barstool since its early days as a site. Before Twitter, Facebook, and Instagram descended into their current forms of portals to hell, seeing women—especially professional women in sports media just trying to do their jobs—continually called "sluts" and "cunts" was genuinely shocking. Even more disturbing was watching armies of young men cheer on Portnoy and his colleagues.

In 2016, on what started out as a normal day, I tweeted that I didn't appreciate Dwayne "the Rock" Johnson slut-shaming a female wrestler on *WWE Raw*, given that so many children, and especially young girls, were watching. Somehow, my tweet caught Portnoy's eye, and the next thing I knew, my mentions were overrun with young white men with little regard for common decency and an oversize sense of entitlement. They called me every name in the book, speculated about what kind of sex my kids were having (they were thirteen and eleven at the time), and tried to find out where I lived and where my kids went to school. It lasted for days. I first protected my Twitter account, but after I got nearly two thousand follow requests overnight, I wound up deactivating my account all together. *That* led to a subreddit in my name, where hundreds of Stoolies gleefully celebrated the chaos they had injected into my life. All this for criticizing the Rock.

I'm far from the only woman to have had a run-in with the Stoolies. In 2019, the Boston Bruins distributed rally towels for Game 2 of the NHL's Stanley Cup Final. The towels were sponsored by Barstool and featured the Barstool logo underneath a Boston Bruins 2019 Playoffs design. Given the NHL's claims that "Hockey Is for Everyone" and at least their lip service to making the game more inclusive, the sponsorship raised more than a few eyebrows.

By that time, Barstool's particular brand of misogyny and racism was no secret to many sports fans. After multiple fans reached out to question why an NHL franchise was partnering with Barstool, Marisa Ingemi, who covered the Bruins for the *Boston Herald*, reached out to the Bruins PR department for an answer.

"This PR guy told me, 'Email us and we'll send you an official comment,'" Ingemi told me. "So I sent an email. I tweeted, 'I've asked the Bruins for a comment,' just because a bunch of people that messaged me wanted to know . . . and people flipped out. I didn't really even know why because I didn't say, 'Oh yeah, Barstool is bad, by the way.' I just said, 'I asked the Bruins about a comment about the promotion tonight. I'll let you know when they give me a comment.' People got really mad."

By "people," Ingemi is referring to Stoolies, who coordinate mass attacks on anyone who dares disparage the Barstool name by "snitch-tagging" on Twitter. Snitch-tagging is exactly what it sounds like. As soon as a Stoolie sees someone (usually a woman) discussing Barstool in anything less than glowing terms, they usually reply to or tweet the comment, including the Twitter handle of one of the Barstool leaders to notify them. This happens so often that I've speculated that Stoolies have some kind of reward program going—when you snitch-tag ten times you get a free sub or something.

By snitch-tagging, the Stoolie hopes that one of the Barstool leaders will either (A) retweet their tweet, thus alerting the Stoolie army that it's open season on whoever their target is, or (B) respond to the target personally, thus alerting the Stoolie army that it's open season on whoever their target is. This is how Stoolies manage to come down on critics like a nuclear bomb within minutes of whatever the target said.

Ingemi eventually received a response to her query from the Bruins, which amounted to a "no comment," but the mass harassment was already well underway. Her Twitter mentions were so bad that her editor checked in to see if she was okay. And it just kept getting worse.

"A couple of days went by and it was still going on. So I sent out a response [to the harassment]," she told me. Ingemi said she had several people she trusted in the industry look over her statement before she posted it. In a heartfelt attempt to stop the harassment, Ingemi wrote on Twitter, in part:

*Barstool, though its content is deplorable, has become a carica-
ture of a certain type of person that can hide behind a brand or
ideal that is nurtured by their content. Their logo has been a representation of the kind of people that create anonymous accounts
or restricted numbers to harass women.*

*Every single comment sent my way has been in regard to my
appearance or something about me and nothing about the content I produce. I'd wager to guess they've never read anything I
wrote. . . .*

*There are consequences for being a woman. It's doing your job
and men calling you to say they wish you were aborted before you
were born, or to be kicked off the beat, or far worse things. It's the
culture that we're living in that, frankly, men's sports thrive on.*

Below her message, Ingemi included screen caps of some of the
tweets that had been sent her way in response to her tweet about
the Bruins rally towels. "Lose some weight fatty," tweeted @Rancid
Heeb. "Women commenting on sports should be banned," came from
@SwiggityG. "I find it offensive that it says in your bio that you're
a 'women's hockey reporter' and not just a 'hockey reporter,'" was
the incredibly genuine tweet from @TomVeducci. While @Rancid
Heeb and @SwiggityG's Twitter accounts have since been suspended, @TomVeducci's account remains an active follower and
retweeter of multiple Barstool accounts.

Unfortunately for Ingemi, Stoolies can't be shamed or reasoned
with. After her statement, Ingemi said, "[P]eople got even more
mad, and it blew up. I basically spent the whole [Stanley Cup] Final
with people just tweeting at me. Someone found my address and
tried to tweet it out. A bunch of people found personal information
about my family and tweeted it out."

Because she was covering the Final, Ingemi felt it was mandatory that she keep her Twitter account public. But as soon as the NHL season was over, she locked her account. That finally calmed things down. But while Ingemi was on the receiving end of a troll army attack, Portnoy went on Tucker Carlson's FOX News show to defend Barstool and their sponsorship of the towels.

"The PC community, people who don't watch hockey, people who are just mad at life," Portnoy said of those who had complained about the towels. "I had a quote that I read from 2011, which remains true. People who don't like life, laugh, they don't like to laugh. They don't like fun. They don't like men. They don't like America. Those people, they hated this. They absolutely hated this. They pulled their hair out. They demanded answers from the Bruins. It turned into World War Three. A lot of good press for us. Because I don't care, any press is good press."

Meanwhile, Ingemi continued to deal with the Stoolies.

"A couple of days after all this, during development camp, which is the last thing before I finally get off-season, some random person, I've never found out who, started tweeting at all the other Bruins writers weird personal information from me as a kid, and my family and stuff. Some of it not true, some of it half true," she said. "I went into the bathroom, was crying and stuff. I was like, 'Wow, this really sucks for no reason.'"

"Any press is good press" seems to be a concept Portnoy has taken to heart. Over the years, Barstool has been involved in numerous dustups with others working in sports media (including me), but it was the 2017 revolt at ESPN that resulted in the network canceling *Barstool Van Talk* that Portnoy took advantage of the most.

Back in 2014, Portnoy wrote in a now-deleted post that ESPN reporter Sam Ponder was a "BIBLE THUMPING FREAK" and that her only job was to "make men hard." In a subsequent Barstool podcast, Portnoy called Ponder a "fucking slut" and continued with: "We want to see you sex it up and be slutty and not see some prude fucking jerk who everybody hates and who's married to the worst quarterback who wears the ring and 'God first' and this and that. Shut up. That's not what you're there for."

As soon as the deal with ESPN was announced, Ponder took to Twitter to call out Barstool. What followed was described to me as a "silent revolt" at ESPN, with several employees letting management know exactly what they thought about ESPN's partnership with the site. In the end, ESPN, which definitely should have known better, called the whole thing off after one episode of *Van Talk*. The cancelation only led Portnoy to dial his "they hate us because they ain't us" mantra up to eleven and retreat to his familiar "Barstool against the world" attitude, which the Stoolies eagerly lapped up.

There's probably an entire book to be written just on all the people Barstool has harassed. Journalist Laura Wagner, who covered Barstool for *Deadspin*, was a frequent Portnoy target and thus a target of everyone else as well. Comedian Miel Bredouw was targeted by Stoolies after she publicly called out Barstool for stealing one of her videos and distributing it via social media under the Barstool banner (something Barstool does regularly). A Michigan mom is suing Barstool for posting a video of her and her son that was filmed without her knowledge, leading Stoolies to reply with comments like "Bro your mom is an attention whore and she's a real whore on top of it," "Poor child to have such a sh*t mom," and "This kid is going to be a future mass shooter."

Robert Silverman, one of the few men in media who has dared to take on Barstool, was publicly doxxed and said he couldn't use his phone for "about four days" after Stoolies obtained and shared his number. Silverman wrote arguably the definitive piece on Barstool for the *Daily Beast* and said that, in the days that followed the publication of his first piece, Barstool's contributors responded by writing dozens of pieces that were either directly or indirectly about his story. It wasn't until Silverman's article that I saw the tweet from Kevin Clancy, a Barstool staffer who writes under the name KFC, that said, "If I was Julie DiCaro I'd be sleeping with one eye open. Id be watching my back. Because the universe is coming for that ass." (Typos are his own.)

I have no idea what this implied threat was referencing, but this is the kind of thing you stumble across if you end up on Barstool's radar.

While most reporters have stayed away from writing publicly about Barstool, knowing what lies in store for them if they do, journalist Soledad O'Brien made Barstool's reputation for racism, sexism, and online harassment the focal point of a *Real Sports* segment in 2019. To report the story, O'Brien said that they reached out to fifteen women and asked them to speak publicly about their experiences being harassed by Barstool. All fifteen women declined.

"Which I fully understood, because to some degree, it's to what end, right? Like, I'm going to set myself up, for the people who you were asking; they're going to set themselves up to feel like they could be an object of an attack. And I understand that," O'Brien told me.

I was one of the women *Real Sports* reached out to. I shared screenshots of harassing tweets from Stoolies and talked about my experience at length with *Real Sports* producers. But in the end, having had several run-ins with the Stoolies, I decided that I couldn't risk my mental health or that of my children—who, as teenagers, are keenly aware of what Barstool is and exactly how many of their friends are enthusiastic followers. There was no way I was going to risk my kids' friends seeing my name pop up on Barstool social media and sharing it with them. To add to my angst, my older son is at a university five hours away, limiting my ability to get to him in a hurry if Stoolies were to target him—not an outlandish concern to have, given their previous attempts to dig up my personal information.

Even so, I was disappointed in myself. I've always prided myself on standing up to bullies, and if you've ever seen what a Stoolie attack looks like, you have no doubt that you're looking at a bunch of guys who get off on bullying people in general and women in particular. I've stood up to Barstool before, and I've paid the price for it with both my reputation and my mental health. You can only beat your head against the wall for so long, you know?

So if Barstool has this reputation for doxxing and bullying and harassing people, why are so many companies willing to get into bed with the brand? A brand that's at least indirectly responsible for harm done to so many people? As I mentioned before, the Boston Bruins allowed them to sponsor their rally towels during the Stanley Cup Final. In 2019, when Barstool's reputation for being misogynistic jerks was already well-established and just a few months after they had created a "2018 Sex Scandal Teacher Starting Lineup," NASCAR announced a partnership with Barstool, which journalist Alanis King described in a piece for *Jalopnik*: "This partnership tells anyone who might be a subject of Barstool's hate and harassment—women, people of color, the people who defend them—that while their money is just as good as anyone else's for getting in the gates, it doesn't mean they deserve to be welcomed and fully embraced as fans."

If you're a person who has never experienced social media in America in 2021, you might think King's heartfelt plea to NASCAR and other sports leagues contemplating ties with Barstool would have made a dent in the cynical world of sport media and caught someone's attention, but you would be wrong. The only attention it caught was that of Stoolies. NASCAR didn't even respond to her request for a comment on the partnership. Instead, she got an extended harassment campaign by Stoolies.

"A lot of men watch NASCAR; typically all the people in the cars are white men almost, and a lot of the people who watch it are white men," King told me. "NASCAR just has a bad track record with diversity and with being open to people who are not part of its core fan base, people like me. You look at the things that people at Barstool, Barstool's followers, have said about women, people of color, and it's just all a bad look and there's encouragement of harassment and doxxing. So I wrote a column about it, and I knew going into writing the column about it that it would not be good, and that I would get a lot of backlash because I obviously had colleagues who had written about Barstool Sports."

I'm not sure "backlash" is the right word here, as it implies King did something other than write a factual piece about Barstool's history of homophobia, sexism, and racism. At least King knew what was coming. "When you say anything critical of Barstool Sports, it, its followers, or if the people leading it get any wind of it, that's about it," she said. "You're going to get bombarded on the internet with tons of rude tweets and all of these horrible posts, and you might get doxxed. You have to lock down all of your information. Before I posted the story, all of my information was locked out, and I actually got my company to pay for a subscription to having my family's information removed from the internet."

King says that as soon as the article went up, she was inundated with the typical Barstool fare. "So people were like, 'Cry more. Are you going to cry?' 'You're the reason Hillary lost.' 'You're a joke.' 'You're a dumb fuck.' 'Fuck off with this bad victim horseshit.' 'Cry more.' 'Cry me a river.' 'Shut the fuck up.' 'Oh fuck off,'" King said. "It's just you get these every twenty seconds."

In February 2020, King was again subjected to mass harassment by Stoolies, after she stood up for a fellow NASCAR reporter who was *also* getting bombarded by Stoolies in response to a tweet from Portnoy, directing Stoolies to "Attack!"

In 2018, freelance writer Britni de la Cretaz wrote a piece on why the New York Yankees, Chicago White Sox, and New York Mets decided to host "Barstool at the Ballpark Night," which began in 2015. De la Cretaz said they wanted to be as fair as possible, seeking input from both Barstool and the female Barstool fans who attended the events. But when the piece was published, all hell broke loose—despite, de la Cretaz says, the fact that they were extremely up front with the Barstool men, Kevin "KFC" Clancy and "White Sox Dave" Williams.

"They accused me of trying to defame Dave Portnoy, and they were going to sue me. I had to take the contact form down off my website because they started flooding my in-box to the point that I had to disable it right away," they told me. "I was out of the house, and I called my then husband and gave him my website password, and he took it down within ten minutes. But I had gotten thirty emails within the course of a three- or four-minute span."

Yet the list of companies eager to join with Barstool keeps growing. In January 2020, the gaming company Penn National entered into a $163 million deal in which it acquired 36 percent of Barstool. When they announced the deal, senior vice president Eric Schippers told Billy Penn, "We have done our due diligence and are confident that [Barstool Sports] understands the importance of our new relationship and has the right guardrails in place to ensure that their comments won't negatively reflect on PENN or the gaming industry in general." That meant, Schippers said, no more "comments that might be deemed as harassment or discrimination of women or minorities, for example."

Clearly, Penn National isn't very familiar with Barstool.

The next month, *USA Today* sportswriter Hemal Jhaveri took Bauer Hockey to task for announcing a partnership with Barstool, especially given Bauer's history of support for women's hockey in the United States. Wrote Jhaveri:

> *With this partnership, Bauer Hockey is practicing the worst kind of corporate hypocrisy. It is trying to burnish its reputation as an advocate for women's sports while upholding, with explicit support of Barstool, an environment that is extremely hostile towards women. For a little bit of revenue and market exposure gained from a handful of t-shirts sales, Bauer Hockey is cosigning away everything that it otherwise hoped to achieve in making the game of hockey a welcoming and empowering space, not just for women, but for everyone.*

It's worth mentioning that the Barstool podcast with which Bauer was specifically partnering, *Spittin' Chiclets*, had only weeks earlier gotten into a verbal spat with former NHL player Daniel Carcillo. While women are most often the target of Barstool's ire, they do go after men now and again. The harassment Carcillo encountered at the hands of the Stoolies proved to be so severe that Carcillo reached out to police for protection. One Stoolie directly threatened Carcillo's wife and child, responding to one of Carcillo's tweets by writing, "I KNOW where you live hahahaha I will find you and Austin and Ela."

With so many of Barstool's specific incidents of bigotry so thoroughly documented, it's still surprising to the innocents that so many companies want to associate themselves with the brand. But Barstool's main account has 2.4 million incredibly dedicated Twitter followers, the vast majority of them white men under the age of thirty. That's a coveted demographic among brands associated with sports, and, as many have suggested to me, tends to be exactly the kind of person that permeates sports marketing departments.

"It's twenty-, thirty-year-old white kids," Robert Silverman told me. "And *they* like it. And then when they have to pitch it as a possible thing to a brand, what they do is show [Barstool's] social media engagement rate."

It remains a stunning prospect to me that so many people in sports and sports media still cock their heads at me like a confused dog and ask, "What's the problem with Barstool?" But most people beyond the die-hard Stoolies don't bother to check out the site. For them, Barstool means those guys who share funny (though often stolen and uncredited) videos on social media. The coordinated harassment of women, the racist comments, and the homophobia and transphobia remain hidden a few clicks away.

O'Brien, who profiled Barstool and Dave Portnoy on *Real Sports*, talks about the compartmentalization by those who aren't the targets of Barstool's attacks. "At the end of the day they bring an audience and they bring a coveted audience. They bring the twenty-year-old dudes. And people want that audience," she said. "And you're like, 'Great.' But they also have this other side of them and they're able to compartmentalize very well. 'I like this; I don't care for that. So I support this part of it. I don't support that part of it.' I think brands do a similar thing. 'We like this; we don't like that particularly, but hey, the upside for us is they bring an audience that we're trying to figure out how to get and can't otherwise get.' And I think sometimes that translates into dollars. And I think when things translate into money and access, then it's really hard for brands to say no to that."

"Why do people think this is okay?" asked Silverman of Barstool's behavior. "The reason I think isn't just ingrained sexism in America. It's that, too, but I think for most people, the reason people don't understand is because explaining to someone what a Twitter dogpile is is beyond the scope of most casual consumers."

It's hard to describe the emotional trauma of being harassed online on a mass scale to those who have never experienced it. As I said in chapter 5, being in the eye of a Twitter storm is one of the most isolating things I've ever experienced. It's doubly isolating when the people attacking you also provide popular Twitter content and have the support of many in sports media. And then there are a lot of guys who, even if they don't support them, won't risk criticizing them publicly. Again, that leaves mostly the women to object to Barstool, and we're their favorite target.

I've tried many different analogies to try to get people to understand what mass harassment feels like, and here's what I've settled on:

Imagine you're naked, standing in the midst of thousands of people. Everyone from your cousins to your neighbors to your coworkers are there. And while you stand there, people dig through your past, find every bad thing you ever did or said, even out of context, and flash them up on a large screen for everyone to see. You don't get a chance to explain or even defend yourself. Strangers are screaming and calling you all sorts of offensive names, talking about the many ways in which they want you to die, and trying to locate your family so they can harass them, too. People start walking away, disgusted by the image of you the harassers have created, even though it's deeply inaccurate. No one comes to your aid. You wonder how long this is going to last.

And then it's over. The trolls get bored, find a new target, and move on to something else. They leave you standing there, traumatized, while they go back to life as usual. Only you can't go back to life as usual. You'll never really be the same again.

Whenever a woman comes to me in the middle of mass harassment by Stoolies, I always tell her to hang on, it'll end eventually. When you're in the eye of the storm, it feels like it will go on forever. But it won't. They always move on. And in some ways, that's one of the most odious aspects of the Stoolies: The mass harassment, which changes people's lives and impacts their mental health negatively, is just any other day for them. Just another victim. And they do it over and over and over.

So what is Barstool's appeal to the masses? To the average nineteen-year-old single white guy? Jemele Hill, a former ESPN anchor who admits to liking Barstool's popular *Pardon My Take* podcast, thinks the site's racism and misogyny is a feature, not a bug.

"When you ask [Stoolies] some of the things that they like, there are always certain code words. Because I hear the same thing when people talk about Donald Trump," she told me. "They say, 'Oh, I like the fact that they're not politically correct.' Well, what does 'politically correct' mean? What's not being politically correct? And then when you dive a little bit deeper and then they say, 'Well, I like that they just say what they think.' I would say there's a huge collection of people who might mark out Barstool because they disrespect people, because they disrespect women, and because that they have some personalities there who say things that would definitely get the shit knocked out of them on any other medium."

Hill went on to say that Stoolies aren't always sincere about what, exactly, they like about the site: "First and foremost, people who do consume their product in a certain way have to be honest about what it is they're liking. Politically incorrect is fine. What's not fine is being racist and misogynistic. That's what's not fine. So it's like if I tell [a Stoolie] to stop disrespecting and dehumanizing me, then don't look at me like you just told a fart joke."

The one question women ask me more than anything else when it comes to Barstool is "Why are these guys *like* this?" Author and gender studies scholar Rebecca Martínez, PhD, says the roots of men behaving the way Stoolies behave goes back decades. "The backlash of the civil rights and feminist movements of the sixties and seventies, along with the slow and steady erosion of the social contract (e.g., Reaganomics) to the current Trump era, tell us much about the cultural climate in the US that has shaped the misogynistic, hypermasculine, and so-called anti–politically correct media platform that is Barstool Sports," she told me. Martínez believes that as marginalized groups like women, BIPOC, and the LGTBQ+ communities have made gains in policy and legal protections, "largely white heterosexual men have claimed so-called 'reverse-racism,' 'reverse-sexism,' and that they are being persecuted by 'political correctness.' They also claim that civil and women's rights have gone 'too far,' which really means that they are afraid of losing their structural power in US society.

"The same men who would claim that white people experience more bias against them than do people of color . . . are also the ones attracted to Barstool Sports and amplifying it through social media.

They enjoy the sexism and homophobia, as it solidifies to them that they are really the true victims in society because they don't have a 'special month,' aren't 'allowed' to say the N-word, feel censored, claim that women and minorities are taking their jobs and spots in colleges," Martínez said.

And as far as people and brands who claim they are unaware of Barstool's offensive history? "Personally, I don't think those people are unaware," Jemele Hill said. "I just think they don't give a fuck."

All too often, I've pointed out Barstool's misogyny to fans, only to be told something along the lines of "If they're so sexist, why do they have a woman CEO? And why do so many women who work there love it? And why do so many women go on their podcasts?"

It's true that Barstool has a female CEO. Erika Nardini has been in charge of Barstool since 2016, when the Chernin Group bought a 51 percent stake in the site, though Portnoy maintains creative control. Nardini has been as steadfast in defending Barstool as Portnoy is, insisting that Barstool does not and has never encouraged online harassment.

Soledad O'Brien interviewed Nardini for her profile of the site on *Real Sports* and told me she's not the least bit surprised by Nardini heading up the site. "I certainly don't think Barstool is the only one who does that," she said, of Barstool hiring a female CEO. "It's an old twist from the playbook. Here's a person who is more than happy to be the face of our conversations around sexism. So I'm not surprised at all."

Martínez agrees. "'Oh,' you say, 'but the CEO of Barstool Sports is a woman! They can't be sexist!' Unfortunately, that doesn't make a bit of difference in this case, because Erika Nardini is simply going along with the sexism. Some women find this gives them cred in the sports world. Women can and do engage in structural sexism by internalizing it and either ignoring it or partaking in it and amplifying it. Ms. Nardini is doing that in her position, and at the same time providing cover for the rampant culture of sexism that goes on there."

There was a time when Barstool was a single site with a lot of followers. As I've already pointed out, they've always been racist, sexist, homophobic, and generally offensive, but they were containable. If you didn't like what they stood for, you could just choose not to follow them on social media or to go to the site. But in recent years, the Barstool empire has exploded exponentially. There's a Barstool Twitter account for every pro and college team in every major sport. There are Barstool podcasts, even one formerly headed up by two women. There are Barstool gaming sites. The company has gotten so big, they're nearly impossible for someone working in sports to avoid.

In March 2020, Kirk Minihane, a former WEEI (Boston sports) radio jock who now hosts a podcast for Barstool, went on hiatus to seek mental health treatment. Reportedly, Minihane was experiencing depression and suicidal thoughts. As someone who has been in treatment for depression since my early twenties, I felt for Minihane. I know how hard it is to ask for help, especially as depression lies and often makes us feel like we're not worth saving. At the same time, I couldn't help but remember that Minihane had gleefully joined in harassing me while at both WEEI and Barstool. In talking to those who have been victimized by Barstool and their Stoolies, Minihane's name has come up over and over again in their tales of harassment.

In the fall of 2019, I was going through a particularly bad bout of depression. No one other than my husband knew, but I could definitely feel the darkness creeping in. All day I felt exhausted and muted, not taking pleasure in anything. At night, I lay awake for hours, feeling nothing but adrenaline-fueled anxiety coursing through my body. Each morning, I would finally drift off just as the rest of the world was waking up, and I'd do the whole thing again.

Around that time, I noticed an uptick in obnoxious tweets lobbed in my direction from the Barstool crowd. Normally, this happens after I tweet something critical about the site, but this time, I couldn't figure out what I had done to "provoke" them. There are good days and bad days when it comes to dealing with harassment, but depression peels off a few layers of armor at the same time as it numbs you. I remember taking some of those tweets about my looks, my weight, my qualifications for my career, harder than I normally would. They certainly didn't help at a time when I was already struggling.

While researching for this book, I came across a Kirk Minihane podcast in which a cohost had prank-called my weekend show with my cohost, Maggie Hendricks. The call didn't even register with us as a prank at the time—we work in sports radio. A fair number of the calls we get don't make sense to begin with. From time to time, we get Barstool callers who just want to say "Barstool" or "Dave Portnoy" on our show, which apparently counts as a huge victory for them. High five, dudes.

Before he played the call on his Barstool podcast, Minihane described me as a "humorless asshole," mocked my #MoreThanMean video and campaign, and repeated a claim from Barstool's Dan Katz that I'm "manipulative" and "a liar." Then he played the "prank" call, which honestly was a big nothing burger. The Jerky Boys this was not. They were celebrating just calling into our show and getting on the air. High five again, dudes!

Can I prove that the Stoolies who were harassing me during my last major depression were inspired by Minihane's podcast? I can't, though I certainly have my suspicions. But the whole thing got me thinking that no accommodation was made for my struggles with depression, nor that of any of the other women who have been trolled by Minihane or Barstool. We didn't have the option of taking a hiatus to deal with the Stoolies and practice self-care. We simply had to get through it, largely on our own, and too often while watching male friends and coworkers casually interact with the brand that brought us so much misery.

I tweeted to that effect, which was probably a mistake from a personal-protection standpoint, but getting righteously indignant and tweeting without thinking things through is kind of my brand. In the days that followed, my radio show was inundated with calls and texts from Stoolies, demanding that I apologize, urging my station to fire me, and wanting to know why I hated those struggling with mental illness. When I promoted my radio show via Twitter and other social media channels, Minihane's podcast cohost and fans would send out the bat signal that I was on the air, complete with the numbers to my station's phone and text lines, urging Stoolies to call in and harass me. Night after night, our phone lines lit up with numbers from area codes in the Northeast, where Minihane's core audience is based. I did the show several nights in a row without being able to take calls from listeners or use the show's text line to keep the conversation with my listeners going, which is a huge disadvantage when doing a show late at night.

My producers, God bless them, did their best to shield me from the harassment, but they could only do so much. In one night alone, I took sixty pages of screenshots of our station's text line, which was full of things like "Bitch," "Whore," "Cunt," and the less violent but more bizarre "you look like you smell like bologna." It went on for over a week. The stress of doing a show that was so compromised by ill will started to affect me physically. Those long, sleepless nights continued. I started developing TMJ from clenching my jaw with stress and anger. One night, while driving home on a busy Chicago interstate at 1:00 a.m., I had a full-blown panic attack and had to pull over. I had no idea if or when my show, or my life, would go back to normal.

Was tweeting about Minihane a mistake from a moral standpoint? Maybe. I don't always get it right, and I, too, often tweet in anger, as my long-suffering husband would be the first to tell you. But I'm not sure I wouldn't do it again. Something about seeing Minihane talk about his own struggle with depression while caring not at all what the women he's gone after over the years have had to deal with sent my last vestige of self-control spinning into the stratosphere. Anyway, I've always been way better at sticking up for other people than for myself. In my view, Minihane had legitimately hurt people.

And I wasn't the only one Minihane had gone after. Marisa Ingemi, who was trolled during the 2019 Stanley Cup Final, told me that Minihane somehow got ahold of her cell number and started bugging her to come on his show while she was enduring harassment at Barstool's hands. It's something Minihane had done to me whenever I criticized Barstool previously.

Britni de la Cretaz had a run-in with Minihane after they published a piece for *DigBoston* in 2017 that mentioned the often racist, sexist, and generally offensive comments shared on WEEI during the *Kirk and Callahan Show*, hosted by Minihane and Gerry Callahan.

The day after the piece was published, de la Cretaz said, "[Minihane] essentially had a complete meltdown on air. He called Sam Kennedy, the president of the Red Sox and John Henry, the owner of the Red Sox, who then were essentially his bosses, too, because he worked for WEEI, 'pandering vomits.'" Minihane was then taken off the air for the rest of the week. But it was just the beginning for de la Cretaz. "I got death threats that were pretty bad. The harassment from that was to the point that I wrote [about] it for a local weekly, and my editor offered to pay for private security detail for my house."

The *Kirk and Callahan Show* began calling them "that hairy-legged *woman*" (they identified as a woman at the time) once Minihane returned to the air, and their derision spawned plenty of their listeners to create memes and blog posts mocking de la Cretaz, who is openly queer, by using the pronoun "it" and openly deriding them for writing about their sexual experiences and having herpes, which they've written about with eloquence and sensitivity. The show had high praise for a blog post written by a Stoolie who goes by Turtleboy (who, fun fact, also wrote a deranged piece calling me a "Ginger Bee-Sting Allergy Chelsea Clinton"), a Minihane superfan. Take a deep breath before you read its title: "Feministo Journalist Who Ripped Boston and WEEI for Being Racist Also Bragged About Having Herpes, Not Having Sex with Her Husband or Shaving Her Legs, and Made Up a Fake Rape Story for Twitter Points." All of this, de la Cretaz said, took a major toll on their mental health, something Minihane probably never considered.

"Kirk is open about his own mental health struggles, but he

seems unable to understand how his behavior might be affecting other people. I don't think he sees any connection to the way in which he engages with the world and its effect," she said.

Incredibly, all of this took place not on some niche podcast but on one of the biggest radio stations in Boston. The worst segment has been removed from the WEEI site. Minihane has since cut ties with WEEI and, after a short stint at Entercom's Radio.com, landed at Barstool, where Minihane fans picked up right where they left off.

Despite Penn National's assurance that Barstool's days of mass harassment were over, no one stepped in to stop Minihane's fans from going after me. They began going after me in February 2020, and, in August of that year, Minifans were still in my mentions on a regular basis.

Like I said, I'm going to regret writing this chapter. I can already hear the howls of indignation from the Stoolies who, in their minds, only engage in righteous pushback against the "hypocrites" who criticize their beloved site. I can already imagine the protests from Dave Portnoy and Erika Nardini, insisting that Barstool absolutely, totally does not tolerate or promote harassment. And yet I can't think of another mainstream site that has incited as many disturbing incidents as Barstool has, and continues to do. As Robert Silverman asked, "Has anyone ever said to them, 'Why do you think you are the only "sports website" that has to do this? That has to constantly tell your fans, Hey, don't target this person'?"

It's true that, as far as we know, no one at Barstool tells Stoolies to attack most of the time. At least not in so many words and at least not where everyone can see it. But over the years, Stoolies have gotten the message that whomever the site, Portnoy, or the other Barstool leaders criticize is fair game. Many women in sports media even believe there are subreddits and other sites dedicated to sharing personal information about harassment targets. It's also true that, after the pack has already struck, one of the Barstool leaders, usually Dan Katz (BarstoolBigCat) or Eric Sollenberger (PFT Commentator) will eventually tweet out something vague telling Stoolies to leave that day's target alone.

This good cop–bad cop shtick is tired by now. You can't unring a bell, and the powers that be at Barstool damn well know it. Robert Silverman poses a fair question: Why *don't* other sites constantly have to tell their followers to stop harassing people? Possibly because other sites haven't established a culture whereby their followers win the approval of the leaders by harassing people on their behalf.

And it works. The Stoolies' calculation is obvious: one critical comment of anyone involved with Barstool means days and weeks of being bombarded by men telling you how terrible you are, how ugly you are, how you have no right to exist. And so many of us deal with it alone. Barstool is so notorious that if you're in the middle of being attacked, people treat you like you're radioactive. They'll express support and sympathy privately, but no one in their right mind is going to wade into the toxic sludge pile voluntarily to defend you. And that's another dynamic Stoolies use against their victims. "How come no one is coming to your defense? People must not like you very much. You must have no friends."

For the women who work in sports, it's often painful to see colleagues treat some of the men who have made our lives miserable as just another buddy on Twitter. I will never forget the pain of having a guy I considered a friend invite one of my worst Barstool trolls as a guest on his show. When I asked him about it, he deflected: "I know you two have beef."

But it's not beef. "Beef" implies two people with equally justifiable complaints about each other. I'd never met or interacted with this guy. He started harassing me one day out of the blue as part of the Stoolie cabal. I don't think I've ever even replied to any of his jabs. And despite being an open sexist who harasses women, he's been embraced by the Chicago sports community, regularly appearing on local talk shows.

Don't make the mistake of thinking women don't know which of our male colleagues have failed to stand by us while Stoolies bat us around as fodder for their hobby of harassing (mostly) women. As de la Cretaz said, "I remember the name of every single male journalist that laughed along while I was being called awful names. I'm sure none of them remember who I am. But I, of course, *I* remember, and it has made me feel really ostracized from the Boston sports media community as a whole."

At the end of the day, the message of mainstream brands, teams, and journalists who promote or partner with Barstool is one of exclusion. Exclusion of people of color, of women, of the LGBTQ+ community, of anyone who isn't a straight white male with a mean streak. All of us "others" can keep raising hell about how terrible Barstool is, but it's up to those with the most power in the industries—straight white men—to shout down Barstool and everything it stands for. I hope that by bringing out so many receipts, I can contribute to that reckoning.

CHAPTER 7

REVOLUTIONARY ANGER

Emotion and Injustice on and off the Court

The last time I cried at work was the worst.

I was sitting in my studio at my day job in September 2017, waiting for my cue to do a ninety-second radio score update during an afternoon show with two male hosts. Their guest that afternoon was former NFL player and current commentator Michael Irvin, a man accused of sexual assault by multiple women. Irvin was set to be a regular weekly guest on the show, and I had raised my objection to his appearance with the station and my boss. But like so many objections based on the way men treat women, it went roundly ignored.

In the days before Irvin's first weekly appearance on that particular show, he had been accused of sexual assault a third time and was under investigation by the NFL. The two men who hosted the show started off the segment by joking around and talking about football with Irvin. Eventually, out of obligation, they got around to asking Irvin about the most recent allegation against him.

What followed was a nearly seven-minute rant from Irvin, in which he repeatedly denigrated his accuser, implied she was a liar, and painted himself as the real victim in the situation. His monologue went largely uninterrupted by the hosts, and afterward they went back to talking about football. In subsequent appearances, they would go on to describe Irvin as "honest, open, and fun."

I've written and spoken openly about my own sexual assault many times and, for the most part, I'm now able to do so dispassionately. But that my station, which employed at least one sexual assault survivor (me) and has tons of female listeners, allowed a man who had been accused of sexual assault by three different women unfettered airtime to denigrate his accusers was too much. That day, I burst into white-hot tears of rage, devastated by the unfairness of it all. I was so upset, I wasn't able to do the score update and ran to tell our sports director that I needed a minute to compose myself.

My absence immediately spurred one of the hosts to barge into my studio, demanding to know why I'd left. One gross comment led to another, and soon the host and I got into a shouting match, in which I told him, "That interview was *fucked*." He laughed with derision and refused to acknowledge that he or his cohost had done anything wrong by palling around with Irvin. At one point, I said to the host, "You have no idea what it's like to live through a sexual assault." Because we were arguing pretty loudly—me through a wall of tears—our HR rep was eventually called down.

The HR rep spent the next twenty minutes lecturing me about

my reaction to the show segment—clearly more upset with me than he was with the host for bursting into my studio, my domain, and screaming at me. He asked me more than once, "How do you know [the host] has never been raped?" He leaned into that point over and over. Clearly, my implied assumption that a man with a cavalier attitude about sexual assault has never been raped was the *real* problem with the whole incident.

I was so angry, the world felt so unjust, and the tears would not stop coming.

Michael Irvin was eventually bounced from his weekly spot on the show, but only after he was named in a 2018 sexual harassment lawsuit against the NFL Network. By 2019, he was a Radio.com insider and back on my station's airwaves.

So many women have had a moment like this in the workplace: something profoundly unfair happens, rage swells inside you, and the next thing you know, the waterworks have started. It's embarrassing and frustrating, and we all wish there was a way to stop it. The fact that tears are an unstoppable physiological response to strong emotions (grief, rage, happiness, et cetera) is cold comfort when you're trying to hold it together in front of a group of men. Particularly if it happens at work.

For so many of us, the tears of anger come, unbidden and unwanted, when we feel we are being treated unjustly. Crying is an automatic reaction to feeling enraged and helpless, not a ploy for sympathy. Soraya Chemaly, media critic and author of the book *Rage Becomes Her*, believes that there's a social component to it as well, and that women are taught to express anger through tears at an early age. "I do think that it has everything to do with early childhood socialization, particularly with white femininity and certain things, because the crying is coded as vulnerable and weak and feminine," she told me. "But it's also coded as 'I am in need of protection.' And so crying doubles down on sort of status quo ideas about how people should behave and if a woman cries, she is in fact rewarded in a way that she would not be rewarded if she demands change, right? When you're angry, you've identified a problem or a threat or a risk or an indignity, and your feeling is that it has to be addressed and that someone around you in your community or relationships should be helping you do that."

And this isn't something we only do at work. Chemaly found that women, especially white women, tend to transform their rage into something else when anger pops up in a relationship.

"I find it interesting that in intimate settings, in intimate relationships, particularly in heterosexual couples, women will display their anger through fear or sadness before they display it as anger. . . . Men see women's anger as selfish, and so that dynamic is really destructive."

Chemaly wrote an entire book on women and anger and says she still cries when she's angry. "When I get very angry, I kind of feel as though I lose the ability to speak. And I think it really does have to do with the way we're taught not to do that. Not to assert yourself with rage." What's more, Chemaly says women may be socialized not to exhibit anger in more forceful ways because of what anger means to others. "Anger is really associated [with] the idea that you can control things in a way that sadness isn't. Crying is clearly associated with sadness, but sadness is not a control emotion. It's a retreat emotion. It's literally more of an emotion of resignation, whereas anger is an emotion of determination."

And that resignation can have harmful effects on women who experience it. A 2003 study by Deborah Cox, Karin Bruckner, and Sally Stabb found that women who divert their anger into other behaviors, rather than expressing it assertively, are more vulnerable to symptoms such as depression and anxiety than women who use an assertive approach to coping with anger. A 2007 study by Lauri Hyers, PhD, at West Chester University discovered that women considered responding "assertively" in 75 percent of cases of everyday discrimination but actually spoke up only 40 percent of the time. In yet another study, Raymond DiGiuseppe, PhD, chair of the psychology department at St. John's University in New York, found that men and women express their anger much differently, with women staying angry longer, and feeling much more resentment, than men. That steady simmer is likely familiar to many women, and it's not difficult to imagine how this societally enforced behavior causes long-term harm.

Which brings me to Serena Williams.

Perhaps no athlete in recent memory has endured as much abuse for longer than Serena Williams. Since she and her sister Venus burst onto the pro tennis scene in the mid-1990s, the hits have never stopped coming: her hair, her body, her fashion choices, her race, her gender.

Williams is often celebrated for her bold fashion choices on the court, but it wasn't always so. When the young sisters debuted their signature beaded braids, there was plenty of tsk-tsking among the majority-white tennis community and sports fans at large, who dismissed the beads as "ghetto," rather than as an homage to the

Compton neighborhood where the Williams sisters grew up, where the hairstyle was a common one for young girls. In 1999, Venus was even penalized by a chair referee for losing a strand of beads during an Australian Open match against Lindsay Davenport. Despite Venus's attempt to fight back tears during the match, this is how the Massachusetts daily *Southcoast Today* covered the event:

> *Venus Williams had a bad hair day at the Australian Open.*
>
> *Williams' rainbow of beads came undone and so did her game yesterday in a 6–4, 6–0 upbraiding by top-seeded Lindsay Davenport in the quarterfinals.*
>
> *Williams complained to the umpire that he was splitting hairs when he called a let in mid-rally the first time a strand of beads flew from her head and scattered on the court.*
>
> *But when it happened again a few points later, and the umpire penalized her a point for causing a "disturbance," Williams really wigged out. That penalty cost her a service game and put her behind 3–0 in the second set.*
>
> *Fighting back tears with her voice quavering, she argued and screamed as her remaining beads clattered.*
>
> *"There's no disturbance. No one's being disturbed," she shouted at Australian umpire Denis Overberg.*
>
> *"I can't guess if it's disturbing your opponent," he replied.*

At the time, Venus was just eighteen years old. Stories like this one, including the groan-inducing jokes about Venus's hair in the opening paragraph, were an indication of the onslaught of judgmental coverage coming the sisters' way. It's also another reason we need more women and BIPOC working in sports media.

Then there's the infamous event at Indian Wells, California, where the Williams sisters were booed by fans and accused of match-fixing when Venus withdrew from a semifinal match in 2001. According to their father and coach, Richard Williams, the jeering at his daughters soon turned into a hail of racial slurs, with one man telling Richard he wanted to "skin him alive." Serena boycotted the annual tournament at Indian Wells until 2015.

Of course, it's impossible to talk about Serena Williams without delving into the unending stream of comments about her physical appearance from the dregs of humanity, i.e., men on Twitter who spend their time criticizing and objectifying women's bodies.

But plenty of mainstream personalities take part, too. For example: in 2009, Serena Williams was twenty-seven years old and had eleven Grand Slam titles under her belt, which wasn't enough for sportswriter Jason Whitlock. He felt the need to weigh in on why Serena, in his eyes, continued to underachieve. After chastising Serena for not living up to her potential—including unfavorable comparisons to noted tennis players such as (checks notes) Michael Jordan, Muhammad Ali, and *Rosa Parks*—Whitlock had this to say about her physique and motivation:

> She'd rather eat, half-ass her way through non-major tournaments and complain she's not getting the respect her 11-major-championships résumé demands. She complains about being ranked No. 2 in the world when she's not bitching on Twitter or her blog about new rules that forbid Wimbledon players from eating in the locker room.
>
> Seriously, how else can Serena fill out her size 16 shorts without grazing at her stall between matches? I know, you think I'm a hypocrite. No, I'm not. Sports writers are supposed to be plump and lazy. I'm fulfilling my destiny.

Anyone who has laid eyes on the physical manifestation of Jason Whitlock's form knows these comments are, yes, hypocritical and obnoxious, but also hysterically funny. Or would be, if men like Whitlock didn't so often get away with this kind of stuff.

But Whitlock wasn't done (of course he wasn't).

> *And you probably think I don't like Serena. You're wrong. I love her. She's the main reason I watch tennis. She's fascinating. Her power and skill are breathtaking. And when she's in shape, she's every bit as sexy as Beyoncé.*

I'm sure it's a relief to Serena that Jason Whitlock finds her sexy when she's "in shape." Thank you, Jason, for your valuable input. By the way, Whitlock's contract with FOX Sports was not renewed after it expired in 2020. You hate to see it.

Of course, this wasn't the first time a male sportswriter decided the world needed to hear his opinion on Serena's body type. In 2006, Matthew Norman of the UK paper the *Telegraph* wrote a piece entitled "Serena's Loyal Supporters," in which he wrote these delightful lines:

> *In a meeting reminiscent of one of those catchweight wrestling contests that used to delight Kent Walton, Serena submitted to the whippet-like Daniela Hantuchova, raising again the question of her commitment to tennis. As with Venus, her commitment to acting is in less doubt, and if anyone decides to remake Gone With The Wind Serena will be in perfect shape to reprise Butterfly Mc-Queen's Oscar-winning role.*
>
> *Generally, I'm all for chunky sports stars. Nothing is more*

reassuring for the portly TV spectator than the sight of Robert Key trundling out to bat for England, or Monty eyeballing an American crowd after cries of Mrs Doubtfire. But tennis requires a mobility Serena cannot hope to achieve while lugging around breasts that are registered to vote in a different US state from the rest of her.

And in case you were wondering: yes, Matthew Norman is still gainfully employed as someone whose opinions people presumably want to read.

To chronicle the full range of abuse that's been heaped on Serena by the media is a Sisyphean task, so I won't even try, but the racism that bleeds into these comments, and their ubiquity in itself, bears consideration. In 2017, announcer Doug Adler was fired by ESPN for reportedly comparing sister Venus to a "gorilla," though he says he meant "guerrilla," as in "resistance fighter." Right. And from the "who needs enemies when you have friends like these?" category, we have Serena's "friend," Danish tennis player Caroline Wozniacki, who impersonated Serena in a 2012 exhibition match against Maria Sharapova by stuffing her bra and shorts to imitate her friends' physique. It was the always-magnanimous Serena who came to Wozniacki's defense, pointing out that Andy Roddick and Novak Djokovic had also made fun of her body type.

There is something heartbreaking about the way all of these taunts and slurs and mocking lines have been brought to Serena's attention, how she is always asked to explain and answer for the malicious behavior of others, and how consistently she seems to float above the criticism and the hate. Which is why the 2018 US Open final was so tough to watch.

Seeing Serena as the US Open title slipped away from her that day, her face crumpling as she fought to hold back tears of rage and injustice, I felt sick. It was a struggle many women recognized.

Chair umpire Carlos Ramos had punished Williams for the same actions we see men get away with on the court regularly: smashing her racket and arguing with the umpire.

"It's not fair," Williams insisted to the umpire who had accused her of illegally receiving coaching during the match. "You're attacking my character. I don't cheat to win. I'd rather lose." Moments later, Williams was assessed a game penalty for calling umpire Carlos Ramos "a thief" and demanding an apology for his actions.

This wasn't the first time Ramos, who has a reputation for sticking players with ticky-tacky rules infractions, has gotten an earful from players. I know you'll be shocked to learn that the men he officiates haven't earned the same wrath of Ramos and the masses as Serena did.

That very year, at the 2018 Wimbledon quarterfinal between Novak Djokovic and Kei Nishikori, Djokovic was issued a warning after both he and his opponent smashed their rackets into the ground. Nishikori was not issued a warning, prompting Djokovic to say to Ramos, "Double standards, my friend, double standards." And in 2017, after Ramos issued Rafael Nadal a warning for taking too much time between games, Nadal replied, "You will have to give me a lot of warnings during this game. Give me the warnings you can because you will not referee me anymore." Ramos took no further action.

Both Djokovic and Nadal got away with telling Ramos off.

Serena Williams did not. After the match, Serena refused to apologize for her remarks to Ramos, which only further served to infuriate her critics. They had grown used to hearing Serena apologize, not just for her own missteps but for those of others.

"I've seen other men call other umpires several things," Serena said after the match. "I'm here fighting for women's rights and for women's equality and for all kinds of stuff. For me to say 'thief,' and for him to take a game, it made me feel like it was a sexist remark. He's never taken a game from a man because they said 'thief.'"

Adding to the frustration is the fact that we've seen high-profile male tennis players verbally abusing umpires for decades (Jimmy Connors once called a chair umpire "an abortion" and John McEnroe . . . well, John McEnroe exists), but being dressed down by a Black woman was more than Carlos Ramos could take. Whether his treatment of Williams was driven by misogyny, racism, his ego, or something else entirely, we may never know. Easier to suss out, probably, are the motivations of the hundreds of men who cheered on Ramos via social media, expressing solidarity against Williams while lecturing women about playing the so-called gender card.

Perhaps worst of all, two days after the incident, Australian cartoonist Mark Knight gleefully shared his latest work online. It depicted a dark and hulking Serena, with an exaggerated nose and lips, jumping up and down on a broken racket. A pacifier lays nearby. Her opponent, Naomi Osaka, for some reason depicted as a white woman (she is of Japanese and Haitian descent), politely talks to the chair umpire in the background who asks, "Can you just let her win?" The cartoon quickly drew condemnation across the globe as both racist and sexist, but both Knight and his paper, the

Herald Sun, doubled down on defending the image, saying it had nothing to do with race. Somehow these hateful-seeming depictions get the benefit of the doubt, but Serena's momentary anger was deemed worthy of widespread ridicule.

In typical fashion, Serena's flash of anger didn't last long. By the time the match was over, she'd composed herself, putting her arm around winner Naomi Osaka and asking the audience to stop booing the result. By that time, though, the damage was done and the moment ruined. Both Osaka and Williams were in tears. One over the unfairness of it all, the other because her dream of facing and even defeating her hero was tarnished by events beyond her control.

The silver lining in all this is that the match sparked conversations between men and women, online and in real life, about the constraints on women in our society. Watching Serena's familiar stoicism collapse under the strain of the latest injustice she was forced to deal with hit close to home for many women, including tennis legend and longtime women's advocate Billie Jean King, who penned an op-ed for the *Washington Post* on the sexism endemic to the world of sports:

> *Did Ramos treat Williams differently than male players have been treated? I think he did. Women are treated differently in most arenas of life. This is especially true for women of color. And what played out on the court yesterday happens far too often. It happens in sports, in the office and in public service. Ultimately, a woman was penalized for standing up for herself. A woman faced down sexism, and the match went on.*

As in so many other moments in her career, Serena seemed to recognize that she had started an important conversation. "I just feel like the fact that I have to go through this is just an example for the next person that has emotions, and that want to express themselves, and want to be a strong woman," she said after the match. "They're going to be allowed to do that because of today. Maybe it didn't work out for me, but it's going to work out for the next person."

Some women who felt that Serena's penalty was uncalled for did express it in a more constructive way than others. Tennis great Martina Navratilova weighed in at the *New York Times* Opinions section, saying that Serena's behavior on the court warranted her losing a game point. Navratilova wrote:

> *In her protests against an umpire during the United States Open final on Saturday, [Serena] also got part of it wrong. I don't believe it's a good idea to apply a standard of "If men can get away with it, women should be able to, too." Rather, I think the question we have to ask ourselves is this: "What is the right way to behave to honor our sport and to respect our opponents?"*

While Navratilova's goal of elevating one's behavior for the good of the sport is laudable, it also smacks of the well-meaning men who tell women, foisted into a storm of online harassment, not to "feed the trolls." It's unfair and unrealistic to expect women to always take the high road, especially in situations where they are being treated unfairly. There is value in standing up for oneself and making one's voice heard, even if it's not the daintiest of behaviors. Sometimes, letting a bully have it is the only way to stay sane.

And for the most part, the reaction to Serena Williams's anger on the court that day really did break down along gender lines, with so many women identifying deeply with her anger and frustration, and so many men, like cartoonist Mark Knight, seeing her tears as nothing more than a woman trying to get her way. This belief pervades all corners of pop culture: take, for example, George Costanza's declaration on *Seinfeld* that when a woman cries, he feels like she's on fire and just wants to "put her out." And too often in professional settings, women's tears, so shameful and unwanted by us, are seen by men as emotional blackmail and attempted manipulation. Even in private, women who dare to cry are often seen by coworkers as weak, overly emotional, fulfilling the dreaded "hysterical woman" trope.

The lesson we learned that morning in Flushing Meadows was that even Serena Williams, arguably the greatest female athlete of all time, can't get away with being angry at work if that anger is directed at a man in a place of authority. And while this revelation isn't news to the millions of women who have been labeled "hysterical," "difficult," or "a bitch" for exhibiting the same emotions as their male colleagues, it is devastating. Because if Serena Williams is punished for standing up for herself at work, what chance do the rest of us women have?

For many women, daring to express anger at work means risking a job they can't afford to lose, especially in male-dominated workplaces. Too often, it means finding the courage to speak up, then rushing to the bathroom to hide the tears that come. To see Serena do what so many women wish they could do—to tell a man he had wronged her and that he owed her an apology—was a powerful moment. And then to watch the fallout, as Serena was punished by the very man who had been unfair to her in first place, and to watch her realize there was nothing she could do about it, was mortifying. Finally, to see Serena, predictably, labeled a "cry-baby," a "sore loser," a "spoiled brat," and, worst of all, "difficult," was especially infuriating. Even Super Serena isn't allowed to stand up for herself when a powerful man is involved.

Still, while a good chunk of the criticism of Serena's came from men, a fair portion of it, predictably, came from women. That women continue to police one another and enforce behaviors and norms that harm all of us is a source of endless disappointment. It would have been a glorious thing if, on that day, white women had stood up in solidarity and defended Serena, shutting down any fathers, husbands, brothers, sons, and drunk uncles who put forth the idea that a woman's rage is any less legitimate than a man's, and that a Black women's rage is the least legitimate of all.

I'd be remiss if I framed Serena's anger as only a gender issue. There's also an undeniable racial aspect to the way she's treated and the way our culture responds to her anger. Because for every viewer who was upset at seeing a woman tell off a powerful man on international television, there were many more who were appalled at seeing a *Black* woman do so.

In her book *Good and Mad*, feminist author Rebecca Traister talks about "the kinds of privileges and incentives certain women—white women—have been offered in exchange for shutting off or turning down their anger, and about the price other women—nonwhite and especially Black women—have paid, always having had reasons to be angry and rarely having been offered reprieve or reward for the act of suppressing it."

In some ways, for those watching the US Open final, it felt as if Serena, who has always had so many justifiable reasons to get mad both on and off the court, and who always, *always* had risen above the fray, had finally *had it*. That all the aggressions, micro and macro, all the sexism, racism, fetishism, objectification that she had suffered from the time she was a teenager, all the disrespect, had finally coalesced into a big, steaming pile of "I'm *done*," and that she simply wasn't going to stand for it anymore.

While I empathized with her tears to the point of tearing up myself, I cheered Serena's ability to yell at a man and demand an apology in full view of millions of people. She must have known even in the moment that she was going to pay for it in public back-lash, but she was getting to do what so many of us women, white women and especially Black women and women of color, almost never get a chance to do: yell and rage at the injustice of it all. The moment was as beautifully cathartic as it was upsetting.

Brittney Cooper, professor of women's and gender studies at Rutgers University, wrote in her book *Eloquent Rage*, "Rage is a fundamentally more reasonable response to America's cultural in-vestment in the disrespect of Black women than being respect-able. . . . Rage is a kind of refusal. To be made a fool of, to be silenced, to be shamed, or to stand for anybody's bullshit. It is a real refusal to lie that Black women's anger in the face of routine, everyday in-justice is not legitimate." That day, Serena *refused*.

In her post-match interview, Serena Williams said she was "fighting for women." But given that Serena not only cracked the glass ceiling when it comes to women's rage, she took a sledgehammer and busted right through it, the least we can do is help her take up the fight.

What if women agreed to stop suppressing righteous anger at unfairness and injustice? What if, instead of snickering behind the back of an outraged female coworker, we all decided to stand behind one another and insist that anger isn't illegitimate just because it emanates from a woman? And what if, each time we heard a man call an angry woman "difficult," "hysterical," or worse, we shut him down immediately, even if it was a man we loved or a man in a position of authority?

There's no doubt that one of the "women" Serena fights for is her young daughter, Olympia. What if we allowed our daughters to express their anger, even as small children, when they perceive something to be unjust, instead of discouraging them from making a scene? What if we encouraged every single girl to stand up for herself, consequences be damned? What if men and boys started to learn that women and girls were just as likely to get angry and act on it?

Maybe then, what Serena Williams stood for, alone, that day in Flushing Meadows, would start more than a conversation. It would start a revolution.

CHAPTER 8

HEY, WHERE'S *OUR* #METOO?

An Overdue Industry Reckoning

Every woman I talked to when researching this chapter cried.

I've been asked often what I want people to know about sports media and the #MeToo movement, and that's what I'll tell them from now on. That when I was writing about #MeToo and sports, every woman I talked to cried.

The #MeToo movement was widely popularized on social media in the fall of 2017. In the wake of the disturbing sexual assault allegations against Hollywood producer Harvey Weinstein, actress Alyssa Milano tweeted out the recommendation of a friend, who said, "If all the women who have been sexually harassed or assaulted wrote 'Me too' as a status, we might give people a sense of the magnitude of the problem." Immediately, women all over the world, from high schoolers to Hollywood stars, began tweeting out simply "#MeToo." I was one of them.

The #MeToo movement was actually founded back in 2006 by

sexual assault survivor and activist Tarana Burke, who coined the phrase and founded the movement to help young women, particularly young Black women and women of color, feel less alone in the aftermath of sexual trauma. That Burke is now universally recognized as the founder of the #MeToo movement is due to the tireless work of Black women to ensure that her decades of work weren't co-opted by the white women who had only come across the hashtag because of Milano and other prominent white women.

In the weeks and months that followed the discovery of #MeToo by the masses, we watched some of the most powerful men in media felled by the women they had left in their wake. Harvey Weinstein. Charlie Rose. Matt Lauer. Mark Halperin.

By October 2018, the *New York Times* reported that #MeToo had relieved 201 powerful men of their jobs, and that nearly half of their replacements have been women. As we watched #MeToo sweep through Hollywood media, political media, financial media, and beyond, many of us braced for the impact on sports media. In December 2017, Sean Gregory wrote a piece at *TIME* called "How The #MeToo Movement Is About to Change Pro Sports," which included predictions that the movement would initiate a wave of women coming forward against some of the industry's most powerful players. He quoted Michael Kimmel, founder of the Center for the Study of Men and Masculinities at Stony Brook University: "One big difference in 2017 is that women are being believed. Women are not on trial. Their credibility is not the issue. Men's behavior is the issue. That is the biggest change right now."

And so we waited.

As of the time of this book's publication, we're still waiting.

That's not to say that there aren't plenty of #MeToo moments happening in sports and sports media all the time, because there are. But neither industry has been able to get any kind of traction when incidents do come up. Still, the whisper networks in my field are just as active as those in Hollywood, and as motivated as the contributors to the infamous "Shitty Media Men" list that circulated online in 2018. We know which men to avoid.

"On one hand, the original hashtag and Tarana Burke's visions of #MeToo have made it much, much easier for survivors to speak out about what they have experienced and seek the help they need," PhD candidate Nicole Bedera told me. "Rape crisis centers have never gotten so many calls. Reporting rates are up. Everyone knows they know a survivor. Every survivor knows they aren't alone." But (I bet you knew there was a "but" coming) there's also been a downside to #MeToo.

"The media coverage of #MeToo has focused a lot on perpetrators," Bedera said. "There has been a swift backlash to this feminist activism, leading people to empathize with the rapists instead of the victims. This is called 'himpathy,' and it's the kind of powerful tool that can stand in the way of progress for survivors. As we move forward, it's crucial that survivors are the center of the conversation. We can't lose this moment to the perpetrators."

Many of us in sports media thought the dam was set to burst in late 2017, when Jami Cantor, a stylist for NFL Network, accused several men at the NFL-owned outlet of sexually inappropriate conduct and flat-out sexual assaults over the course of a decade. While much of Cantor's allegations were reduced to "groping" and "sexually-charged language" in media reports, her lawsuit itself reveals harrowing attacks on her person on multiple occasions. Cantor alleged that NFL Network executive producer Eric Weinberger repeatedly pushed his crotch against Cantor's shoulder while she worked at her desk, urging her to "touch it," and that he shoved his hands down her pants to see if she was wearing underwear.

According to Cantor's lawsuit, ex-player Marshall Faulk, working for NFL Network as an analyst, "greeted her" by fondling her breasts and groping her behind, and once pinned her against the wall and demanded oral sex while he pulled his pants down. Cantor made similar allegations against other former players at the network, including Heath Evans, Warren Sapp, Donovan McNabb, Ike Taylor, and Eric Davis. The NFL eventually settled with Cantor and fired Evans, Taylor, and Faulk. McNabb and Weinberger, both of whom had already left the network at the time Cantor's allegations became public, were fired by their subsequent employers.

It's worth mentioning that in their initial response to Cantor's lawsuit, the NFL alleged that the incidents Cantor "complained about were consensual or brought about by Cantor's actions," which is the legal equivalent of saying "this never happened, and even if it did, she wanted it." Not a great position for a league that boasts a female fan base of nearly 50 percent.

Cantor's allegations against the culture at NFL Network were quickly validated by similar claims from a makeup artist, Erin McParland, who talked to Tim Rohan about her experiences in an essay for SI.com. McParland accused Eric Davis of rubbing his genitals against her leg and groping her on more than one occasion, and she said that ex-player Michael Irvin—the man whose invitation to my own workplace spurred a fight between me and my coworker—also made inappropriate comments and gestures to her. Davis was subsequently fired by ESPN, but Irvin was back on NFL Network after a month-long "investigation." He's also frequently back on the radio station where I worked as a Radio.com insider.

But after Cantor and McParland came forward, the #MeToo

movement in sports media seemed to grind to a halt. While many women in sports media had stories similar to Cantor's and McParland's, nothing happened.

In December of that same year, two women at ESPN tried to jumpstart a reckoning in sports media. Jennifer Decker and Adrienne Lawrence, both of whom had interacted with ESPN, spoke with a member of the *Boston Globe*'s famed Spotlight investigative team about their experiences with sexual harassment at the Worldwide Leader in Sports. Decker in particular has spent the last decade and a half in sports media and has been demeaned and objectified by men, and especially famous men, every step of the way. Adrienne Lawrence worked in law before she worked in sports media; she's also the author of a brilliant book on how to survive sexual harassment in the workplace called *Staying in the Game*. These are brave, intelligent women who are not shrinking violets by any stretch of the imagination. And yet.

Just in case it isn't crystal clear yet how deeply misogyny is embedded in this media landscape, let's talk for a moment about how Decker was first "discovered." She rose to fame in 2005 during a twelve-second video clip of her at an FSU football game during her senior year. The image prompted Brent Musburger, a veteran sports announcer who has a creepy history of pointing out beautiful young women in the stands, to quip on ABC: "Fifteen hundred red-blooded Americans just decided to apply to Florida State." Thanks, Brent.

Decker, formerly known by her maiden name, Sterger, went on to work for the New York Jets as a sideline reporter. While working for the Jets in 2008, Decker received illicit texts, images, and suggestive voice mail messages by an unidentified man in the Jets organization. The person claimed to be Jets quarterback Brett Favre.

It's worth noting here that the Hall of Fame quarterback was sued in 2011 by two Jets masseuses for sexual harassment. The women claimed Favre sent sexually suggestive texts to another masseuse and that they were fired when they complained about it. That case was settled in 2013 for an undisclosed amount.

Jen Decker has never met Brett Favre. The texter claiming to be Favre obtained her phone number internally from the Jets organization, even after she changed it. Decker says she had passed Favre in the hallway, but never actually interacted with him. She describes the texts she received as "cyberbullying"; they continued long after she asked the texter to stop. At one point, Decker says she asked the texter, "You could do this to anyone. You literally can have anyone you want. Why won't you leave me alone?" She says the texter responded by saying, "I want what everyone else wants but can't have."

After she left the Jets to work at *Deadspin* (full disclosure: my current employer), Decker confided in the site's then editor in chief, A. J. Daulerio, about what had happened while she worked for the Jets. Without her knowledge or consent, Daulerio went public with Decker's story in 2010. "He told me he was going to publish it," Decker said. "And then when it came out, he was just very like, 'Hey, I'm running this tomorrow. Sorry to fuck you over, but it's too big of a story. Bye." Daulerio, Decker said, "basically ruined my life."

Months after the initial article ran at *Deadspin*, Daulerio obtained the pictures that the person claiming to be Favre sent to Decker, along with her private information and nudes of herself, from a third party. Decker says she found out about her private hard drive being hacked when a stranger messaged her years later to tell her he was in a private chat where other men were sharing her nude photos.

After that, Decker's life exploded.

"In 2010 it wasn't good," Decker said. "I would get death threats mailed to my house. One guy sent it from prison in Jacksonville, and he basically told me that he was going to murder me and then he was going to fuck me after he murdered me." People, Decker said, blamed her for dragging Favre into the lurid tale. "They just wanted to tell me what an absolute whore I was, how dare I fuck with his marriage. And it was like, 'I didn't fuck with his marriage. I've never even met him.' But that never was able to come out because I wasn't allowed to speak for months."

Ten years after the story broke, Decker is still hesitant to talk about it. "It was made very clear to me that if I pursued any kind of action moving forward, there was going to be a lot retaliation."

In 2006, long before Decker was outed by *Deadspin*, she underwent a months-long audition for an on-air position at ESPN. Decker said that while she was trying out for ESPN, an executive at ESPN showed her a copy of a *Playboy* magazine she was featured in. Later, Decker was taken to a strip club following a dinner with prospective ESPN employees, one of whom was current ESPN fantasy football guru Matthew Berry. Decker didn't know where she was going until the party arrived. The men teased her about being uncomfortable while at the club. According to the *Boston Globe* report:

Sterger [Decker's name at the time] and Berry say they were both admonished for the strip club outing, but Sterger did not get a job at ESPN while Berry did. . . . Berry is now ESPN's senior fantasy analyst and one of the most influential personalities in fantasy sports.

Decker said, "All the guys involved in that outing ended up keeping their jobs; I was the only one that was removed." Decker, who also teaches sports media, says she tells her students she hopes what she went through with the Jets in 2008 makes it not happen to someone else. "If it even puts a policy into place that would have prevented it from happening to someone else, I'm okay with being the first person through the walls. Unfortunately, it's just that it's usually the first person through the wall that's the bloodiest."

Decker said Berry made additional sexual comments to her in 2007, when she interviewed at ESPN for another position. Berry admitted that he was "talked to" about an issue that year but denied making the sexually inappropriate comments.

"We all just want to be able to do our work. We want to be able to prove that we can do the work just as well as the guy and we shouldn't have to deal with all of those other distractions that only come to us because we're women," Decker said. "[Men] don't have to worry about walking into a room and being sexually harassed; they don't have to worry about their job being threatened because they didn't want to play along with the sexual innuendo game. They don't want to feel like if they're not one of the guys that they can't be taken seriously in the workplace. I've compromised too much of myself to fit in and just feel I was one of them and I could do the work. I'm so mad at my younger self for doing those things, because I feel they set me back."

My own career, spanning multiple outlets, is riddled with the things I've decided to keep quiet about, either because they weren't worth compromising relationships for or because I just didn't have the energy on that given day. Whether it's walking into a radio studio and seeing "Titties" written on a whiteboard or walking into a room where my male colleagues are all huddled around a screen just in time to hear one of them say, "Did she show her pubes?" or finding images of naked or barely clad women on shared work computers, there are too many moments I've kept to myself to count. And this is the same for every woman I know working in sports media—from the NFL reporter who had a beloved and respected member of an NFL team single her out and waggle his dick at her in front of an entire locker room of people (I mentioned this briefly in chapter 1) to the NFL general manager who propositioned another reporter when she was only eighteen years old—we all have our stories. And, for the most part, we do our jobs, day after day, keeping our mouths shut while we watch very flawed men in both sports and media elevated to the role of demigods in our sports-obsessed culture.

Adrienne Lawrence, though, is not one to keep things to herself, nor to allow those around her to get away with acting like they work in a frat house instead of at a major media outlet. A lawyer by training, Lawrence worked at ESPN as part of a two-year talent development program. In March 2018, Lawrence sued ESPN in federal court for sexual discrimination and sexual harassment, claiming the company was "rife with misogyny." Lawrence's claims are too numerous and too nausea-inducing to list in their entirety, but she alleged, among other things, that ESPN male executives kept scorecards and ranked female ESPN employees by attractiveness, that women at ESPN are expected to put up with men openly watching porn and sexual predation and grooming by the male employees, and that *SportsCenter* anchor John Buccigross tried to "lure" her into a sexual relationship by making sexual advances toward her and texting her shirtless pictures of himself. Lawrence further alleged that ESPN's HR department covered up the sexual misconduct and that women who pressed their case were subject to retaliation by the company. ESPN's record of handling online harassment is strong, but it seems that no company is immune to the pervasive misogynistic culture of sports and sports media.

Lawrence has since settled her lawsuit with ESPN but believes that until many more women work in sports media, it will continue to be a playground for sexually inappropriate conduct.

"In environments that are white male–dominated or male-dominated, the threat of otherness, especially a woman who doesn't 'know her place,' is what attracts these predators and individuals who want to either exercise benevolent harassment and/or hostile harassment against you," Lawrence told me. She believes there is no safe space for women in sports media, even for those who never make waves: "I found that there was an 'as long as I'm taken care of, everything is fine' mentality. The reality is that the machine is still working against you. So even if you are 'taken care of,' there are individuals in positions of power who still will mistreat you. Because, as we saw, plenty of women [at ESPN] who were loved and very much praised were put out on their butts and retaliated against when they tried to push back in any way or exert their rights to be treated fairly."

Both John Buccigross and Matthew Berry continue to have big, public-facing roles with ESPN, despite the allegations against them. As with seemingly all men in sports media accused of sexual misconduct, the public eventually forgives, forgets, and then lashes out at those who remind them. Some of these men go on to become the faces of sports coverage for their outlets. Mike Tirico, for example, was disciplined by ESPN decades ago for one of the most egregious allegations of sexual harassment/assault I've heard of, in addition to multiple allegations of stalking and harassment by other female colleagues.

In his book *ESPN: The Uncensored Story*, Michael Freeman recounts Tirico's inexplicable behavior toward a work colleague at a house party. After ignoring the woman's pleas that he leave her alone, Tirico, who had just met the woman for the first time, continued to follow her around the party and insist he was in love with her. When the woman, fed up with Tirico's harassment, left the party, he followed her out to her car and attempted to block her from leaving. When she rolled down the driver's window to tell him to get out of the way, Tirico reached into the car and shoved his hand between her legs. In another case, Freeman writes that Tirico followed a woman's car after she rejected his proposition to "throw you on the table right here and fuck your brains out."

This wasn't the only harassment allegation against Tirico. In the book *Those Guys Have All the Fun*, James Andrew Miller and Tom Shales write that at least six other women came forward with stories about Tirico. In 1992, ESPN suspended him for three months and told him to seek counseling.

After that, Tirico began a meteoric rise at ESPN, eventually becoming the host of ESPN's crown jewel, *Monday Night Football*. Tirico was put front and center by ESPN, despite his disturbing history, and I often think of the women he left in his wake as he went on to call NBA and college basketball games, US Open tennis matches, and World Cup soccer.

In 2016, before #MeToo exploded on Twitter, Tirico left ESPN for NBC, which would, the following year, fire Matt Lauer for similarly predatory behavior. Like at ESPN, Mike Tirico became the face of NBC Sports, replacing Bob Costas as the lead studio host for coverage of the Olympics. And, in an impressively tone-deaf move by NBC, they had Tirico interview snowboarder Shaun White about a sexual harassment lawsuit against White. When asked, NBC admitted they knew of Tirico's past but dismissed it as something that happened long ago.

If people perceive you're good enough at something, there's nothing sports won't let you get away with. That's true for those in media as well as for athletes. Those who make programming decisions in sports have convinced themselves there's no one else who can do what Mike Tirico does, so therefore whatever he's done to women in his past doesn't matter. In reality, there are probably dozens of people, both men and women, who could easily fill Tirico's shoes. I don't know what bothers me more: the fact that NBC refused to cut ties with Tirico as the allegations against him resurfaced during #MeToo, or the fact that people still can't seem to muster up enough effort to care. Either way, I've taken to tweeting out media stories about Tirico's ESPN suspension every time I see him on my TV.

All of this brings me back to my original point on #MeToo: Why hasn't sports media had its #MeToo moment? Why didn't Cantor's lawsuit or Decker and Lawrence's story bring women in the industry crawling out of the woodwork with stories of their own? Why haven't we seen multiple Shitty Sports Media Men bounced from the industry for acting like overgrown frat boys?

The answer, I fear, is a depressing one. There simply aren't enough women working in sports media to make an impact.

"It's still a boys' club at the end of the day," Decker said. "We are vastly outnumbered—it's like [the movie] *300*.... If we ever wanted to have an honest #MeToo moment in sports, there would have to be more women in positions of power, and men will never allow that to happen."

There's a sad amount of truth in what Decker said. In my last radio job, I was the only woman with a regular, weekday job at my station. Most days, I didn't even lay eyes on another woman unless I was in the lobby or ran into someone in the bathroom. When I look at #MeToo cases that got results, they all seem to consist of multiple women banding together to accuse predatory men. We never hear about the case where a lone woman goes to HR, tells her story, and then gets ignored by HR and retaliated against by her coworkers. And no one wants to put herself in that situation.

One of the rare #MeToo moments in sports that has resulted in significant change is the case of Larry Nassar, a doctor who treated gymnasts at both Michigan State University (MSU) and USA Gymnastics. In 2018, Nassar was sentenced to 175 years in prison for the systemic sexual assault of more than 265 gymnasts, though he ultimately pled guilty to only seven counts of sexually assaulting minors. The case was so big, portions of the victim impact statements were shown live on TV. Since that time, more than 300 lawsuits have been filed against Nassar and various entities that he worked for; the entire eighteen-member board of USA Gymnastics, MSU president Lou Anna Simon, and MSU director of athletics Mark Hollis have all resigned.

And while it was gratifying to see a #MeToo moment result in some measure of justice, it was one of the very few moments we've had in sports media. And the case against Larry Nassar was the result of hundreds of women all finding strength and security in one another.

"The reason why the Larry Nassar case really took off . . . is scale," Title IX attorney Nancy Hogshead-Makar told me. "It's very difficult for most abusers to abuse hundreds of victims. It's almost impossible."

For her part, Lawrence thinks there's a lack of support for women in sports media by the public. "I think society on the whole has this idea that sports is a man's world. And if you walk into it, that's on you. It's kind of the 'you go into a man's room, whatever happens, is on you.' That's still the underlying current in society. 'Well, what did you think would happen?' And I want to say, 'That I'd be treated like a human being and respected.' So I think changing society's mentality when it comes to that is necessary; they have to see women in sports as being worthy of being treated fairly and right," she said.

While those of us in sports media wait for our #MeToo moment, it's athletes who are leading the movement when it comes to sports in general. The case against Larry Nassar has boiled over to USA Gymnastics, where even Simone Biles, the best gymnast the United States has ever produced, has publicly demanded changes at USA Gymnastics. An investigation into the wrestling program at Ohio State University found that team doctor Richard Strauss abused 177 student athletes over the course of twenty years. At the University of Michigan, dozens of former student athletes have come forward to accuse Dr. Robert E. Anderson of sexual abuse dating from the 1970s to the 1990s, while he worked for the school's athletic department. Of course, the biggest sex abuse scandal before Nassar was on the radar happened at Penn State University, where offensive coordinator Jerry Sandusky, who worked under the legendary Joe Paterno, was eventually convicted of sexually abusing dozens of boys (forty-five, to be exact, though he was charged with fifty-two) over the course of fifteen years. Ten years later, there are those who still defend Sandusky and accuse the victims of lying.

Hogshead-Makar, a former Duke swimmer and Olympic gold medalist, now heads up Champion Women, where she uses her skills as a lawyer to advocate for women and girls in sports. According to her, athletes are particularly susceptible to sexual predators.

She says that most of the sexual abuse she sees in sports involve athletes in "inappropriate relationships" with someone in a position of authority over them, like a coach or doctor, while about 20 percent of the cases involve peer-to-peer abuse. Worse, the layers of protection that exist for others in society—employment laws, Title IX, criminal laws, and professional licensing—simply don't exist for athletes outside of the university system.

"If you were a pedophile and were wondering, 'Where in society should I go?,' you would want to go into coaching, because there's no licensing," she said. "You can't take someone's coaching license away the way you can with other professions."

As for the criminal justice system: "It's particularly awful when the child is postpuberty; age twelve and up, and the abuse wasn't violent but was the result of manipulation. And there are all kinds of tricks on how they do that. For example, they have the kid drink, knowing the parents will get mad at them for drinking. Or they have them watch porn, so the kid feels guilty about having watched the porn. There are all these ways of that they're able to do it."

While I spoke to Hogshead-Maker, I thought back to my own gymnastics club, where rumors abounded that our barely-eighteen-year-old star gymnast was "dating" our fortysomething coach. The parents gossiped about it, the gymnasts all whispered about it, but I don't recall anyone saying, "This is wrong and needs to stop." The fact that the girl was eighteen was probably enough to cause everyone to shrug and look the other way, but I'd be shocked if it hadn't started much sooner.

In a piece I wrote for the *Washington Post* in 2018, Hogshead-Maker told me, "Parents have to teach kids that they have bodily autonomy, to know what's theirs, and to trust their inner gut. We don't want parents telling their kids, 'Do whatever the coach says.' Athletes have to be empowered to say no. . . . Athletes and coaches should not be in an authoritarian relationship."

For Hogshead-Maker, the end of the sexual abuse of athletes begins with empowering them.

"If you give athletes power, if they have authority over their own bodies, if they can say 'no' to the coach without losing a scholarship or getting shamed," Hogshead-Makar said, that's what keeps them safe. She talks about the NCAA's fight to keep athletes from profiting off their own images and likenesses. "It's not just losing money. It is that [the NCAA is] used to having all-consuming power over the athletes, where they go, what they eat, who they date, what they're doing. They follow them around in the evenings to see where they are, at restaurants or at fraternity parties or sorority parties. They have incredible control over the athletes. And if the athletes have their own source of income, then [the NCAA] can't rely on them to be obedient and compliant."

It's clear that when it comes to the #MeToo movement, both sports and sports media have a long way to go. In sports media, we need much more than for HR to make us watch a video once every couple of years or click "acknowledge" on a company website. Because while media outlets may be going through the motions when it comes to improper sexual conduct, empowering women to feel that their jobs are safe if they turn in one of their colleagues is a much harder, and ultimately more important, task.

It's worth noting that while several women talked to me privately for this book about men in sports media who have sexually harassed them, none were willing to go on the record as the first woman to publicly accuse their harasser. One woman sent me emails between herself and the owner of a National Women's Soccer League team, in which he struggled to understand what went wrong that led her to being sexually assaulted by a team employee, and refused to take responsibility for hiring another employee with a public history of harassing and stalking women.

It's hard to blame women for staying silent, given that men like Tirico, Buccigross, and Berry continue to rise in the industry, while women like Decker and Lawrence are left to wonder why so few cared about their plight. I'd like to believe that the few brave women who have come forward about sexual misconduct in sports and sports media are just the first, and bloodiest, through the wall, to be followed by a long line of others.

But I'm not holding my breath.

CHAPTER 9

CARE ABOUT WOMEN'S SPORTS MORE THAN ONCE EVERY FOUR YEARS

Elite Athletes' Fight for Equal Pay and Support

Nothing got the text line at my radio station fired up like talking about women's sports. I often did three- to four-hour shows, 90 percent of which was dedicated to talking about the big four men's pro sports leagues: the NBA, NFL, MLB, and NHL. But as the only woman with a nightly show on my station, I felt an obligation to talk about women's sports, too. More than that, I *wanted* to talk about women's sports—they're exciting!—especially when the US Women's National soccer and hockey teams were competing in international tournaments.

I suppose I should have expected backlash. After all, it's not like sports talk radio is a bastion of progressivism and equality. But no matter how many times I knew it would happen, I was never prepared to have adult men *screaming* at me over the phone or hurling sexist slurs my way online because I spent ten minutes out of a three-hour show talking about women's sports. These dudes just had to express their nuanced opinions: "Women's sports are boring," "I don't tune in to a sports station to hear you talk about women's sports," and "No one cares about women's sports."

I heard that last one a lot, both from a certain faction of my listeners and from my colleagues at the station. It seems that way from inside an echo chamber full of bros, but statistically speaking, it's just not true. More than one *billion* people tuned in to watch the Women's World Cup in the summer of 2019. The two most-watched soccer games in US history are both games played by the US Women's National Team (USWNT). In fact, the 2019 World Cup final between the United States and the Netherlands pulled in more than twenty million viewers inside the United States. For comparison, the finale of *Game of Thrones* had 19.3 million viewers, and the first two episodes of *The Last Dance*, the highly anticipated documentary on the 1997–1998 Chicago Bulls, averaged 6.1 million viewers. We certainly wouldn't say that no one cares about *Game of Thrones* or Michael Jordan. Oh, and the most-watched soccer match ever in the United States? It was the USWNT against Japan back in the 2015 World Cup final. It pulled in an audience of a whopping twenty-four million people, 22 percent more people than watched the men's final the previous year.

So why, twenty-five years after the WNBA was founded and thirty years after the USWNT hoisted America's first World Cup trophy, do women's sports still struggle so much to gain a foothold in the United States?

Obviously, misogyny and sexism play a massive role in the "women's sports are boring" narrative. I defy anyone to say that the 2019 Women's World Cup final or the 2018 US Women's National Hockey Team's gold medal win were "boring" matches. It's difficult to recall a more exciting game, men's or women's, in any sport, than

Notre Dame's women's basketball team winning the 2018 NCAA championship over Mississippi State, which hinged on a shot from Aríke Ogunbowale with 1.7 seconds left on the clock. That day, it seemed like everyone I knew was watching the game and talking about it, including a bunch of NBA players, who seemed as excited about it as they would have been about the NBA finals.

When we think about the progress women's sports has made in America, it's worth remembering that Title IX, which mandated that girls have equal access to educational programs and activities that received federal funding, was enacted in 1972. It was only after that point that girls' sports teams started popping up in earnest at high schools and colleges. Despite its location in the soccer mecca of northern Illinois, my high school didn't have a girls' soccer team until 1988. Before that, one or two lone girls had to hack it on the boys' team. While the first boys' high school state basketball championship in Illinois was played in 1908, the girls didn't get a state tournament of their own until 1979. That year Niles West and trailblazing ESPN reporter Melissa Isaacson, who would go on to inspire me to get into sports journalism with her coverage of the Chicago Bulls in the nineties, took on and beat East St. Louis, led by their star player, Jackie Joyner. Joyner went on to marry her track coach, Bob Kersee, win a bunch of Olympic gold medals, and become one of the greatest track-and-field athletes of all time.

By the time I reached high school in the early nineties, a generation of daughters of Title IX had been born. We grew up watching and playing sports, just like the boys. Balancing schoolwork with practice, games, matches, and races was as woven into our DNA as it was for any of our male counterparts. Yet it was only every four years, when the Olympics rolled around, that we got to see female athletes perform at the highest level. And with that came an inescapable sense of finality. For us, no matter how good you were at soccer, volleyball, softball, or track, there was just nowhere to go. Even if we were lucky enough to get to play in college, there was also a recognition, with very few exceptions—namely the Olympics—that that was the end of the journey. There was nothing else.

Our daughters, on the other hand, have grown up in a world with a USWNT, with a thrilling USA-Canada rivalry in women's hockey, with a WNBA, with pro beach volleyball players they see in commercials as well as on the court. And, of course, they get to celebrate Olympians like Lindsey Vonn and Simone Biles on their television sets just like we did, too.

Julie Foudy was there for the beginning of the movement for women's sports on a national scale. She played for both the 1991 USWNT that won the United States its first World Cup trophy and the better-known team that captured America's hearts in 1999. Foudy believes the 1999 team, which also included household names like Mia Hamm and Brandi Chastain, proved that women's sports were viable in the United States.

"It was a reaffirmation that our instincts were right. For so long, we had said, 'There is a market, we're just not tapping into it,' or 'There are fans who care,' or 'Yes, girls do want to play. We're not crazy.' And so I think what we realized with all of this is that, with a little bit of investment, [women's sports] would blossom," Foudy told me.

But while the 1999 USWNT seemed to be everywhere commercially, there still was no good professional option for the players in the United States, and it would be a long road to creating one. Hoping to capitalize on the USWNT's popularity, the Women's United Soccer Association (WUSA) was founded in 2001, only to dissolve in 2003. After that, many US women, who played for the best team in the world, were forced to go overseas to play for European clubs. Similarly, the ill-fated Women's Professional Soccer league (WPS) was set up in 2008 and shuttered by 2012. It wasn't until the current National Women's Soccer League (NWSL) was formed in 2013 that a league with any real staying power took hold in this country. Yet with the global pandemic that swept America in 2020, even the NWSL's future may be on shaky ground.

"I fear we're going to take huge strides backwards. We're already in a marginalized space. People have always argued that we cost more than we make. We were finally at the point of saying, 'Actually, that's not true.' There's a market we're starting to tap into," Foudy said, pointing out that the men's game for superclubs, like Manchester United, Chelsea, and Real Madrid, may no longer be able to justify financially supporting their women's clubs, which are in early stages of growth. "A few million lost a year was pennies in the bucket. But now it's a much different equation. Clubs have to justify losing hundreds of millions of dollars and might ask themselves, 'Can we afford to have this expenditure on the women's side?' And I fear they're going to retreat. They're going to drop women's teams because there's no revenue coming in and on top of that you have no gate revenue because people can't congregate to go to games."

The Euro superclubs, like those I mentioned before, are consistently named the most valuable franchises in sports. In other words, they have more money than God. So any claim that they can't afford to keep women's teams afloat seems somewhat disingenuous. Real Madrid, for example, was worth approximately $4.64 billion in 2019, having made $100 million as a result of winning the Champions League in 2018. In March 2019, Madrid signed a $1.6 billion deal with Adidas. Even with COVID-19 shuttering soccer stadiums around the globe, it's hard to imagine that Madrid and other big-time clubs don't have the funds to keep women's teams going.

Meanwhile, despite their excellence, the commercial viability of women's pro teams in the United States remains a constant struggle, and one that is often held over the heads of female athletes as a reason why their jobs shouldn't exist. Kendall Coyne Schofield, one of the stars of the United States Women's hockey team, takes exception with that approach to valuing women's pro sports. "The first thing that comes to my mind is 'If you build it, they will come.' I challenge those organizations and those people who would say, 'Well, they don't bring in as much money.' My question is, have they put in the same amount of marketing dollars? Do they put in the same amount of energy to promote that women's event as they did that men's event? Do they put the same amount of resources to market their female athletes as they do their male athletes?

"I feel strongly about it," Coyne Schofield told me. "I've seen it from a USA hockey standpoint that the marketing behind our events is not good enough. We can only do so much as players. We're players; we're advocates; we're marketers, we're role models. We wear every hat, but sometimes you need someone to wear another hat for you and to build it and believe in it."

Casually chatting with Coyne Schofield about women's pro sports while driving into my radio job one night was a thrill. In addition to crossing over into providing analysis for the NHL's San Jose Sharks, Coyne Schofield made many across America sit up and take notice during the 2019 NHL All-Star skills competition, when she took the place of a late scratch in the fastest skater competition. She finished less than a second behind the fastest skater in the NHL, Connor McDavid of the Edmonton Oilers, and ahead of three other NHL players.

As she crossed the finish line, the crowd erupted in a chorus of "USA! USA! USA!" I still get chills remembering that moment. I think every girl and woman in America who had ever been able to keep up with the boys, but was told she and her sport were lesser, felt seen.

The moment was even sweeter given that just two years earlier, the circumstances for USA Women's hockey were so poor, they threatened to boycott the world championships, demanding they earn a livable wage. That year, USA alternate captain Monique Lamoureux-Morando called into my radio show to talk about what the team was fighting for, revealing that the members of the women's national team earned just $6,000 *every four years*, spread out over a six-month period.

"Typically, you are training five to six days a week for one to three hours depending on the day," Lamoureux-Morando said. "Then we skate, so you are at the rink for an additional two hours. I live in close proximity to the rink and where I train, so I'm lucky in that aspect compared to teammates who have to commute. Then you have the whole nutrition, recovery, and mental aspect that goes into being an elite athlete. It's literally a full-time job. If I wasn't working on top of training, I would devote more time on the ice and in the gym, but I don't have the time."

Lamoureux-Morando also spoke about players moving back in with their parents or working three jobs just to be able to play hockey. Coyne Schofield agrees that the average fan has no idea what women's national team players go through to be able to represent their country on the ice: "You're a full-time employee by day, and your hobby is pro hockey player at night. . . . I don't think people really deeply understand what we're going through on a regular basis, what our daily schedule looks like. They think about the [2017] boycott and they're like, 'Oh, you guys just want money.' But we're trying to set this team up for success in the future."

In a rare display of solidarity in sports, Team USA not only boycotted training camp, they managed to convince every postcollege, college, and high school player in the country not to cross the picket line to fill the USA's roster. The 2017 team not only forced USA Hockey to blink, inking a four-year deal that provided travel accommodations and insurance provisions in line with that the men's team was provided; they also went on to win the 2017 Women's World Championship, beating rival Canada in overtime. And while the financial details of the new deal weren't disclosed, part of the settlement included USA Hockey allocating more money into developing the girls' game, along with the creation of an advisory panel to advance the progress of women and girls.

These victories, achieved under pressure by the 2017 and 2018 US Women's teams, set up Coyne Schofield's skate at the NHL All-Star skills competition. Schofield says she didn't find out she was skating until four hours before the competition, due to the Colorado Avalanche's Nathan MacKinnon dropping out because of a bruised foot. "As a competitor, I was just telling myself, 'Don't get last . . .' I was representing a big group of women and girls in hockey in that moment. I just didn't want to stumble because I knew the narrative would change to 'I told you so. They don't belong,'" she said. "And people don't remember, but Miro Heiskanen fell right after me. No one says 'boo' about that. He's still one of the best skaters in the

NHL. I fall, and it's a totally different story." But she didn't fall. In fact, Schofield kept up with the fastest male skaters in the game, finishing less than the time it takes to blink behind Connor McDavid.

As I drove toward downtown Chicago, Coyne Schofield still describing her trailblazing skate for me, I flew past the United Center and Fifth Third Arena, where the Chicago Blackhawks play and practice, respectively. High above the Eisenhower Expressway, a giant billboard for the short documentary *As Fast As Her*, about Coyne Schofield's infamous skate, loomed over me. It was the first time I could recall seeing a female athlete featured there.

Later, I pulled up a clip of the competition to watch the moment again. It was over so quickly, in just over fourteen seconds. Watching the camera panning NHL players with their mouths hanging open, Coyne Schofield's earrings flashing as she bursts across the finish line, the crowd loudly celebrating the US Women's hockey player . . . it's so emotional, such a feel-good moment, that you can almost forget that the most elite women's hockey players in the United States *still* aren't paid well enough to be truly full-time professional athletes.

Of course, the US Women's hockey team isn't the first or only team to have to fight for some semblance of a living wage. After winning their fourth World Cup in 2019, the USWNT has had to pivot to a legal battle with US Soccer, claiming that the governing body has violated the Equal Pay Act, Title VII of the Civil Rights Act of 1964, and the Fair Labor Standards Act. And while the lawsuit, in which every member of the USWNT is a party, has evoked the usual cry of "this is just a money grab," which always seems to rear its head when women seek legal redress for past wrongs, the case is about much more than money. It's about the best soccer team in America (and the world, for that matter) being treated as second-class sacrificial lambs for the sake of a subpar men's team.

In addition to seeking $67 million in back pay, which is what the USWNT players claim they would have been paid under the pay structure set out in the US Men's National Team's collective bargaining agreement, the women also claim US Soccer discriminates against them with regard to travel and training conditions. In the USWNT's complaint, the players allege that US Soccer chartered flights for the men's team on seventeen occasions in 2017, while forcing the women to fly commercial for every match. The USWNT also points out that they have been forced to play on artificial surfaces, generally thought to be inferior and less safe than natural grass, around 21 percent of the time in 2017; in the same year the men's team had to do so in only 2 percent of their matches. And despite the fact that the USWNT has won *half* the Women's World Cups played to date, the USWNT lawsuit claims US Soccer spends far less time promoting women's matches than men's games.

After mediation between the USWNT and US Soccer fell through, it became clear the case was headed to trial. And that was before US Soccer lobbed a hand grenade into the proceedings by claiming there should be no comparison between the men's and women's teams, and thus no basis for equal pay, because "men are bigger, stronger, faster." You can imagine how well that went over with the USWNT and women in general.

Biologically, men may tend to be bigger, stronger, and faster, but it's the women's team who put US Soccer on the international map. In fact, all four stars on the national team jerseys, worn by both the men's and women's teams and representing how many World Cups the United States has won, are courtesy of the US women. The outcry over US Soccer's tone-deaf response was swift and wide-ranging, and when a lukewarm apology from US Soccer president Carlos Cordeiro failed to quiet the backlash, he was eventually forced to step down. The new president, Cindy Parlow Cone, played for the USWNT from 1995 to 2006 and won two Olympic golds and a World Cup playing alongside USWNT legends like Mia Hamm and Julie Foudy.

"I know there are a ton [of people] within US Soccer who were horrified by that legal approach, and I'm not just talking women," Foudy said. "I'm talking men who have been there for years who said, 'I was in tears when I read that. How could we put this out there?' . . . Culturally, I think we're going to see a shift within the organization."

But it's not as if such feelings never existed when it came to the USWNT, Foudy said. "It was very apparent that mind-set lived back when we were playing. I mean, you didn't have a GM on the team who was a woman; you didn't have a president who was a woman. . . . They looked at us like we were crazy."

It's ironic that the two teams that have been demeaned the most by US Soccer—the Julie Foudy–era USWNT behind the scenes and the current USWNT squad publicly—have done more to boost interest and pride in the US game than any iteration of the men's team ever has, and the women have the receipts to show for it. According to the *Wall Street Journal*, the USWNT outdrew the men's team in ticket sales, bringing in $50.8 million to the men's $49.9 million, from 2016 to 2018. In 2016, the year after the women won the 2015 World Cup, they brought in $1.9 million more in revenue than the men. And that's not taking into account that the UWSNT's lawsuit alleges that US Soccer spends fewer resources marketing their matches and that their tickets are priced lower than the men's. Why would fans want to pay more to see a team that hardly ever wins and didn't even manage to qualify for the 2018 World Cup? Only US Soccer knows.

In the spring of 2020, US District Court judge Gary Klausner dealt the US Women's lawsuit a stunning blow, dismissing their Equal Pay and Title VII claims before they even got to trial, leaving only the issues like playing surface and travel accommodations. The US Women's team has vowed to appeal, but their equal-pay-for-equal-work movement, which galvanized a nation, hangs in limbo for the time being. Whether the changes at the top of US Soccer and the public backlash that preceded them will be enough to shift decades' worth of entrenched sexism about women's sports remains to be seen.

While both women's national teams and pro sports leagues scratch and claw their way toward some semblance of equal pay and respect, one league is miles ahead of the rest. In January 2020, the WNBA's Players Association (WNBPA) inked a new collective bargaining agreement (CBA) that secured long-sought provisions to prioritize the women's game in the United States.

For years, WNBA players have been decrying their low salaries. They're so low, in fact, that many players have been forced to play for teams in Europe in their off-season in order to earn a living wage. In April 2019, WNBA star Breanna Stewart ruptured her Achilles tendon playing in Hungary for her EuroLeague team,

Dynamo Kursk. She injured herself and collided with *another* WNBA star, Brittney Griner, who was playing for *her* EuroLeague team, UMMC Ekaterinburg. As a result, the WNBA's Seattle Storm lost Stewart for the season. But it could have been worse. The WNBA could have lost two of its biggest stars in a single play, thousands of miles away from their homes in the United States.

Prior to the new CBA, the average WNBA player made around $75,000 per year. That's not chump change for the average American, but it is hardly enough for WNBA players who have to live or rent apartments in large urban areas where their teams are located, keep themselves conditioned and maintain a nutritious diet, and sometimes support a family. The best players in the league could earn around $115,000, while rookies have made only around $40,000. For comparison, players with select contracts in the NBA's development G League can make $125,000 for five months of work. In fact, the WNBA paid its players so little that superstars like Diana Taurasi and Maya Moore had opted to sit out their WNBA seasons in order to keep their bodies ready for their far-more-lucrative overseas teams. Other players missed WNBA reporting deadlines for team camps, as they were contractually obligated to remain with their Euro teams for the playoffs, which sometimes overlapped with WNBA training camps.

All that will likely change now that the new CBA is in place. In addition to nearly doubling the max league salary to $215,000, the average WNBA player is expected to make around $130,000. Perhaps more important, the new CBA marks the first real effort to keep US players at home during the off-season, providing that by 2024, players with at least three years of WNBA experience must play the entire WNBA season. Players who fail to do so because of play for another team will forfeit their WNBA season and their salary.

Like the USWNT and the US Women's National hockey teams, the WNBA was also sick of flying coach. With the average height of a WNBA player being five foot eleven, coach seats, which seem to get smaller every year, just can't get the job done. Per the new CBA, WNBA players will fly in only "premium" airline seats and will get their own rooms when staying in hotels. Imagine being one of the best athletes in the world and having to double up with a friend at the Marriott, especially when traveling with children! To the envy of working mothers everywhere, players will also receive fully paid maternity leave, a $5,000-per-year childcare stipend, and accommodations for nursing mothers. Imani McGee-Stafford of the Dallas Wings was happy with the CBA, saying, "It's a great step forward. We are finally getting the institutional investment we've been asking for."

For obvious reasons, the WNBA's new CBA is the gold standard for women's pro sports leagues. But is it really such a stretch for the best players in the world? Howard Megdal, editor/founder of *The IX* newsletter and *High Post Hoops*, both of which focus on women's sports, says the new CBA is just a jumping-off point for the league: "The new CBA is great as progress, though not a destination, as both sides would acknowledge. It gives players more incentive to prioritize their WNBA careers over their overseas play and rewards them more financially at both the rookie and star levels. It forces the teams to invest more on the marketing end. It gives everyone the incentives to fully buy into what the league is building. It's a huge change in that way alone."

In talking about the WNBA's new CBA on my radio show, one thing became clear. A certain faction of men was personally offended by the new deal, protesting, with more emotion than grown men should have over what other people are paid, that WNBA players don't deserve living wages for playing in a league that isn't profitable. McGee-Stafford offered a simple reply: "Why do you care? The money doesn't come from your pocket."

But more to the point, the WNBA is far from the only league that struggled with revenue. In fact, the NBA itself operated at a net loss of $15 to $20 million as recently as 1982. There was real fear that year that a looming players' strike could sink the league for good. Megdal says the WNBA is really only beginning its journey toward becoming a sustainable league. "So it's important to think of the WNBA relative to, for instance, the NBA. 1982 was roughly thirty-five years into the NBA's history. We're entering year twenty-four of the WNBA. And much of the WNBA has taken place amid a tilted-toward-men sports media marketplace that has suffered massive, unprecedented cuts to staffs. So just getting the story out has been difficult for most of the league's history."

The WNBA has only been around since 1997, and I'm not sure anyone can argue in good faith that the NBA has provided the league with the resources and marketing on par with the men's game. As Megdal points out, half the WNBA teams already turn a profit, and roughly half the NBA teams lose money. "So what are we really talking about here?" he asked.

Perhaps it was due in part to the lack of sports because of the global pandemic, perhaps it was due in part to the strides the WNBA has made in recent years, but the 2020 WNBA draft seemed bigger, felt bigger, in the public consciousness than ever before. That's due in large part to the amazing women who covered the draft for sites like *The Athletic*, *High Post Hoops*, and *Swish Appeal*. For the first time in my career working in sports, I had texters and callers to my radio show wanting to talk about the WNBA draft. There weren't lots of them, but they were there. It seemed everyone on Twitter was watching and commenting on the draft. At one point, the list of trending topics was almost all players and team names. I got me wondering: maybe the new CBA, which treats women's players like honest-to-God professional athletes for the first time, caused a sea change in the public consciousness.

Almost every woman I know who works in sports media feels a personal responsibility to talk about and help promote women's pro sports and national teams, even if they aren't necessarily assigned to cover them as part of their job. Many of us were athletes in our youth and didn't have female pro leagues to aspire to after high school and college. For us, it's important that these leagues not just succeed but also thrive. And while it's anecdotal, I felt a pushback when talking about the WNBA on my radio show that I didn't get when talking about the USWNT or the US Women's National hockey team, making me wonder: What exactly is at play here? For his part, Megdal says the two biggest obstacles facing the WNBA are "a crumbling media sector and an unwillingness in too many circles to properly spotlight a majority women-of-color enterprise of any kind, even one as insanely entertaining as the WNBA." As marginalized as white women are in sports, there's no doubt that Black women and women of color have it much worse.

So how do those of us who want to see women's pro sports and national teams flourish go about supporting them? Julie Foudy is quick to offer an easy way to help, even from afar. "Just click on articles, right? Read, pay attention. If you're a fan, just spreading [stories about women's teams] makes your point, right? You're showing that 'okay, I can't show up right now,' but as we all know in the media, it matters how many clicks you're getting and who's reading and who's paying attention." And while the global pandemic prevents fans from getting out to the parks and stadiums to support their teams, Foudy said, "As much as you can, just be talking about it and make it part of the conversation. I'm hearing more and more now with my kids, for example, where their friends are saying, 'The NWSL was supposed to start tomorrow and I'm so bummed it's not happening.' So it's in their conscience."

The WNBA's McGee-Stafford had a similar request for the media: "Give us your space and time and tell our stories." I often wonder how much of the "women's sports are boring" talk is driven by the fact that the stories of women athletes just aren't as well-known as the men's stories are. When we watch the NBA, everyone knows who is back playing the old team after an acrimonious departure, who has beef with who, what pitcher and batter have a history of going at it. If viewers knew those stories about women in the NWSL or the WNBA, would the games be just as interesting to them as the men's games are? There's no way for us know until those stories are as common for women's teams as they are for their male counterparts.

Kelsey Trainor, an attorney, producer, and sportswriter, believes that women's sports need to change the way they reach their audiences. "We need to understand that men's and women's sports and leagues shouldn't be marketed and branded the same way," Trainor said. "While the target audiences are similar, the product is different and has different components." While the WNBA often gets criticized for not being as fast-paced as the NBA, there are plenty of fans, including the late Hall of Fame basketball coach John

Wooden, who love the "purity" of the women's game, the shooting skill, and the defense. While the NBA is marketed largely to young men, perhaps the WNBA's core audience are young women and the parents of girls who hoop?

"Another way [to support the WNBA] is to simply put our money where our mouth is, which is easier to advocate for than to do," Trainor said. "But if you 'support' women, then buy tickets. Take your kids or friends to games. People don't know what they don't know. If you bring them into the women's sports world, they may not fully understand or support it, but they will know it exists, which can lead to interest."

But when it comes right down to it, maybe the best way for women to support women's sports is simply to demand that we see more of them. *The Atlantic*'s Jemele Hill points out that it's not just men prioritizing men's sports. "There are a lot of female sports fans, but they're coming up and taking their cues from what they've seen men do. A lot of female sports fans don't actually support women's sports," she said. "If you look at the women's college basketball numbers, it's overwhelmingly men [who are watching]. Some women haven't been able to support women's sports, but some aren't vocal about women being on TV because I don't think they care all that much, either. So that's got to be the first place it comes from. We don't need any more women doing the work of the patriarchy. Unfortunately, I feel there are too many women who get into [sports media] and feel the need to prove they can be just like men as opposed to adding the value of what women bring to the table."

Lamoureux-Morando thinks visibility is the biggest problem for women's sports: many women's teams pick up rabid fans for a couple of weeks every four years for the Olympics or World Cup who then go back to watching the men after the closing ceremonies. "Obviously they do that because that's what's on. Women's sports are not nearly as visible and they aren't marketed as much. One of the big pieces to this puzzle is closing the investment gap," she said, pointing out that leagues need to invest in women's sports to get them to grow. "I'm not a genius, but I do know that a business that doesn't promote, market, or invest in its product is not going to be successful. If those things can be done, more revenue will be generated, you can pay your players more, more girls and boys will start playing, the sport grows, and everybody wins."

Maggie Hendricks, my Saturday radio show cohost who covered the WNBA for *The Athletic*, thinks we're making all of this too complicated. "Cover [women's sports] like sports," she told me. "There's this tendency among, particularly men but not limited to them, sports media to want to focus on the social importance of women's sports, and it's true. The WNBA and the NWSL and the WTA [Women's Tennis Association], et cetera, are important to society. But when people only focus on that, and not the fact that these are actually thrilling sports with playoff races and job implications and all of the things we see in men's sports, they get turned into a charity. They're not a charity, and watching the WNBA isn't a charitable endeavor."

Hendricks points out that when the 2019 WNBA All-Star team was announced on *The Jump*, a transcendently popular ESPN staple hosted by Rachel Nichols, the show didn't treat the league the same way it would have treated the NBA. "It was the summer, and free agency had already been happening for a week or so, so NBA news was at a minimum. When they announced the [WNBA All-Star] rosters, they said the names, and the panel—all NBA people—said maybe two sentences. 'The WNBA is so good. We should watch it.' And then returned to the NBA. They did no analysis, no snubs, no 'Why is this person a starter?'—nothing about the actual games and players. That's treating the WNBA like a charity, instead of giving them fair coverage."

And then there's the reality that local TV and radio stations don't bother to give the scores of women's games in their daily sports recaps. In fact, when I started including Chicago Sky and Chicago Red Stars scores in my updates, our station's text line immediately blew up with men, enraged that their ears had been assaulted with the knowledge that women's sports were even happening. "WHO CARES ABOUT THE CHICAGO SKY?" "NO ONE CARES ABOUT WOMEN'S SPORTS." The texts came in fast and furious. But I felt it was up to those of us in the industry to normalize hearing about women's sports. During the Saturday *Julie & Maggie Show*, we kept an eye on the scoreboard for Sky and Red Stars games and made sure to update out listeners as to what was happening. After a while, it became normal. Our listeners knew we were going to talk about Chicago's women's sports, and it was just part of our show. The texts that came changed after a while. We heard from a lot of parents who thanked us because their daughters heard two women on the radio talking about women's sports.

And the end of the day, maybe it really is that simple. To really raise women's sports to be on par with men's, maybe we all need to care more, be louder, and demand that women's pro sports be seen.

CHAPTER 10

AROUND THE WORLD, HERE COME THE GIRLS

Sports as Empowerment for Girls Everywhere

I n the spring of 2018, I got a cryptic email, offering me the chance to "change the narrative" about women in Pakistan with an organization called Women Win. The details were vague, but the thing that stood out was the offer of a trip to Pakistan, which, in my American ignorance, seemed only slightly less dangerous than traveling to North Korea. I deleted the email and forgot about it.

A few weeks later, I was talking with my radio cohost, Maggie Hendricks, about unsolicited PR pitches when I happened to mention that some organization invited me to go to Pakistan.

"You're going to do it, right?" she said.

"What? Go to Pakistan?"

"When else are you going to get a free trip to Pakistan?" she asked. "I'd look into that."

Her comment niggled at me for a few days. At one time, I had imagined a life full of travel to faraway places as an international human rights lawyer, only to find myself driving a grocery-laden (but still sexy!) station wagon in the suburbs as a sports radio host. My husband, it would turn out, would get to do all the traveling for his job while I was stuck holding down the home front.

A week later, I dug back through my trash folder and found the original email. I reread it. I responded. Long story short: I went to Pakistan. What I saw there renewed my faith in the power of sports and cemented my belief that access to sports and play are essential to growing women's voices and influence around the globe.

I arrived in Karachi on a sweaty May night. The humidity kicked in somewhere over Dubai, and by the time we landed, I was covered in a thin sheen of sweat that stayed with me the entire time I was there. Surprising, considering Americans tend to think of Pakistan as being an arid desert climate.

The organizations that brought me to Pakistan to see how young women were benefiting from sports were called Women Win and Right To Play. Both are well-respected nongovernmental organizations that travel to some of the most marginalized places on earth to get kids running and playing and, well, acting like kids. Right To Play, in fact, began as an organization dedicated to getting child soldiers into schools and onto playgrounds. It doesn't get much more noble than that.

When it comes to Pakistan, the challenge is to overcome centuries of religious and cultural beliefs that have fed into the idea that girls playing sports are less feminine or harming their reproductive health. (You may recognize these as beliefs some American institutions held about women who took part in sports not so long ago.) In some ways, the United States and Pakistan are fighting the exact same battles when it comes to fairness for women's sports: a lack of equity and respect.

Feminist scholar and MMA fighter L. A. Jennings was with me on the trip, and she was taken aback at how similar the coverage of women's sports is in the United States and Pakistan.

"Most of my research has been about the portrayal of female athletes in the media, and the numbers here are pretty staggeringly low in the US. I think just in the last year it's risen finally from three percent to four percent of all sports media coverage. And I think that, based on my experience as a woman in the US, even though I knew those numbers, I knew how atrocious they were, I still felt like we were doing a better job than Pakistan."

We are, but not by much.

"I really don't feel like we are that far removed from Pakistan, from a country that [many] Americans like to think that we are so much better than morally, ethically," Jennings said. "Yet, there really isn't much of a tremendous differential. The only difference here is that in the US we can highly, highly sexualize our female athletes, and that's not going to happen in the same way in Pakistan."

After a brief organizational meeting about how to dress (relatively conservative, head scarves not necessary), act (Americans hug everyone. Don't hug everyone!), and eat (drink bottled water and don't eat fruits or vegetables washed in tap water). That last one didn't matter much because, frankly, Pakistan is full of transcendent and delectable foods and none of us were exactly thinking of salads. I've never eaten so gloriously in my life.

Our first trip was to Karachi United, a local soccer club that started teams for women and girls in 2010. Before then, there were 442 teams in the Karachi Football League. All were comprised solely of men.

The heat and humidity in Karachi are oppressive for Americans from north of the Mason-Dixon Line, and probably for Southerners, too. It felt like all we did during our time in South Pakistan was sweat, and the pictures on my phone confirm that was an accurate assessment. It seemed like everywhere we went, people were waiting for it to cool down "for the Americans."

Having played soccer through high school, I knew just how much intense cardio was involved in any given practice, and I couldn't imagine the young girls sitting outside in the one-hundred-degree-plus heat were actually going to play. "We're just waiting for the temperature to drop a degree or two before we get started," one of the older girls told us. They quickly shuttled the melting Americans into a darkened conference room festooned with oscillating fans. While we fanned ourselves and sucked down bottle after bottle of water, the girls began warming up outside in the heat. Our hosts brought out a platter of *chikoo*, the most amazing fruit on the planet, which tasted like a combination of pears and strawberries and had the added benefit of keeping the Americans from talking about how hot it was out because we were too busy clearing our plates and licking our fingers.

Twenty minutes later, we were watching the girls play *futsal*, small-sided soccer games that are more popular overseas than in the United States. Their field was dusty and filled with rocks, nothing like the pristine pitches I had played on back home, but soccer is soccer wherever you go. The juggling, the passing drills, the shots on goal—all too familiar to someone who grew up playing the sport. None of us were dressed for playing. We'd been told to dress modestly, and while we didn't wear head scarves, we did all sort of look like we'd just stepped out of a Chico's or J.Jill. Lots of long flowing skirts, lots of palazzo pants, lots of linen. Sensible shoes for hours of walking every day.

But these girls. *These girls*. They played the game with such joy. They were shy playing in front of us at first. But eventually they were laughing and yelling trash talk at one another. It's funny how you *know* its smack talk even if it's in Urdu. It was impossible to simply sit on the sidelines. I got up and played in my sandals. Have you taken a shot on goal with open-toed sandals? It sucks. And it was still a billion degrees out. But I didn't care. I was in baggy linen pants and sandals, and I ruined my pedicure mixing it up with these amazing young women, but it was so worth it. *This is they why call it "the Beautiful Game,"* I remember thinking. Once a soccer player, always a soccer player. And that incredible game allows you to connect with other players anywhere in the world.

More than 35 percent of Karachi is under the age of fourteen, which means there are approximately five million girls in the city alone, and that's not counting the millions of undocumented immigrants estimated to be living there. A huge percentage of children in Pakistan have no access to a safe place to play. Many girls have never had the chance to try sports or even "play," the way we think about it in the West. We met girls in their mid-teens who had never run, jumped, or chased a ball until sport-as-development organizations like Women Win and Right To Play came into their lives.

While girls and women in Pakistan are slowly gaining a foothold through clubs like Karachi United, women's sports get little serious consideration in the media, and female athletes are largely ignored. Representation matters to young girls of all nations, and the lack of athletic role models appears to be due to a lack of imagination everywhere as well as good old-fashioned sexism.

As part of my visit, I attended a conference in Islamabad on media coverage of women's sports, with dozens of women athletes, sportswriters, and broadcasters in attendance. During a panel discussion, two of the very few men in the room decided to enlighten the womenfolk on the reason for the dearth of coverage of women's sports; they told us, "If women want us to cover them, they have to do something interesting." It seems that once male sportswriters got past the obligatory "a Muslim woman is playing sports!" profile, they were plumb out of ideas, which, frankly, sounded way too familiar to the Americans in the room. If I had a dime for every time an American guy suggested women's sports were "boring," I could buy the goddamn New York Knicks.

Aggravated, I suggested a story of how Pakistan's women athletes train during Ramadan as an example of another angle. One of the men snorted with laughter. "Women don't train during Ramadan." In unison, about a dozen of the athletes at the conference spun around and shouted, "*I* train during Ramadan!" He sat back down.

The problems for women and sports in Pakistan go far beyond a lack of media coverage, though not seeing themselves represented on the sports pages certainly doesn't encourage girls to give sports a go. In a country ranked 151st out of 153 nations in gender equality (beating only Iraq and Yemen) according to the World Economic

Forum's 2020 Global Gender Gap Report, the larger issue is that there is no culture or infrastructure to funnel young women into sports (and lest we Americans get too judgmental, the United States only came in at number 53). In effect, Pakistan looks a lot like America might, had we never enacted Title IX. Can you guess how many colleges and high schools would field women's teams in the United States if they weren't required by federal law to do so? So can I.

Like women everywhere, Pakistani women who want to excel at their sport are fighting an uphill battle for resources, decent competition, and acceptance. Only in Pakistan, it's even harder.

Sana Mahmud, who has served as the captain of the Pakistan national women's soccer and basketball teams, says the lack of safe spaces for female athletes in Pakistan is an ongoing issue. "A challenge that has really affected me is that you don't have female-friendly spaces and female-friendly avenues. I was injured and I only had this male physiotherapist for the longest time. And after a year I realized that something was not right. This person seemed to be taking advantage of me and was harassing me, and so I had to leave that doctor to find another one. And I would never find another suitable doctor. So (A) we don't have enough medical experts, but then (B) if you're a female athlete and you don't know much and you're only guided to the one central sports complex with the sports physio, and that person ends up harassing you, you have no recourse. And then later I found out that he's had a reputation of doing this." While the United States has had its fair share of sexual abuse and harassment scandals, societal and religious forces in places like Pakistan make it even more difficult for women to come forward with stories of abuse. Going to a female physiotherapist wasn't an option Mahmud had.

Many of the young women we met in Pakistan talked about a lack of safe spaces for women in general, not just in sports. Because traditionally, young girls were expected to remain at home, they risk harassment walking down the street, taking public transportation, and essentially existing in the same spaces with men who aren't members of their families. They expressed frustration with the idea that, somehow, by breaking traditional norms, *they* were responsible for being harassed, rather than the men who do the harassing.

It's easy to see how the lack of safe space and play space limits how many girls can take part in sports. The women at Karachi United told me that when they first began practicing, passersby threw garbage over the fence onto their practice field to protest their "immodest" training gear: shorts, high socks, and T-shirts. Pakistani parents are fiercely protective of their daughters, and a culture of street harassment of young women by men of all ages is endemic. While more progressive families may be okay with their daughters playing in shorts and a T-shirt, conservative families, especially in rural areas, demand their daughters remain covered from head to toe. I was in awe of the girls who played in more modest clothing, including long skirts and head scarves, especially remembering how we bumbled around in nonathletic clothes and battled the heat. My God, the heat. Americans faced with such temperatures would strip down to sports bras and hot pants. The drive and determination of these women, not to let their lack of athletic apparel stop them, was inspiring. No more complaining about uncomfortable sports bras from me.

Most of the safe places in big Pakistani cities like Karachi and

Islamabad are behind fences and gates. Especially in a sprawling, crowded, endless sea of construction like Karachi, sports clubs have had to fight to gain control over green spaces and practice fields. When Naseem Hameed, easily the most popular woman athlete in the country after winning the one-hundred-meter dash in the 2010 South Asia games, opened a sports academy for local girls in a derelict stadium near Karachi's Korangi Town, she had to withstand threats from organized crime syndicates who tried to terrorize her off the property. Sports clubs have had to pull out of other neighborhoods as they became unsafe for female athletes.

The lack of safe places to play in places like Karachi means families who do allow their girls to take part in sports have to figure out how to safely get them to and from games and practices. Public transportation is largely unsafe for young women traveling alone in Pakistan, which means that parents either have to escort their daughters to safe play spaces or have to release them to the wind, hoping they'll return home safely. On average, it costs parents three times as much to get their daughters to sports facilities as their sons. A few of the girls we met at Karachi United told us their fathers regularly take time off their day jobs to shuttle them to practice.

It's even more complicated, because a city like Karachi has been around, literally, for millennia. The entire city is a huge, sprawling tangle of roads and wires, and it's constantly under construction. Everywhere we went, we saw buildings being reconstructed right on top of whatever had been there before. So to have access to sports, girls first have to live within commuting distance from a place that (A) has green space and (B) allows women to use it. And because of the aforementioned problem with young women taking public transportation alone, they either need a parent who can take off work to escort them to practice and games and a way to get there. All this means that families in more advantaged neighborhoods, who can provide their own transportation, are more likely to have daughters who take part in sports.

There are also myriad cultural, religious, and gender stereotypes that keep girls out of sports. The legal age for marriage in Pakistan is sixteen, and a whopping 21 percent of girls there are married by age eighteen, according to UNICEF, though other reports put that number as high as 37 percent. Girls in conservative families who are not married in their teens are often expected to be homemakers. Cooking, sewing, and waiting on men are expected of girls from a young age in traditional families, leaving little time for athletic pursuits. Some of the young women we met in Pakistan told us that, when they weren't cooking or cleaning at home, they were expected to sit quietly and wait to be spoken to.

Of course, Pakistan, like any other country, has big modern cities, educated and uneducated citizens, and people who run the gamut of political affiliations from progressive to conservative. The vast majority of its citizens who practice Islam, the national religion, do so in many different ways. I, in my myopia, expected to find a country of oppressed women in burkas. What I found was a vibrant, lively, and courageous nation of women pushing the boundaries of expectations and dragging Pakistan, in some cases kicking and screaming, into the twenty-first century of women's sports.

Luckily, there are organizations like Women Win, Right To Play, Karachi United, and Go Girl Pakistan to help them do it. While on the streets we saw groups of women walking with their heads down and avoiding eye contact, at Karachi United we saw girls running, yelling, and attacking one another on the pitch with good-natured aggression. We visitors agreed to a game of *futsal* but most of us cashed it in after a few minutes. It was just too hot to run. The Karachi United girls, though, played hard for another hour. As we left, several fathers watched, beaming, as their daughters took shots on goal.

At Karachi United, dozens of girls found kindred spirits, other women who were not content with their lot in life and who demanded to be allowed to do the things they saw girls in other countries doing. Today's youth may be separated by geography, but they all have cell phones and are connected by technology. Many of them told us that their parents initially resisted allowing them to play soccer. But kids and parents are largely the same everywhere, and their pleas of "but everyone else is doing it" eventually wore their parents down.

On the ground, the benefits of sports couldn't have been more clear—and the evidence that they have in developing nations isn't just anecdotal. One Win Leads to Another (OWLA), a joint partnership between UN Women and the International Olympic Committee (IOC), found that girls who took part in their sports-as-development program in Brazil showed real gains in self-esteem and real-world skills. Before the program began, only 46 percent of the girls in the program saw themselves as leaders. Afterward, a full 89 percent of girls considered themselves leaders. Perhaps as important as instilling confidence in young women is teaching them things they may not learn in school or from their parents.

Seventy-nine percent of girls left the program knowing how to prevent pregnancy, whereas only 25 percent had known when the program began. Ninety-three percent of the girls leaving the program said they knew where and how to report domestic violence. Perhaps most importantly, 99 percent of the girls left the program believing they would one day have a job.

Billie Jean King's Women's Sports Foundation echoes these findings, reporting that high school girls who play sports are less likely to experience a teen pregnancy and more likely to get good grades. Girls in sports also have a higher level of self-esteem and a more positive body image than those who don't take part in sports. Soraya Chemaly, author of *Rage Becomes Her*, says taking part in sports during youth may affect how successful women are in careers later in life.

"Women who do sports are socialized differently and are socialized in ways that we traditionally think of as male socialization. They learn to compete, they learn to be aggressive, their hormones shift with their behavior, right? If you are physically expansive and you are physically dominant, you actually get surges of testosterone that [are] measurably happening. Women and girls who engage in sports have a different physiological response and they also get used to on-field and off-field behavior," Chemaly said.

"It's kind of like an emotional code-switching. Boys learn to be competitive in sports really early on. They learned to have camaraderie and competition coexist. Whereas for girls, competition is really looked down on, because we're supposed to be communal and nice and nurturing and smiling. I really think that you cannot overstate the importance of the socialization of girls through sports to their stature in society or to their ability to express themselves in traditionally masculine ways."

As Jennings previously said, as much as we'd like to think of ourselves as better on issues of gender equality than places like Pakistan, the hard truth is that we still rely on the same kinds of sports programs in the United States to give women confidence and teach them to speak up. In the big picture, the United States also does a rotten job of empowering women from a young age. One day, perhaps women of all races and ethnicities will have the confidence that white men seem born with. Until that day, participation in sports is a tried and true method of teaching girls to stand up and speak out in "traditionally masculine ways."

You know, traditionally masculine ways like defending yourself, asking for what you want, and having career ambition. These are all traits that women are punished for in the workplace in the Western world and even more so in countries where women have been traditionally more marginalized than in the United States. But as more young women discover their voices through sports, not just in the United States but around the world, perhaps this can change. Maybe, someday, so many women in so many places will be using their voices to scream from the rooftops that women pushing back becomes the norm, just as it is for men.

Wherever we visited girls playing sports in Pakistan, they seemed more outspoken and confident than their peers. To a one, they looked us in the eyes, shook our hands firmly, and asked question about how the West views Pakistani women. They asked what kind of training American girls got. They wanted to know how often they practiced, what they ate, what else they did to keep their bodies in shape. They wanted to know if they were as good as American athletes. For many of these girls, who came from poor neighborhoods with little in the way of opportunity for women, sports are about so much more than dribbling and juggling and corner kicks. It opens up an entire world of travel, continuing education, and having a career. It's not enough for many of them to kick a ball around for practice. They're hungry to improve, to compete, and to test themselves against who they perceive to be the best in the world. The women we met were so curious and excited; you could sense them feeling the world opening up before them.

A few days after visiting Karachi United, we rolled into the slum of Bari Imam in Islamabad, not far from the US embassy. We were there to visit the Mashal Model School girls' cricket team, but our usually boisterous group was silent on the ride through town. The poverty we saw outside the windows of our cushy, air-conditioned van was the most crushing we'd seen. Earlier that morning, we had learned that the fortresslike US embassy, just a mile or two down the road, was spending a vast sum of money to build a baseball diamond in their compound, in addition to the basketball courts they already had. Now, the knowledge of such excess in proximity to such hopelessness left us feeling deeply ashamed.

The Mashal Model School, though, was an oasis. Inside the crisp, white walls of the school, children recited multiplication tables, learned computer programming, and drew crayon pictures of butterflies and SpongeBob SquarePants. Because the school is funded solely by private donations, the kids were used to visitors. They all rose and smiled in practiced unison, greeting us and striking perfect poses for our pictures. While the school is ostensibly for girls who live in Bari Imam, male siblings are also welcome. We saw several little boys running around in one group—and while they took part in the schoolwork, we never did find out if they take part in the school's sports program.

The affirming, progressive learning environment isn't all that makes the Mashal Model School special: it also fields its own girls' cricket team. A school solely for girls in the middle of a slum is rare in any country, but assembling the girls into a cricket team gained the school national acclaim. On the day we visited, the team was already practicing in matching white hijabs on a sunbaked patch of dirt, strewn with rocks that I kept tripping over, but which they nimbly avoided. A six (the cricket equivalent of a home run) is scored when the ball sails over the barbed wire fence into a cow pasture next door, where local women sometimes gather to watch the girls play. The smallest girls have to crawl through the fence to retrieve the ball.

On the day of our visit, it was so hot the cricket coaches asked the girls to vacate the only patch of shade so the Americans (overheated once again) didn't get sunburned. The girls were dressed modestly, wearing head scarves and covered from head to toe but, like the soccer players in Karachi, seemed immune to the heat. They invited us to play and couldn't suppress their giggles as we struggled to convert baseball rules to cricket. "Run!" they shouted. "Get the ball!" "Throw it!" Like the other young athletes we'd seen, they had no reservations about shouting instructions at a group of strangers.

While chasing a ball across the hard-packed dirt, I got my sandal caught on a rock and, next thing I knew, I was airborne. I quickly realized I had two choices: tuck and roll or land face-first. I somersaulted out of my dive, looking like a complete fool. They whooped with laughter and applause, the group of little brothers perched on a nearby stone way yelling encouragement at us. Little brothers are the same wherever you go; they wanted us to beat their sisters. The girls spoke only a few words of English, and we spoke no Urdu, but we spent an hour playing and laughing, a kind of communication that didn't require words. Though we were journalists, we were also women who had been lucky enough to grow up playing and loving sports. The girls of the Mashal Model School cricket team were girls who were growing up playing and loving sports.

We all got it.

And so it is that thousands of girls across Pakistan and other countries with a history of gender inequality (read: every country) are finding their voices through sport, in part thanks to organizations that are changing minds about women's sports and parents who seek equal opportunities for their daughters. When Go Girl Pakistan held their first clinic to introduce girls to different sports, more than one hundred fathers showed up with their girls in tow. Rishad Mahmood, a sportswriter for *DAWN*, Karachi's biggest newspaper, says that fathers have told him they sometimes lie about taking their daughters to the mosque, taking them to practice instead. It's not just the girls who fear the judgment of their community.

But lest we give too much credit to outside organizations, women athletes in Pakistan have a major role in opening doors for the next generation of women in sports. The members of Pakistan's national women's cricket team were met with death threats and lawsuits when they first formed in 1996. The next year, the government ruled that women were not allowed to play sports for religious reasons. With no state support and no sponsorship, national team members and sisters Shaiza and Sharmeen Khan sought recognition from the International Cricket Council, the sport's governing body, and got it. The Pakistan women's team now tours the world and won the Asian Games in both 2010 and 2014. They're currently ranked 7th in the world.

When swimmer Kiran Khan turned twelve in 2002, training in her hometown of Lahore became difficult. She was forced to wait until all the men had vacated the pool, because she wasn't allowed to be seen by men while in her swimsuit. Of course, when the men vacated the pool was solely up to the men. (Even in 2018, our Western hotel in Karachi had separate pools and workout areas for men and women; you can guess which group was awarded the far more luxurious spaces.) Frustrated at the limitation on her training schedule, Khan convinced her parents to build her a training pool in their home. To date, Khan has brought Pakistan seven international gold medals and trains other young swimmers in her private pool. She's a fierce voice for equality in sports in Pakistan, which hasn't endeared her to many of the male sportswriters who cover her.

"I believe parents still look at sports as a joke. Other than cricket, no one makes a living out of it. Kids and women are pushed into studies and other fields. In my opinion, you can play a professional sport and manage to study at the same time," Khan said. "Without your parents' support, you can't actually do much. Only a few schools provide a good, healthy environment for girls and boys in sports. But after eighteen, no one wants to carry on with it or doesn't have their parents' permission." It's an issue that faces female athletes in the United States, as well. Unlike men, who vie for hundreds of spots in the MLB or the NFL, women athletes simply don't have as many options, though there are more now than ever before. Upon entering college, many parents encourage their daughters to give up sports and focus on their schoolwork, especially if an athletic scholarship isn't paying for school.

The list of women fighting for acknowledgment in Pakistan's sports scene continues to grow. MMA fighter Anita Nisar, table tennis star Iqra Rehman, Sana Mahmud, and former national cricket team captain Sana Mir are just a few of the women leading the charge for the next generation of athletes in their country.

I heard plenty of stories in Pakistan that broke my heart: fathers who refused to let their daughters play the sports they lived for; entire communities declaring young women "bad girls" (which was horribly upsetting for them) for following their sports passions; girls secretly disguising themselves as boys to find acceptance and inclusion among teammates. But there were far more stories of women volunteering their time, expertise, and resources to lift up young female athletes and teach them to dream.

Of course, Pakistan isn't the only place where sport as development is teaching young girls a different way to move through life. Women Win, for example, has conducted programs for young girls in more than one hundred countries and claims to have positively affected the lives of more than two million girls in developing nations. Pakistan was just the program I was lucky enough to get to see. There, sports are teaching girls to find their voices. Once those voices are raised together, the society that has held them back will never be able to shut them up.

I can't wait to see it.

CHAPTER 11

ALL TOGETHER NOW

On Solidarity among Women in a Sexist World

I t's never easy being the only woman in a room. Objectively, we all know this, right? I would often go to my radio job and not see a single woman the entire time I was there. It helps to have someone there who knows what you're going through, for example, when your employer closes the only women's bathroom on your floor for several months and tells you to either use a bathroom on another floor (not possible during the four-minute breaks my show afforded me), or "feel free to use the men's." Not cool.

While there were times I desperately wanted another woman around to confide in, I also knew that any other woman who came on board at my station might not be the soul mate I was looking for. Saturdays at my station were heaven. That was when I cohosted the *Julie & Maggie Show* with my dear friend, sportswriter Maggie Hendricks, as good of an ally as I could have hoped for. But any woman who has worked with other women, especially in environments where women are tokenized (like the *Highlander*: there can be only one), knows that having more women around doesn't necessarily guarantee solidarity. There are plenty of women who are willing to throw their sisters under the bus in a heartbeat if it means they'll advance their careers.

My friends and I use the term "cool girl" to describe women who don't support other women. In sports media, like any other industry, there are plenty of women who prefer to be the only woman in the room. But because there are so few women in sports media overall, it feels like they make up a bigger segment of the industry. When I walked into a room that wasn't comfortable for me, which happened a lot in sports talk radio, I typically looked around for another woman. On more than a few occasions, the woman in my sights was coolly polite before moving into a group of men, leaving me on my own.

While women in sports media share many experiences rooted in sexism and misogyny, there's often a strain of competition that runs through our interactions. The reason is pretty simple: we know the odds are slim there will ever be more than one of us at the table. Outside of shows like *Around the Horn* and *Outside the Lines*, both ESPN properties that often have more than one woman on a panel, it's rare that any show has more than one token woman. We all want to be that woman. And rather than asking ourselves why there have to be four men (or worse, shows composed entirely of white men), we target the women who we perceive to be our strongest competition and align ourselves with the men who dominate the space. (And this can go all the way to the top: remember, the CEO of Barstool Sports is a woman. . . .) The entire thing is backward and counterproductive.

Nicole Bedera, a PhD candidate at the University of Michigan who studies gender inequality, said there's a reason women don't always support one another in male-dominated fields. "When resources are scarce for women, they often compete with each other instead of focusing attention on the patriarchal systems that keep them from getting what they need," she told me. "It feels easier in the moment. It can also lead women who want to push back against the competition between women to refuse services they need." Bedera also told me that, in her research, she found that sexual violence survivors often avoided victim advocacy services or terminated services early because they were afraid they were taking something from a survivor who "had it worse." "It's horrifying that women are so used to taking things away from each other in structures of scarcity that it's hard to even imagine that getting what you need doesn't hurt someone else," she said.

When I was laid off from my radio show because of the coronavirus pandemic, I, feeling very shitty and emboldened by having nothing to lose, said to my boss's boss, "So, just to be clear, there are no longer any women on the station."

She made an audible choking sound before asking me what I meant.

"I mean," I said, "that women make up damn near fifty percent of the fan base in every major sport, and there is no longer a single woman on this radio station."

She mumbled something at me about how she doesn't make decisions based on gender, which was probably true. But it was clear she didn't take gender (or any other kinds of representation) into account, either. The ESPN station across town was also womanless. The two sports talk radio stations in Chicago, a city full of rabid female sports fans, have zero women on the air. In what other industry can you just say, "There are no women"? *That's* why women in sports media compete with one another. Because we're lucky if there's a single woman at the table. Even when other women are doing the hiring and firing.

And this feeling doesn't stay in the background; the attitude permeates fandom, too. For example: it's not just male sports fans who balk at the sound of a woman's voice on the airwaves. Remember the outcry over Jessica Mendoza becoming the first woman ever to announce on *Sunday Night Baseball*? When ESPN announced it was moving Mendoza into other roles, I saw far too many women saying, "Oh *thank GOD!* I hated the sound of her voice!" Despite women making up a huge portion of the MLB fan base, we literally had *one woman* calling national games, and yet some women celebrated seeing her go. Internalized misogyny remains undefeated when it comes to women cheering the perceived failure of another woman.

And while 90 percent of the trolling I get comes from men, some of it comes from women who have decided that I don't deserve my job, my platform, or any respect. One woman in particular was so upset about a column I wrote back in 2016 that she's still chirping away at me, having gone so far as to record a podcast episode on all the reasons I don't deserve to exist. There are women who have gone to organizations I worked with and told, if not straight-up lied about, extremely one-sided stories about disagreements we've had in an effort to sever the working relationship. I've learned to ignore it, but it doesn't mean it doesn't hurt just a little bit more coming from other women.

This isn't to say that I haven't been unfairly judgmental about women in the media myself. I remember the days when I was just a Cubs blogger and desperately wanted the recognition that came with being a "legit" sports journalist. Rather than judging the men covering the team who made gaffes of players' names or who whiffed on citing a statistic, I remember being laser-focused on the women, cataloging every single mistake as proof that I was more qualified for their job than they were. Without looking back (because God only knows what I'd find), I can say for certain that there were times I criticized a woman's appearance or sports knowledge. Sometimes, our dragging of other women is a projection of how we feel about ourselves. Like in junior high, laughing at the cool kids was driven by desperately wanting a seat at the lunch table.

I wish I cared less what other women said about me, but the fact of the matter is that I do care. And no matter how many times I read *The Life-Changing Magic of Not Giving a F*ck*, I will probably always care. It's depressing that, every time I make news, a certain group of women comes out of the woodwork to start reminding people of all the reasons they shouldn't like me, most of which are (A) made up entirely or (B) taken wildly out of context. Examples abound in chapter 5 about this dynamic. It's easy to say, "Ignore them." It's more difficult when you start seeing them convince people that what they say is true. Do I push back and defend myself? Or do I ignore them and hope others do, too?

Now in my forties, staying true to myself seems like such a no-brainer. But back when I left the world of law practice, in which I had rarely felt overt sex discrimination (I worked at one firm that was composed solely of badass women lawyers), I immediately felt the pressure to objectify and demean women—including myself!— to fit into sports media. My first choice for the name of my Cubs blog was *The Baseball Bimbo*. Shout out to all the men in my life who talked me out of it, reminding me I was so much better than I was willing to make myself for the sake of attracting followers.

I'm lucky enough to be asked to speak to women on high school and college campuses fairly frequently. Without fail, I always get asked, "What advice do you have for women who want to get into sports media?" My first thought is always to thank God that the first part of my talk, which focuses on the feeling of being the only woman in a room and online harassment, hasn't scared all the women in the room away from sports media entirely. I always struggle to answer this question, because there are so many things I want to tell them about walking into this industry and so many ways I want to prepare them. But you can't inject a twenty-two-year-old with the same confidence you have at forty, and you can't gift her the thicker skin you know she's going to need.

I always wind up going with one of two answers: First, learn to ask for what you want. Too often, women are socialized not to be pushy or greedy, which too often means they are left with no advocate. If you won't advocate for yourself, who will? But the other thing I tell young women is to find a strong group of women in the industry and hold on to them for dear life. Because at the end of the day, they are the only ones who are going to understand what you're going through. And they're going to be the ones there for you when you need someone to pick you up, brush you off, talk you up, and point you in the direction of your goals.

I've been really lucky to have had some long heart-to-hearts with my hero Andrea Kremer, who, by some cosmic miracle I'm still in awe of, decided to befriend me and treat me like a colleague instead of a hanger-on, which is always how I feel when in her presence. Nancy Hogshead-Makar and Kathy Redmond are always willing to listen to me complain about the toxic stew of violence against women that permeates sports, as are Laura Okmin and my former radio cohost Maggie Hendricks. Both CJ Silas and Amy Lawrence have given me priceless advice on being a woman in sports radio. When I look back over the sports media part of my career, I can't imagine having survived without their support.

Over the course of the past several years, there's been a shift in the way women in the industry look at one another. At least it feels that way. Social media has allowed women, so often excluded from the whisper networks at their jobs, to create a whisper network of their own. There are Twitter chat groups and secret Facebook and Instagram groups made up of women in the industry supporting one another and sharing their experiences. It's as if a huge group of us woke up one day, took a look around, and realized that other women aren't the enemy. Maybe if we support each other, promote each other's work, pick each other up when we fall, we can all rise together.

ESPN's Mina Kimes said, "I think a lot of the competition in our industry, and I'm sure this is true of any industry, is driven by a perception of limited opportunity. And as that opportunity expands, as the presence of women not only in host roles but in a variety of roles becomes normalized, it's better for everyone. And I think it encourages people to be more supportive because it doesn't feel like we're all competing for scraps."

It's not just a theory. A recent study detailed in the *Harvard Business Review* suggests that women who have a circle of close-knit female allies are more likely to succeed in their chosen field. According to the author of the study, Brian Uzzi, "Because women seeking positions of executive leadership often face cultural and political hurdles that men typically do not, they benefit from an inner circle of close female contacts that can share private information about things like an organization's attitudes toward female leaders, which helps strengthen women's job search, interviewing, and negotiation strategies." In other words, your girls will give you the deets no one else will.

This idea has become readily apparent in recent years; increasingly, women are using private Facebook groups and chats to advise one another on what to ask for when pitching freelance stories, negotiating raises, and applying for jobs. We've also begun sharing our salaries and rates with other women in their fields. Thanks to sportswriters like Britni de la Cretaz and Sheryl Ring sharing what they've been paid, I realized I was seriously undervaluing what my writing was worth. I started asking for more for freelance pieces and got it. And if it hadn't been for my radio partner, Maggie Hendricks, telling me that she was making *twice* what I was making for our radio show, I never would have known. The same day she told me, I confronted my boss and asked about the reason for the disparity. When he couldn't give me one, he doubled my pay to match hers.

In addition to these organically grown networks, there are women like veteran NFL broadcaster Laura Okmin, who is teaching young women how to support each other through her GALvanize program. Okmin said that one of her biggest challenges in getting large groups of young women together is to stop them from immediately sizing one another up.

"From the second they walk in the room, I don't even allow them to talk," Okmin said. "I don't even allow them small talk. There are exercises, there are things that they have to do so that they aren't judging themselves. The first boot camp I did, I was signing girls up in the front and they were just walking into the room. And I kind of had an ear in the room and I could hear what they were saying. 'How much experience do you have? Who do you know?

Where did you go to college? What's your sorority?' I kept thinking, 'This is going to take me all day to undo.' Because everybody was judging. You know what judging is? It's not even about judging the other woman. It's about sizing *yourself* up."

And while young women sign up for Okmin's GALvanize program to learn the tricks of the trade from a seasoned vet, Okmin sees a value far beyond what her students can use on the sidelines.

"How I begin GALvanize is by saying, 'I know why you guys are here. I know you signed up to be better on camera, but look around this room.' And I make them," Okmin said. "I make them make eye contact with everybody in the room. 'I want you to know that, for the rest of your life, this is what you'll remember. You will never again, in this business, be in a room of women and be this supported and feel this loved." Okmin gives the hard truth to her students right out of the box: There are women in our industry who have risen up the ladder by aligning themselves with where the power lies: with the men. I often wonder how much further we could go if only we treated each other like sorority sisters instead of rivals.

By teaching the women in her program to be there for other women, Okmin hopes to change how they interact with each other in the real world. "Take all the love and support you feel to another room, or to your office, or to your sorority, or to your college, or to your job. Go find every woman in that building [where you work in sports media]. I promise you there won't be more than a handful. If you go GALvanize, if you go create this, we just changed twenty-five cultures."

Why is Okmin on such a mission to ensure women lift each other up as they move forward in her careers? She's met her share of negative people in the business. "That's life, right? That's sports;

that's politics; that's the world right now. It's like, 'Come on, ladies, get it together,'" she said. "I used to focus so much on those [negative] women; that was probably what colored my relationships, what colored my prism when it came to women in this business. And as I got older, I starting thinking about how I can make sure that doesn't change me. I really focused on my energy at the time. So I never look anymore at 'How is this woman coming at me?' I always look at, as I walk into a room, 'What's the energy that I'm bringing?'

"So I think, 'What can I do every day, [with] every woman I come across, to say, "I'm with you, sister. I support you, sister. You're fantastic. I'm rooting for you!"?' And will that help change how they are to other women? I know that's a very big landscape. You know, you can't change the world, but I really look at it as 'Can I change one woman today?' And maybe she would have gotten online and said something negative, and maybe that day she won't. And if we all did that, that creates a ripple effect, right? Because there's room enough for everybody. There's success enough for everybody."

I can speak personally to Okmin's pay-it-forward theory. I came to sports media later in life. I'd already had a legal career that spanned more than ten years, followed by a mishmash of writing, PR, and social media jobs, before I got into sports. I've always looked with envy at the women who got into the industry in their twenties—so young! So fresh-faced! In a medium where such a premium is put on women's looks (even in radio), they didn't have to worry about crow's-feet or working with producers young enough to be their kids. I've always been insecure about it and still am, to a degree.

But when someone with a résumé like Laura Okmin's reaches

out and tells you how great she thinks you are, you stand a little taller, and maybe you believe in yourself a little more. You carry yourself a little differently. Your confidence inches up a bit and you feel more settled in your job. Once I started feeling that way, it was much easier to see younger women as what they are: women I genuinely want the best for.

Women supporting each other in sports media goes far beyond just how we make each other feel, as important as that is. It also means making sure women's voices are heard that otherwise might not be. Many of us have tried to address the issue by using our platforms to amplify the voices of other women, especially Black women and other women of color, who aren't afforded the same opportunities as their white counterparts. But we have to do more.

Tamryn Spruill, an accomplished WNBA reporter who is also the editor in chief of the site *Swish Appeal* and covered the league for *The Athletic* (more on that in a minute), is tired of the struggle Black women have to keep up with white women in the industry. "Being a Black woman in sports media requires taking one of two unacceptable roads," she told me. "One, swallowing the dismissiveness and disrespect that come with being in a boys' club, or two, speaking out against the practices that marginalize us and cause us to be labeled troublemakers." Spruill says she's paid a steep price for speaking out about racial injustices in the industry and talked to me about some of the frustrations she's faced. For example, a white male editor pulled one of her stories and told her to "stick to sports" after she wrote about racial injustice. The editor told Spruill her take was "controversial." She also recalls her applications for full-time work going ignored, while a white female colleague was hired into one of those jobs at $82,000 a year—$70,000 more than Spruill was making to run an entire site.

And, after many of us praised *The Athletic* for hiring so many women, and especially Black women, to cover the WNBA, the site eventually terminated most of their contracts, leaving no Black women to cover a league where more than 70 percent of the players are Black or Latina. Worse, the women found out via a media report posted on Twitter. No one even bothered to tell them. "The resounding message from the mostly white, mostly male sports media, even in covering women's sports, is that this is the acceptable treatment for Black women," Spruill said. "That we are expected to accept it, and that we should be thankful for these crumbs. The only Black women deserving of respect in this space, it seems, are those on the basketball court. Those who dare to step into the newsrooms white men have claimed for themselves face a much different reality."

It's a dangerous time for everyone in media right now. We're all constantly looking over our shoulders for a pink slip. But why *The Athletic*'s firing of nearly all their WNBA reporters didn't raise a hue and cry from women all over the industry, I will never understand. It's in situations like these that we white women, who in general enjoy far more job security than our Black counterparts, should have raised bloody hell. At the time, I retweeted an article about how unfair *The Athletic* had treated their writers and registered my general disgust, and I'm ashamed that I didn't do more. We all have to do better. Whatever white women have to complain about in their workplaces, BIPOC, especially Black women, have it a hundredfold.

Kelsey Trainor, an attorney and sportswriter, says that the

biggest challenge she faces as a woman covering sports is having to limit her voice—not by choice, but because authority figures in media won't give her the same leeway they might give male colleagues. "I pitched an opinion piece once and was told there needed to be more folks in women's sports talking about it or else they wouldn't publish it. My first thought was 'Who is a folk in women's sports that would need to say this for this to be worthy?' Then I thought to myself, 'You are a folk in women's sports.'"

Trainor is far from the only woman to have outlets limit what she can and can't publish. After lots of behind-the-scenes grumbling from other women in the media, I once pitched an article examining the sexist language used at *ProFootballTalk* in articles about domestic violence in the NFL. The site is run by Mike Florio, an attorney who should know better. I was told by the editor at my station that, as Florio was a frequent guest, they wouldn't run the piece. In fact, there were several pieces my station didn't want me to write, not because of a lack of newsworthiness but because they didn't want to deal with the political problems that could result.

But having a network of women supporters means having people who will promote your work, even if your boss or your male colleagues won't. During my time working in radio, my work was rarely shared by the guys I worked with, but it was always promoted by my network of women in the industry. A study by the University of Illinois suggests that I was not alone and that this is by no means a problem exclusive to sports media: it found that male journalists interact with other men on Twitter 90 percent of the time and tend to ignore their female colleagues on the platform. And while women may not talk about that imbalance in support, there's plenty of grumbling about it going on in women-only spaces. But thanks to my group of female friends, I know my work will get shared around and that I'll be heard. As a wise person once said, "On the internet, generosity is currency." Share other women's work, and they'll share yours. A rising tide lifts all boats.

And when things get tough, there is safety in numbers. I've had my share of online harassment due to stories I've written. But when you put a story out there, especially on a hot-button topic like domestic violence or sexual assault, and all your female colleagues share it on social media to help spread your voice, you can't help but feel a bit braver. The braver we all feel, the less women feel the need to self-censor in order to survive. It's like having a badass girl gang behind you, pointing over your shoulder and saying, "Yeah. What *she* said." That's a good feeling. And it seems like the least we can do for each other.

There's also an added benefit to the whisper network of women in sports media. More than once, I've had women reach out and tell me of something happening, usually involving violence against women, that they couldn't write about because of the outlet they worked for. Maybe their parent company had close ties to the NFL, or perhaps someone's agent made a call and threatened a lawsuit. Or maybe they felt that (like all of us have in sports media over the past few years) their best course was to keep their head down and do work that didn't draw any attention to them. Could I write or tweet about it instead? Why yes, yes I could. I've also sent out the bat signal to my girl gang of sportswriters myself—there have been plenty of times, even for me, when sharing a story could put my livelihood at risk.

Our very own secret society is shining sunlight in places it might not otherwise reach and keeping the sports world a little more honest in the process. But make no mistake, when women spend too much time writing about social justice in sports and not enough time making sports "fun" for the reader, we're putting a target on our backs. A friend in the industry once told me that writing about violent athletes as much as we did wasn't helping our careers. Not too long afterward, she was gone in a major purge by her employer. And despite my employer blaming COVID-19 for eliminating my position, I will always believe that I brought just a little too much backlash on the station.

Don't get me wrong, I've worked with some wonderful men whom I consider close friends. They've stuck up for me, defended me, helped me sound better than I was on the air, covered for me while I ran two floors up to the only functioning bathroom during a commercial break. But it's not the same as having a core group of girlfriends around. The only person who knows what it's like to be the only woman in a male-dominated workplace is another woman. End of.

There are so many things women in sports media have to put up with. Online harassment is a huge one (my third bit of advice is always: start working on your thick skin now!), sexual harassment, marginalization (like when all the male hosts at your station get invited to spring training for a week and you get left behind), being left out of gossip, being left out of fantasy football teams and softball teams, just never quite feeling like you belong. It's so important to have that group you can run to, your safe place, even if that group exists only online or in a group text. It's important to have a group of people who know what it's like to be you.

Melissa Ludtke, the first woman to report in an MLB locker room, said there are advantages afforded to women in sports today that her generation didn't necessarily have: "Back in my day, as literally the only woman most nights in press boxes and at the field, I wound up getting to know and having some very close friendships with a few of the men that were covering the game. Today, there are more women around to offer that support. I see it happening, I admire it. I'm envious of it in some ways."

Ludtke made it work by building those relationships with men in her field, but it put limits on what her job could look like. "I did everything I could to be like the guys. I mean, I can remember chewing tobacco with one of the players one day . . . it attracted a lot of attention of people kind of watching me spit into this cup and chew tobacco. But I kind of thought I had to do it," Ludtke told me in a podcast interview. "Anyone wants to try to fit into the environment where they're going to be spending a lot of their time."

When I initially started working at my station, I was ride-or-die for my colleagues. I shared articles they had written, I promoted their shows or funny bits, I talked about how great they were. It was my way of trying to fit in—act like you're in the club and eventually you'll be in the club, right? But the generosity was almost never reciprocated. Some of them even stopped following me on Twitter, and most of them never helped promote my show or my projects, even when specifically asked to by the boss. As I said, I've since learned that men in media have a bad habit of sharing the work of other men and not their female colleagues, but at the time, I took it very, very personally.

"In [the mid-1970s] almost every job that highly educated women were doing in that era were jobs that women hadn't done before," Ludtke told me. "And the guidebook or the playbook, if we had one, was looking at the men do it and do it like they do. Even back then our clothes were designed to make us look like men. Our

outfits came with ties, and it was all designed that we were supposed to look like men, act like men, but do better than the men if
we looked for making advancement in our own careers. So, I would
hope and I do believe, that's what I guess I was saying, I believe
that by now, forty years later, women really have a strong sense of
who they are in this."

It's true that we don't dress like men, at least not those women
who have careers in TV. But I definitely put the sundresses away
and showed up for work in torn boyfriend jeans and hoodies a lot
of the time, because that was how the guys at my station dressed. I
wouldn't do that if I were starting a job in radio now. It's funny—
I've never felt more alone in my life than at my most recent job in
radio, but I came out the other side of it into a better job, a strong
group of girlfriends in the industry, a thicker skin, and a much better sense of what I'll stand up for and who I am as a woman.

And when I lose the courage of my convictions, I think of Melissa Ludtke, of Claire Smith, and of Lesley Visser and all the
women who went before me and made my path a little bit easier. I
think of Jemele Hill, Tamryn Spruill, Maggie Hendricks, Julie
Foudy, and all the other women who are forging this path right
now. And I think of all the young women I've met and how I want
this to be easier on them than it was for us. That's what gives me
the strength to push through.

As Melissa Ludtke told me, "It doesn't always make it easy, but
I think having that spine, having that notion that you can be who
you are, I think that helps a lot. I hope it does. I hope it does."

ACKNOWLEDGMENTS

This book never would have come into being if it hadn't been for the wonderful Josh Gondelman, who, after listening to me lament about an agent I wasn't getting along with, was generous enough to ask, "Do you want me to introduce you to *my* agent?" And just like that, I landed in the lap (figuratively) of Noah Ballard at Curtis Brown. Noah believed in this book from day one and, in addition to having to explain the entire process of selling a book to me, did a ton of cheerleading along the way.

I got so lucky in somehow landing Marya Pasciuto as my editor. She was the perfect combination of trail guide, spiritual healer, and gentle taskmaster, keeping me pointed in the right direction and moving forward, even when I was prostrate on my bed with impostor syndrome. The entire crew at Dutton was a joy to work with. Thanks to the hard work of Becky Odell, Hannah Poole, Caroline Payne, Alice Dalrymple, Dora Mak, Susan Schwartz, Laura K. Corless, Vi-An Nguyen, and my fact-checker, Shannon Flynn, I came out of writing my first book not only not traumatized, but joyful, which feels like a huge win.

I'm so grateful to my parents, Peter and Karen DiCaro, for spending most of their parenting years shuttling me (and my three younger siblings) from sport to sport and for encouraging me to use my voice (though sometimes a little more softly). I wouldn't be the person I am today (or have been able to write this book) without those experiences.

Thank you to Fred Peterson, the best AP English teacher who ever lived, who taught me how to write and to diagram a mean sentence. You handed me a copy of Joan Didion when I was sixteen and told me I'd write a book someday. How I wish you'd lived to see it.

Thank you to every single woman who talked to me for this book—on the record and off. I hope I did you guys proud. Thanks to the DQ crowd—Kirsten, Shannon, Deana Marie, Jamie, Teri, Libby, Tiff, and Kate. Where would I be without you guys?

Finally, thank you to my wonderful boys, A and C, for letting me take a year out of our lives to write and for bringing me endless Diet Mountain Dews to keep me caffeinated and working. And thank you to my husband, Brian, for taking over as both parents while I was closeted away, working on the book. Your love gives me the courage to go on each day.

SOURCES

Chapter 1: Behold: Smashers of Glass Ceilings

Interviews with Lisa Olson, Maggie Hendricks, Melissa Ludtke, Mirin Fader, Nicole Bedera, and Tommy John Jr. conducted by the author.

Sundberg, Annie, and Ricki Stern, dirs. *Let Them Wear Towels* (Nine for IX). ESPN Films. Aired July 16, 2013, on ESPN.

Baccellieri, Emma. "The Everlasting Legacy of Melissa Ludtke, Who Dared Join the Boys Club of the Baseball Press." *Sports Illustrated*, September 28, 2018, https://www.si.com/mlb/2018/09/28/melissa-ludtke-lawsuit-anniversary.

Baer, Bill. "Jack Morris Should Not Be in the Hall of Fame." Hardball Talk, NBC Sports, December 10, 2017, https://mlb.nbcsports.com/2017/12/10/jack-morris -should-not-be-in-the-hall-of-fame.

Barron, Laignee. "NFL's Cam Newton Slammed for Laughing at a Female Reporter." *Time*, October 5, 2017, https://time.com/4970126/cam-newton -jourdan-rodrigue-routes.

Conway, Tyler. "Female Sports Writers Denied Entry to Jaguars Locker Room at Lucas Oil Stadium." *Bleacher Report*, October 4, 2015, https://bleacher report.com/articles/2575731-female-sports-writers-denied-entry-to -jaguars-locker-room-at-lucas-oil-stadium.

DiCaro, Julie. Interview with Melissa Ludtke. "Episode 6—Women in the Locker Room," *Stick to Pods* podcast, fifty-three minutes, thirty-nine seconds, March 1, 2018, https://sticktopods.libsyn.com/episode-6-women-in-the -locker-room.

Herman, Robin. "My Very Small Step for Womankind." *New York Times*, October

12, 1990, https://www.nytimes.com/1990/10/12/opinion/my-very-small
-step-for-womankind.html.

Kenney, Madeline. "Cubs Removed 'No Women Admitted' Art Amid Backlash for
Being Tone-Deaf." *Chicago Sun-Times*, April 8, 2019, https://chicago.suntimes
.com/2019/4/8/18313973/cubs-remove-no-women-admitted-art-amid
-backlash-for-being-viewed-as-tone-deaf.

Robertson, Nan. *The Girls in the Balcony: Women, Men, and the* New York Times.
New York: Random House, 1992.

Sheir, Rebecca. "'We Just Wanna Be a Part of It': The Women Who Fought to
Cover MLB." Only A Game, WBUR, September 1, 2017, https://www.wbur
.org/onlyagame/2017/09/01/women-baseball-writers-saxon-ludtke-claire
-smith.

Zinser, Lynn. "In 1975, 2 Women Crossed a Barrier." *New York Times*, January
23, 2010, https://www.nytimes.com/2010/01/24/sports/hockey/24reporter
.html.

Chapter 2: Women Calling the Shots

Interviews with Andrea Kremer, Amy Lawrence, Rebecca Martínez, Jessica
Mendoza, Beth Mowins, and Laura Okmin conducted by the author.

DiCaro, Julie. "Safest Bet in Sports: Men Complaining About a Female Announcer's Voice." *New York Times*, September 18, 2017, https://www.nytimes.com
/2017/09/18/sports/nfl-beth-mowins-julie-dicaro.html.

Hill, Benjamin. "Tiedemann Becoming a Legend in Booth." MiLB.com, March
15, 2018, https://www.milb.com/milb/news/emma-tiedemann-becoming-a
-legend-in-booth-268732204.

Johnson, Matt. "NFL Says 47 Percent of Fans Are Women, Launches Women's
History Month." *Yardbarker*, March 2, 2020, https://www.yardbarker.com
/nfl/articles/nfl_says_47_percent_of_fans_are_women_launches_womens
_history_month/s1_12680_31460792.

Kleinschmidt, Jessica, and Thomas Harding. "Jenny Cavnar Breaks Barriers by
Calling Play-by-Play on Monday's Rockies Broadcast." Cut4, MLB.com,
April 23, 2018, https://www.mlb.com/cut4/jenny-cavnar-is-first-woman
-to-call-play-by-play-on-mlb-tv-broadcast-c273532718.

Knecht, Bailey. "How Katy Winge Blazed Her Way to an Analyst Position with the Denver Nuggets." *Front Office Sports*, October 29, 2018, https://frnt officesport.com/katy-winge-analyst-denver-nuggets.

Kremer, Andrew. Interview with Doris Burke. *Real Sports*. Episode 251, "Doris Burke Gets the Call." Aired February 27, 2018, on HBO.

Montell, Amanda. *Wordslut: A Feminist Guide to Taking Back the English Language*, New York: Harper Wave, 2019.

Petchesky, Barry. "We Have Found It, the Place All Hot Takes Are Born." *Deadspin*, May 9, 2016, https://deadspin.com/we-have-found-it-the-place-all-hot-takes-are-born-1775539534.

Raissman, Bob. "ESPN Baseball Analyst Jessica Mendoza Called 'Tits McGhee' by Atlanta Radio Host Mike Bell; Station Suspends Him Indefinitely." *Daily News* (New York), October 7, 2015, https://www.nydailynews.com/sports/baseball/espn-jessica-mendoza-called-tits-mcgee-radio-host-article-1.2389109.

Rosenthal, Phil. "Controversial Radio Host Mike North Says He's Done with Sports." *Chicago Tribune*, August 29, 2017, https://www.chicagotribune.com/sports/breaking/ct-mike-north-leaving-sports-radio-20170829-column.html.

Spangler, Todd. "Amazon Bringing Back Hannah Storm, Andrea Kremer to Call 'Thursday Night Football' Games in 2019." *Variety*, January 24, 2019, https://variety.com/2019/digital/news/amazon-nfl-thursday-night-football-hannah-storm-andrea-kremer-1203116650.

Chapter 3: Now, from the Sidelines

Interviews with L. A. Jennings, Mina Kimes, Beth Mowins, Laura Okmin, and Katy Winge conducted by the author.

Allsop, Jon, Kelsey Ables, and Denise Southwood. "Who's the Boss?" *Columbia Journalism Review*, Spring/Summer 2018, https://www.cjr.org/special_report/editors-by-the-numbers.php.

Lapchick, Richard. "The 2018 Associated Press Sports Editors Racial and Gender Report Card." ESPN, May 2, 2018, https://www.espn.com/espn/story/_/id/23382605/espn-leads-way-hiring-practices-sports-media.

Women's Media Center. "The Status of Women in U.S. Media 2019." February 21, 2019, https://www.womensmediacenter.com/reports/the-status-of-women-in-u-s-media-2019.

Chapter 4: #BelieveWomen

Interviews with Nicole Bedera, Michael Feinerman, Soraya Nadia McDonald, and Katherine Redmond conducted by the author.

Adelson, Eric. "How Would Kobe Bryant Have Fared if His Legacy's Darkest Chapter Happened in the 'Me Too' Era?" Yahoo! Sports, December 18, 2017, https://sports.yahoo.com/kobe-bryant-fared-legacys-darkest-chapter -happened-era-155025004.html.

Apstein, Stephanie. "Astros Staffer's Outburst at Female Reporters Illustrates MLB's Forgive-and-Forget Attitude Toward Domestic Violence." Sports Illustrated, October 22, 2019, https://www.si.com/mlb/2019/10/22/houston -astros-roberto-osuna-suspension.

Baumann, Michael. "'An Unacceptable Lack of Judgment': Gabe Kapler and the Dodgers Must Be Held Accountable." The Ringer, February 6, 2019, https:// www.theringer.com/mlb/2019/2/6/18213283/gabe-kapler-los-angeles -dodgers-philadelphia-phillies.

Bair, Scott. "Raiders' Trent Brown Responds to Civil Lawsuit Alleging Domestic Violence." NBC Sports, October 16, 2019, https://www.nbcsports.com /bayarea/raiders/raiders-trent-brown-responds-civil-lawsuit-alleging -domestic-violence.

Blum, Ronald. "Astros Fire Exec Taubman After Rant at Female Reporters." Associated Press, October 25, 2019, https://apnews.com/0c3edc3cf5d743 c8ab687118cd6469b5.

Boren, Cindy. "Details of Slava Voynov's Domestic Violence Arrest Are Bloody." Washington Post, December 15, 2014, https://www.washingtonpost.com /news/early-lead/wp/2014/12/15/details-of-slava-voynovs-domestic -violence-arrest-are-bloody.

Bucholtz, Andrew. "Jonah Keri Arrested Again, Faces Eight New Charges Relating to Alleged Acts from Before His First Arrest in July." Awful Announcing, December 11, 2019, https://awfulannouncing.com/international/jonah-keri -arrested-again-faces-eight-new-charges.html.

Dennis, David, Jr. "Gayle King Doesn't Deserve Your Anger." The Undefeated. February 6, 2020, https://theundefeated.com/features/gayle-king-doesnt -deserve-your-anger.

Farrow, Ronan. Catch and Kill: Lies, Spies, and a Conspiracy to Protect Predators. New York: Little, Brown and Company, 2019.

Folkenflik, David (@davidfolkenflik). Twitter post, October 22, 2019, 4:26 p.m., https://twitter.com/davidfolkenflik/status/1186755725969809408.

Gibbs, Lindsay. "Judge Tells Derrick Rose to Stop Slut-Shaming His Alleged Rape Victim." *ThinkProgress*, September 23, 2016, https://archive.think progress.org/judge-tells-derrick-rose-to-stop-slut-shaming-his-alleged -rape-victim-c817c1b8c675/.

Greenberg, Chris. "Janay Rice Says Ravens Pushed Her to Apologize After Husband's Domestic Violence." *Huffington Post*, December 1, 2014, https://www .huffpost.com/entry/janay-rice-ravens-suggested-apology_n_6248954.

Hogg, Dave. "Jerry Jones Is Still Defending Greg Hardy's Behavior, Somehow." *SB Nation*, November 22, 2015, https://www.sbnation.com/nfl/2015/11/22 /9781052/jerry-jones-greg-hardy-defense-domestic-violence-cowboys.

Jenkins, Bruce. "Giants Hire Gabe Kapler as Their Manager—It's Quite a Gamble." *San Francisco Chronicle*, November 12, 2019, https://www.sfchronicle .com/giants/jenkins/article/Giants-hire-Gabe-Kapler-as-their-manager -14830540.php.

Johnson, Ted. "*Washington Post* Suspends Reporter After Kobe Bryant Tweets; UltraViolet Calls for Her to Be Reinstated." *Deadline*, January 27, 2020, https://deadline.com/2020/01/kobe-bryant-washington-post-felicia -sonmez-1202842926.

Joseph, Andrew. "Ezekiel Elliott's Mom Wasn't Happy to See Skip Bayless Retrieve Her Son's Jersey from the Trash." *USA Today*, December 16, 2019, https://ftw.usatoday.com/2019/12/skip-bayless-ezekiel-elliott-mom-jersey -trash-cowboys.

Kapler, Gabe. "My Statement." Kaplifestyle.com, February 2, 2019, http:// kaplifestyle.com/2019/02/02/my-statement.

Killion, Ann. "'Wrong on Many Levels': Gabe Kapler's Hiring Appalls Some Longtime Giants Fans." *San Francisco Chronicle*, November 16, 2019, https:// www.sfchronicle.com/giants/annkillion/article/Wrong-on-many-levels -Gabe-Kapler-hiring-14840466.php.

Lauing, Jacob. "Jurors Took Photos with Derrick Rose after Clearing Him of Rape." *Mashable*, October 19, 2016, https://mashable.com/2016/10/19/derrick -rose-juror-photos.

May, Jake. "Antonio Brown: 'I'll Never Play' in the NFL Again." *Sports Illustrated*, November 7, 2019, https://www.si.com/nfl/2019/11/07/antonio-brown-lashes -out-social-media-following-nfl-meeting-report.

McGhee, Tom. "Semyon Varlamov Told Ex, 'I Could Have Killed You,' She Testifies at Trial." *Denver Post*, January 26, 2016, https://www.denverpost.com/2016/01/26/semyon-varlamov-told-ex-i-could-have-killed-you-she-testifies-at-trial.

Moskovitz, Diana. "This Is Why NFL Star Greg Hardy Was Arrested for Assaulting His Ex-Girlfriend." *Deadspin*, November 6, 2015, https://deadspin.com/this-is-why-nfl-star-greg-hardy-was-arrested-for-assaul-1739117634.

———, and Lindsey Adler. "Lawyer: Derrick Rose Said He Doesn't Know What Consent Means." *Deadspin*, September 15, 2016, https://deadspin.com/lawyer-derrick-rose-said-he-doesnt-know-what-consent-m-1786681789.

National Coalition Against Domestic Violence. "National Statistics Domestic Violence Fact Sheet." Accessed February 1, 2020, https://ncadv.org/statistics.

Neveau, James. "Addison Russell Non-Tendered by Cubs, Making Him a Free Agent." NBC Sports Chicago, December 3, 2019, https://www.nbcchicago.com/news/sports/chicago-baseball/addison-russell-non-tendered-by-cubs-making-him-a-free-agent.

Payne, Marissa. "'First Take' Host Stephen A. Smith Takes On, then Apologizes to, ESPN's Michelle Beadle over Domestic Abuse Statements Related to Ray Rice's Suspension." *Washington Post*, July 25, 2014, https://www.washingtonpost.com/news/early-lead/wp/2014/07/25/first-take-host-stephen-a-smith-takes-on-espns-michelle-beadle-over-domestic-abuse-statements-related-to-ray-rices-suspension.

Perry, Dayn. "Roberto Osuna on Domestic Violence Suspension: 'Everybody Is Judging Me for Things They Don't Know.'" CBS Sports, August 29, 2018, https://www.cbssports.com/mlb/news/roberto-osuna-on-domestic-violence-suspension-everybody-is-judging-me-for-things-they-dont-know.

Pisciotta, Ann (@Pisicotta08). Twitter post, November 17, 2019, 6:16 p.m., https://twitter.com/Pisciotta08/status/1196220613930692608.

ProFootballTalk (@ProFootballTalk). Twitter post, December 27, 2019, 8:37 a.m., https://twitter.com/ProFootballTalk/status/1210570496309366784.

Rape, Abuse, & Incest National Network (RAINN). "Victims of Sexual Violence: Statistics." Accessed March 15, 2020, https://www.rainn.org/statistics/victims-sexual-violence.

Ross, David. *Teammate: My Journey in Baseball and a World Series for the Ages.* New York: Hachette, 2018.

Russell, Jake. "Three Years after Ouster from Baylor, Art Briles Gets Job Coaching High School Football." *Washington Post*, May 24, 2019, https://www.washingtonpost.com/sports/2019/05/25/former-baylor-coach-art-briles-gets-job-coaching-high-school-football-texas.

Schulman, Henry. "SF Giants CEO Larry Baer Suspended by MLB for Domestic Dispute." *San Francisco Chronicle*, March 26, 2019, https://www.sfchronicle.com/bayarea/article/SF-Giants-CEO-Larry-Baer-suspended-by-MLB-for-13717072.php.

Shum, David. "Exclusive: Blue Jays Pitcher Roberto Osuna Pictured in Holding Cell after Arrest for Assault." *Global News* (Canada), May 9, 2018, https://globalnews.ca/news/4196728/roberto-osuna-holding-cell.

Sigler, Robert T. *Domestic Violence in Context: An Assessment of Community Attitudes*. Lexington, MA: Lexington Books, 1989.

Stern, Marlow. "Kobe Bryant's Disturbing Rape Case: The DNA Evidence, the Accuser's Story, and the Half-Confession." *Daily Beast*, April 11, 2016, https://www.thedailybeast.com/kobe-bryants-disturbing-rape-case-the-dna-evidence-the-accusers-story-and-the-half-confession.

Wells, Adam. "Astros' Brandon Taubman Issues Statement on Rant Directed at Female Reporters." *Bleacher Report*, October 22, 2019, https://bleacherreport.com/articles/2859335-astros-brandon-taubman-issues-statement-on-rant-directed-at-female-reporters.

Witz, Billy. "Cubs Fans Root for Aroldis Chapman While Deploring His History." *New York Times*, August 27, 2016, https://www.nytimes.com/2016/08/28/sports/baseball/chicago-cubs-fans-aroldis-chapman-domestic-violence.html.

Young, Dennis. "Astros Fire Brandon Taubman and Apologize to Stephanie Apstein." *Daily News* (New York), October 24, 2019, https://www.nydailynews.com/sports/baseball/ny-brandon-taubman-fired-astros-apologize-20191024-hymv35t3krbqbkeu7v6dmk2zdm-story.html.

Zucker, Joseph. "Crystal Espinal Says Tyreek Hill Used a Belt and Punched Son in Audio Recording." *Bleacher Report*, April 25, 2019, https://bleacherreport.com/articles/2833191-crystal-espinal-says-tyreek-hill-used-a-belt-and-punched-son-in-audio-recording.

Chapter 5: Don't @ Me

Interviews with Mina Kimes, Amy Lawrence, Kristen Ledlow, Anita Sarkeesian, and Sarah Spain conducted by the author.

Amnesty International. "Toxic Twitter: A Toxic Place for Women." Accessed December 18, 2020, https://www.amnesty.org/en/latest/research/2018/03/online-violence-against-women-chapter-1.

Buckels, Erin. "Probing the Sadistic Minds of Internet Trolls." *Character & Context*, June 7, 2019, https://www.spsp.org/news-center/blog/buckels-internet-trolls#gsc.tab=0.

DiCaro, Julie. "How NOT to Talk About the Patrick Kane Rape Allegations." CBS Chicago, August 10, 2015, https://chicago.cbslocal.com/2015/08/10/dicaro-how-not-to-talk-about-the-patick-kane-rape-allegations.

———. "Threats. Vitriol. Hate. Ugly Truth about Women in Sports and Social Media." *The Cauldron*, September 27, 2015, https://www.si.com/the-cauldron/2015/09/27/twitter-threats-vile-remarks-women-sports-journalists.

———. "Why I Believe Jameis Winston's Accuser." *Deadspin*, December 19, 2013, https://deadspin.com/why-i-believe-jameis-winstons-accuser-1479782169.

Golbeck, Jennifer. "Internet Trolls Are Narcissists, Psychopaths, and Sadists." *Psychology Today*, September 18, 2014, https://www.psychologytoday.com/us/blog/your-online-secrets/201409/internet-trolls-are-narcissists-psychopaths-and-sadists.

Herrman, John. "Two Minutes of Walking on the Internet as a Woman." *The Awl*, October 28, 2014, https://www.theawl.com/2014/10/two-minutes-of-walking-on-the-internet-as-a-woman.

@_Hey_Its_Don (account suspended). Twitter post. December 16, 2019. https://twitter.com/_Hey_Its_Don_.

Just Not Sports. "More Than Mean: Women in Sports 'Face' Harassment." YouTube video, four minutes, fifteen seconds, April 25, 2016, https://www.youtube.com/watch?v=9tU-D-m2JY8.

Lowen, Cynthia, dir. *Netizens*. April 22, 2018, https://www.netizensfilm.com.

Muir, Allan. "Patrick Kane Remains NHL's Most Polarizing Figure." *Sports Illustrated*, March 10, 2016, https://www.si.com/nhl/2016/03/10/patrick-kane-sex-assault-case-reaction-sports-illustrated-story.

Schroeder, Michael O. "The Physical and Mental Toll of Being Angry All the Time." *U.S. News & World Report*, October 26, 2017, https://health.usnews

.com/wellness/mind/articles/2017-10-26/the-physical-and-mental-toll -of-being-angry-all-the-time.

WMC Speech Project. "Online Abuse 101." Women's Media Center. Accessed March 6, 2020, https://womensmediacenter.com/speech-project/online -abuse-101/#why-focus.

Women's Media Center. "What Online Harassment Tells Us About Our Newsrooms: From Individuals to Institutions—A Women's Media Center Report." March 5, 2020, https://womensmediacenter.com/reports/what-online -harassment-tells-us-about-our-newsrooms-from-individuals-to-insti tutions-a-womens-media-center-report.

Chapter 6: Kicking Out the Barstool

Interviews with Britni de la Cretaz, Jemele Hill, Marisa Ingemi, Alanis King, Rebecca Martínez, Soledad O'Brien, and Robert Silverman conducted by the author.

Barstool Sports. "Slut Reporter Drinks Cam Newton's Jizz." Facebook post (deleted). December 7, 2010.

Carlson, Tucker. Interview with David Portnoy. FOX News, May 31, 2019, https://www.foxnews.com/transcript/barstool-sports-founder-responds -to-outrage-over-controversial-towel.

Clancy, Kevin. "Guess that Ass." November 18, 2015, https://www.barstool sports.com/blog/697394/martians-have-officially-been-discovered -on-earth.

Daulerio, A. J. "The 'Big' Penis of Tom Brady's Toddler Son Prompted State Police to Visit Barstool Sports Editor's Home (UPDATE)." *Deadspin*, August 5, 2011, https://deadspin.com/the-big-penis-of-tom-bradys-toddler-son-prompted -stat-5831042.

de la Cretaz, Britni. "Unpacking Barstool at the Ballpark Night." *Hardball Times*, July 27, 2018, https://tht.fangraphs.com/barstool-at-the-ballpark-night.

Deitsch, Richard, and Chris Chavez. "ESPN Abruptly Cancels *Barstool Van Talk* After One Episode." *Sports Illustrated*, October 23, 2017, https://www.si .com/media/2017/10/23/espn-cancels-barstool-van-talk-pft-commentator -big-cat-pardon-my-take.

Dupnack, Jessica. "Detroit Area Mom Sues Barstool Sports for Sharing Video of Her and Son Used without Permission." FOX 2 Detroit, December 18, 2019,

https://www.fox2detroit.com/news/detroit-area-mom-sues-barstool
-sports-for-sharing-video-of-her-and-son-used-without-permission.

Feitelberg. "Martians Have Officially Been Discovered on Earth." *Barstool Sports*,
January 6, 2017, https://www.barstoolsports.com/blog/697394/martians
-have-officially-been-discovered-on-earth.

Feldman, Brian. "A Dispute Between a Comedian and a Sports Site Illustrates
the Insanity of Copyright Law." Intelligencer, *New York*, March 5, 2019,
https://nymag.com/intelligencer/2019/03/barstool-sports-ripped-miel
-bredouw-copyright-dmca.html.

Finn, Chad. "Kirk Minihane to Take Leave of Absence from Barstool Podcast."
Boston Globe, March 2, 2020. https://www.bostonglobe.com/2020/03/02
/sports/kirk-minihane-take-leave-absence.

Gibbs, Lindsay. "Barstool. Hates. Women." *ThinkProgress*, October 25, 2017,
https://thinkprogress.org/barstool-sports-sexism-30cee73eccc4.

Jhaveri, Hemal. "Bauer Hockey Becomes the Latest Brand to Enable Barstool's
Culture of Harassment." *USA Today*, February 28, 2020, https://ftw.usatoday
.com/2020/02/barstool-culture-of-harassment-bauer-hockey.

Jones, Layla A. "Barstool Sports' New Pennsylvania Investor Says No More Harassment. Will the Bro Brand Follow Suit?" Billy Penn, February 24, 2020,
https://billypenn.com/2020/02/24/barstool-sports-new-pennsylvania
-investor-says-no-more-harassment-will-the-bro-brand-follow-suit.

Joy, Russ. "Barstool's Paul Bissonnette Accuses Former Flyer Dan Carcillo of
Using N-Word, Swastika on Robe." *Crossing Broad*, February 17, 2020.
https://www.crossingbroad.com/2020/02/barstools-paul-bissonnette
-accuses-former-flyer-dan-carcillo-of-using-n-word-swastika-on-robe
.html.

King, Alanis. "Progress Isn't the Goal." *Jalopnik*, August 14, 2019, https://jalopnik
.com/progress-isn-t-the-goal-1837210632.

Kingkade, Tyler. "Barstool Sports Rape 'Joke' Sparks Blackout Party Backlash."
Huffington Post, March, 27, 2012, https://www.huffpost.com/entry/barstool
-sports-rape-joke-_n_1293328.

McDermott, John. "The Barstool Sports Founder Got Cucked, and It's Everyone's Fault but His Own." *Mel*, 2017, https://melmagazine.com/en-us/story
/the-barstool-sports-founder-got-cucked-and-its-everyones-fault-but
-his-own.

O'Brien, Soledad. "Interview with David Portnoy and Erica Nardini." *Real*

Sports with Bryant Gumbel. Episode 267. Aired June 2019, on HBO. https://www.hbo.com/real-sports-with-bryant-gumbel/all-episodes/june-2019.

Portnoy, David. "Guess What? I'm Bringing Back the Word 'Cunt,'" (deleted) *Barstool Sports,* https://www.barstoolsports.com/boston/guess-what-im-bringing-back-the-word-cunt.

Putterman, Alex. "WEEI Hosts Call Red Sox Execs 'Cowards' after Team's Pointed Statement about the Station." *Awful Announcing,* July 25, 2017, https://awfulannouncing.com/local-networks/weei-hosts-call-red-sox-cowards-criticism.html.

Rigdon, Jay. "Here's the NSFW Audio that Prompted Sam Ponder to Call Out Her New Barstool Coworkers." *Awful Announcing,* October 17, 2017, https://awfulannouncing.com/espn/heres-audio-prompted-sam-ponder-call-new-barstool-coworkers.html.

Silverman, Robert. "Barstool Sports Slut-Shames Mackenzie Lueck, Murdered 23-Year-Old Female College Student." *Daily Beast,* June 29, 2019, https://www.thedailybeast.com/barstool-sports-slut-shames-mackenzie-lueck-murdered-23-year-old-female-college-student.

——. "Inside Barstool Sports' Culture of Online Hate: 'They Treat Sexual Harassment and Cyberbullying as a Game.'" *Daily Beast,* March 14, 2019, https://www.thedailybeast.com/inside-barstool-sports-culture-of-online-hate-they-treat-sexual-harassment-and-cyberbullying-as-a-game.

Yuscavage, Chris. "Howard Stern Slams a Sports Blogger for Posting a Naked Photo of Tom Brady's Kid." *Complex,* August 17, 2011, https://www.complex.com/sports/2011/08/howard-stern-slams-a-sports-blogger-for-posting-a-naked-photo-of-tom-bradys-kid.

Chapter 7: Revolutionary Anger

Interview with Soraya Chemaly conducted by the author.

AAP. "'Double Standards': Fuming Novak Djokovic Unleashes on Chair Umpire." FOX Sports, July 11, 2018, https://www.foxsports.com.au/tennis/wimbledon/double-standards-fuming-novak-djokovic-unleashes-on-chair-umpire/news-story/b5a0be8b07cb91eda69c38a5114661a1.

Associated Press. "Serena Williams Accuses Umpire of Sexism and Vows to 'Fight for Women.'" *Guardian* (US), September 9, 2018, https://www.the

guardian.com/sport/2018/sep/09/serena-williams-accuses-officials
-of-sexism-and-vows-to-fight-for-women.

Chemaly, Soraya. *Rage Becomes Her: The Power of Women's Anger*. New York: Atria Books, 2018.

Cooper, Brittney. *Eloquent Rage: A Black Feminist Discovers Her Superpower*. New York: St. Martin's Press, 2018.

Daniels, Tim. "Michael Irvin's Sexual Assault Allegations Under NFL Investigation." *Bleacher Report*, September 6, 2017, https://bleacherreport.com/arti cles/2731788-michael-irvins-sexual-assault-allegations-under-nfl-inves tigation.

Dittmann, Melissa. "Anger Across the Gender Divide." *American Psychological Association* 34, no. 3 (March 2003): 52, https://www.apa.org/monitor/mar03 /angeracross.html.

Drucker, Joel. "What Happened at Indian Wells?" ESPN, March 11, 2009, https://www.espn.com/sports/tennis/columns/story?columnist=drucker _joel&id=3952939.

Hyers, Lauri. "Resisting Prejudice Every Day: Exploring Women's Assertive Responses to Anti-Black Racism, Anti-Semitism, Heterosexism, and Sexism." *Sex Roles* 56, no. 1 (February 2007): 1–12, https://www.researchgate.net /publication/238309952_Resisting_Prejudice_Every_Day_Exploring _Women's_Assertive_Responses_to_AntiBlack_Racism_Anti-Semitism _Heterosexism_and_Sexism.

King, Billie Jean. "Serena Is Still Treated Differently than Male Athletes." *Washington Post*, September 9, 2018, https://www.washingtonpost.com/outlook /2018/09/09/serena-is-still-treated-differently-than-male-athletes.

Meade, Amanda. "Serena Williams Cartoon Not Racist, Australian Media Watchdog Rules." *Guardian* (US), February 24, 2019, https://www.theguard ian.com/sport/2019/feb/25/serena-williams-cartoon-not-racist-australian -media-watchdog-rules.

Navratilova, Martina. "What Serena Got Wrong." *New York Times*, September 10, 2018, https://www.nytimes.com/2018/09/10/opinion/martina-navratilova -serena-williams-us-open.html.

Norman, Matthew. "Serena's Loyal Supporters." *Telegraph* (UK), January 22, 2006, https://www.telegraph.co.uk/sport/tennis/australianopen/2331012 /Serenas-loyal-supporters.html.

Sangweni, Yolanda. "Serena Williams Responds to Caroline Wozniacki's 'Racist' Impersonation." *Essence*, December 23, 2012, https://www.essence.com /news/serena-williams-responds-caroline-wozniackis-racist-impersonation.

Santhanam, Anuradha. "French Open 2017: Rafael Nadal Threatens Chair Umpire, Says He Will 'Never Chair His Match Again.'" *Sportskeeda*, June 5, 2017, https://www.sportskeeda.com/tennis/french-open-2017-rafael-nadal -threatens-chair-umpire.

SportsDay Staff. "Former Cowboys WR Michael Irvin Named in NFL Network Sexual Harassment Lawsuit." *Dallas Morning News*, July 25, 2018, https:// www.dallasnews.com/sports/cowboys/2018/07/25/former-cowboys -wr-michael-irvin-named-in-nfl-network-sexual-harassment-lawsuit.

Traister, Rebecca. *Good and Mad: The Revolutionary Power of Women's Anger*. New York: Simon & Schuster, 2018.

Tribune News Services. "'Gorilla' or 'Guerrilla'? ESPN's Doug Adler Apologizes for Venus Williams Remark." *Chicago Tribune*, January 19, 2017, https://www .chicagotribune.com/sports/breaking/ct-venus-williams-gorilla-guerrilla -espn-20170119-story.html.

Wilstein, Steve. "Venus Loses Her Beads, Her Cool, and the Match." *SouthCoast Today*, January 27, 1999, https://www.southcoasttoday.com/article/19990127 /News/301279933.

Chapter 8: Hey, Where's *Our* #MeToo?

Interviews with Nicole Bedera, Jennifer Decker, Nancy Hogshead-Makar, and Adrienne Lawrence conducted by the author.

Abelson, Jenn. "At ESPN, the Problems for Women Run Deep." *Boston Globe*, December 14, 2017, https://www.bostonglobe.com/sports/2017/12/14/women -who-worked-espn-say-its-problems-far-beyond-barstool-sports/L1v9 HJIvtnHuBPiMru6yGM/story.html.

Associated Press. "Brett Favre's Inappropriate Text Message Case Settled." *USA Today*, May 24, 2013, https://www.usatoday.com/story/sports/nfl/jets/2013 /05/24/brett-favre-racy-texts-case-settled/2359211.

———. "Larry Nassar Sexual Assault Fallout: A Look at Everyone Charged, Fired, or Forced Out." *Chicago Tribune*, October 18, 2018, https://www.chicagotri bune.com/sports/ct-spt-sexual-assault-gymnastics-larry-nassar-fallout -20181018-story.html.

Borchers, Callum. "Why Mike Tirico's History of Alleged Sexual Harassment Hasn't Led Him to Matt Lauer's Fate." *Washington Post*, December 10, 2017, https://www.washingtonpost.com/news/the-fix/wp/2017/12/10/why-mike-tiricos-history-of-alleged-sexual-harassment-hasnt-led-him-to-matt-lauers-fate.

Carlsen, Audrey, Maya Salam, Claire Cain Miller, Denise Lu, Ash Ngu, Jugal K. Patel, and Zach Wichter. "#MeToo Brought Down 201 Powerful Men. Nearly Half of Their Replacements Are Women." *New York Times*, October 29, 2018, https://www.nytimes.com/interactive/2018/10/23/us/metoo-replacements.html.

DiCaro, Julie. "How Parents Can Protect Their Young Athletes from the Larry Nassars of the World." *Washington Post*, January 22, 2018, https://www.washingtonpost.com/news/parenting/wp/2018/01/22/how-parents-can-protect-their-young-athletes-from-the-larry-nassars-of-the-world.

Freeman, Michael. *ESPN: The Uncensored History*. Lanham, MD: Taylor Trade, 2001.

Garcia, Sandra E. "The Woman Who Created #MeToo Long Before Hashtags." *New York Times*, October 20, 2017, https://www.nytimes.com/2017/10/20/us/me-too-movement-tarana-burke.html.

Gregory, Sean. "How the #MeToo Movement Is About to Change Pro Sports." *TIME*, December 18, 2017, https://time.com/5064703/how-the-metoo-movement-is-about-to-change-pro-sports.

McCann, Michael. "Breaking Down the Disturbing Details, Implications of NFL Network Sexual Harassment Claims." *Sports Illustrated*, December 12, 2017, https://www.si.com/media/2017/12/12/nfl-network-sexual-harassment-jami-cantor-lawsuit-faulk-mcnabb-weinberger.

McParland, Erin, and Tim Rohan. "NFL Network Sexual Harassment: One Woman's Story." *Sports Illustrated*, December 21, 2017, https://www.si.com/nfl/2017/12/21/nfl-network-sexual-harassment.

Miller, James Andrew, and Tom Shales. *Those Guys Have All the Fun: Inside the World of ESPN*. New York: Back Bay Books, 2011.

Perrett, Connor. "Ohio State University Will Pay Out $41 Million to 162 Men Who Say They Were Sexually Abused by a Longtime Team Doctor." *Business Insider*, May 9, 2020, https://www.businessinsider.com/ohio-state-41-million-richard-strauss-sexual-assault-2020-5.

Pflum, Mary. "A Year Ago, Alyssa Milano Started a Conversation About #MeToo.

These Women Replied." NBC News, October 15, 2018, https://www.nbcnews
.com/news/us-news/year-ago-alyssa-milano-started-conversation-about
-metoo-these-women-n920246.

Stanglin, Doug. "Ex–Penn State Coach Jerry Sandusky Appears in Court; Resen-
tenced to 30 to 60 Years." *USA Today*, November 23, 2019, https://www.usa
today.com/story/news/nation/2019/11/22/jerry-sandusky-ex-penn-state
-coach-sex-abuse-re-sentencing-hearing/4269271002.

Waterman, Cole. "University of Michigan Admits to Sexual Abuse by Athletic Doctor, Seeks to Have Lawsuit Dismissed." *MLive*, May 2, 2020,
https://www.mlive.com/news/ann-arbor/2020/05/university-of-michigan
-admits-to-sexual-abuse-by-athletic-doctor-seeks-to-have-lawsuit
-dismissed.html.

Chapter 9: Care about Women's Sports More Than Once Every Four Years

Interviews with Julie Foudy, Maggie Hendricks, Jemele Hill, Howard Megdal,
Monique Lamoureux-Morando, Kendall Coyne Schofield, Imani McGee-
Stafford, and Kelsey Trainor conducted by the author.

Bachman, Rachel. "U.S. Women's Soccer Games Outearned Men's Games." *Wall
Street Journal*, June 17, 2019, https://www.wsj.com/articles/u-s-womens
-soccer-games-out-earned-mens-games-11560765600.

Cato, Tim. "14 NBA Teams Are Reportedly Losing Money. Here's Why that Does
and Doesn't Matter." *SB Nation*, September 19, 2017, https://www.sbnation
.com/2017/9/19/16334596/nba-teams-losing-money-revenue-profits
-why-matters.

Conway, Tyler. "Report: Breanna Stewart Suffers Torn Achilles Injury after Col-
lision with Griner." *Bleacher Report*, April 15, 2019, https://bleacherreport
.com/articles/2831400-report-breanna-stewart-suffers-torn-achilles
-injury-after-collision-with-griner.

Das, Andrew. "U.S. Women's Soccer Team Sues U.S. Soccer for Gender Discrimination." *New York Times*, March 8, 2019, https://www.nytimes.com/2019
/03/08/sports/womens-soccer-team-lawsuit-gender-discrimination.html.

——. "U.S. Women's Soccer Team's Equal Pay Demands Are Dismissed by
Judge." *New York Times*, May 1, 2020. https://www.nytimes.com/2020/05
/01/sports/soccer/uswnt-equal-pay.html.

DiCaro, Julie. "U.S. Women's Hockey Team Is Fighting for Your Daughter." CBS Local, March 27, 2017, https://chicago.cbslocal.com/2017/03/27/dicaro-u-s-womens-hockey-team-is-fighting-for-your-daughter.

Elsesser, Kim. "U.S. Soccer Says Women Don't Deserve Equal Pay Because They Have Less Skill." *Forbes*, March 11, 2020, https://www.forbes.com/sites/kimelsesser/2020/03/11/us-soccer-says-women-dont-deserve-equal-pay-because-they-have-less-skill/#12a477986bb0.

Fagan, Kate. "Taurasi to Rest, Skip WNBA Season." ESPN, February 3, 2015, https://www.espn.com/wnba/story/_/id/12272047/diana-taurasi-opts-sit-2015-wnba-season.

Hess, Abigail. "US Viewership of the 2019 Women's World Cup Final Was 22% Higher than the 2018 Men's Final." CNBC, July 10, 2019, https://www.cnbc.com/2019/07/10/us-viewership-of-the-womens-world-cup-final-was-higher-than-the-mens.html.

Isaacson, Melissa. *State: A Team, a Triumph, a Transformation*. Chicago: Midway, 2019.

McCann, Michael. "Analyzing the WNBA's New CBA Deal and What It Means for the Future of the League." *Sports Illustrated*, January 14, 2020, https://www.si.com/wnba/2020/01/14/wnba-cba-labor-salary-raise-players-association.

Otterson, Joe. "'Game of Thrones' Finale Sets New Series High with Staggering 19.3 Million Viewers." *Variety*, May 20, 2019, https://variety.com/2019/tv/ratings/game-of-thrones-series-finale-draws-19-3-million-viewers-sets-new-series-high-1203220928.

Young, Ryan. "Viewership Numbers from 'The Last Dance' Prove Michael Jordan Documentary Was a Smash Hit." Yahoo! Sports, May 21, 2020, https://sports.yahoo.com/michael-jordan-the-last-dance-documentary-numbers-viewership-figures-espn-chicago-bulls-224004795.html.

Chapter 10: Around the World, Here Come the Girls

Interviews with Soraya Chemaly, L. A. Jennings, Kiran Khan, and Sana Mahmud conducted by the author.

ESPNCricInfo Staff. "Sharmeen Khan, Pioneer of Women's Cricket in Pakistan, Dies." ESPNCricInfo, December 13, 2018, https://www.espncricinfo.com

/story/_/id/25526464/sharmeen-khan-pioneer-women-cricket-pakistan
-dies.

Girls Not Brides. "Pakistan." Accessed March 1, 2020, https://www.girlsnot
brides.org/child-marriage/pakistan.

Human Rights Watch. "'Shall I Feed My Daughter or Educate Her?': Barriers to
Girls' Education in Pakistan." November 12, 2018, https://www.hrw.org
/report/2018/11/12/shall-i-feed-my-daughter-or-educate-her/barriers-girls
-education-pakistan.

Ijaz, Saroop. "Pakistan Should End Child Marriage." Human Rights Watch, October 12, 2017, https://www.hrw.org/news/2017/10/12/pakistan-should-end
-child-marriage.

UN Women. "Press Release: In Sport and for Gender Equality One Win Leads
to Another." UNWomen.org, August 6, 2016, https://www.unwomen.org
/en/news/stories/2016/8/press-release-in-sport-and-for-gender-equality
-one-win-leads-to-another.

Women's Sports Foundation. "Benefits—Why Sports Participation for Girls and
Women." WomensSportsFoundation.org, August 30, 2016, https://www
.womenssportsfoundation.org/advocacy/benefits-sports-participation
-girls-women.

World Economic Forum. "Global Gender Gap Report 2020." December 16, 2019,
http://www3.weforum.org/docs/WEF_GGGR_2020.pdf.

Chapter 11: All Together Now

Interviews with Nicole Bedera, Melissa Ludtke, Mina Kimes, Laura Okmin,
Tamryn Spruill, and Kelsey Trainor conducted by the author.

DiCaro, Julie. "Episode 12—Jack Johnson." *Stick to Pods* podcast, eighteen minutes, twenty-eight seconds, April 25, 2018, https://sticktopods.libsyn.com
/episode-12-jack-johnson.

Gantt, Darin. "D.A. Couldn't Find Greg Hardy's Accuser, as She Was Out of
Town." *ProFootballTalk*, February 9, 2015, https://profootballtalk.nbcsports
.com/2015/02/09/d-a-couldnt-find-greg-hardys-accuser-as-she-was
-out-of-town.

Uzzi, Brian. "Research: Men and Women Need Different Kinds of Networks to
Succeed." *Harvard Business Review*, February 25, 2019, https://hbr.org/2019

/02/research-men-and-women-need-different-kinds-of-networks-to
-succeed.

Waterson, Jim. "Male Journalists Ignore Female Peers on Twitter, Study
Shows." *Guardian* (US), June 24, 2018, https://www.theguardian.com/media
/2018/jun/24/male-journalists-ignore-female-peers-on-twitter-study
-shows.

INDEX